ORDER RESTORED

ORDER RESTORED

A Biblical Interpretation of Health, Medicine, and Healing

by

Garth D. Ludwig, Ph. D.

Concordia Academic Press

A Division of

Concordia Publishing House

Saint Louis, Missouri

Copyright © 1999 Concordia Academic Press
3558 S. Jefferson Avenue, Saint Louis, MO 63118-3968
Manufactured in the United States of America

Library of Congress Cataloging-in-Publication Data

Ludwig, Garth D.
    Order restored : a biblical interpretation of health, medicine, and healing / by
  Garth D. Ludwig.
        p.   cm.
    Includes bibliographical references and index.
    ISBN 0-579-04272-0
    1.   Health—Biblical teaching. 2. Health—Religious aspects—Christianity.
3. Spiritual healing.   I. Title.
BS680.H413L83   1999
261.8 ' 321—dc21   99-21264
                                                                         CIP

Contents

Foreword

When Marlene Ludwig asked me to write a foreword to *Order Restored*, the last book of my cousin Garth Ludwig, I was both pleased and proud. Garth had planned to ask me to participate, but his illness, which ultimately led to his death, kept him from carrying out those plans, so his wife carried out those plans for him. My background is as an allopathic physician/surgeon, scientist, and researcher with deep roots and commitment to Christianity. I have read and enjoyed Garth's book and learned much from it. The book has provided for me the inspiration to be both a better and more concerned doctor and also a better Christian. I learned much from his positive and enthusiastic approach to life, illness, and disease and his proposal for the Healing Christian Ministry. This book reads as a fascinating story, which begins before the time of Christ and continues to the present. In addition, it is scholarly, practical, and helpful. There are extensive citations of many who have written about health, faith, and God: from George Benson, who grew up in an Orthodox Jewish family, and Henri Nowen, a Catholic priest, to Paul Tillich, Reneé Dubos, Rudolph Virchow, Hans Selye, Bernie Siegel, and many Lutheran theologians such as Martin Scharlemann and Martin Marty. Garth urges a return to the healing ministry by ministers, congregations, and Christians, not by the faith healer's approach, but rather through prayer, faith, and worship. He cites many examples of Jesus' healing where He said, "Thy faith hath made thee whole." I recommend this book to all clergy, congregations, and particularly all Christians who have experienced illness, disease, or both, and would like a better understanding of "the restoration of order" in their lives.

When I first heard my cousin Garth Ludwig preach at the Castor Gardens Lutheran Church in northeast Philadelphia in the early 1960s, I recognized then that he would make a great contribution to our Christian experience. Garth also served churches in Upper St. Clair, Pennsylvania, where he earned his Ph.D. in anthropology at the University of Pittsburgh, and in Tucson, Arizona. Thus he was able to combine his ministerial education and parish experience with his scholarly pursuits to teach at Concordia University, Irvine, California, where he was chairperson of the Division of Social Science.

As part of his continuing education, Garth regularly led anthropological field trips to and visited many sections of the world, including the Middle East, Eastern Europe, Central America, and South America. He was always seeking a fuller knowledge of how different peoples and different cultures look at their community, their faith, their illnesses, and their healing processes. One of his main purposes in undertaking such travel was to enable him to compare the ideas of other societies with those of Christendom from ancient to present times.

Now, shortly after his death, this book, which represents a lifetime of experiences, observations, research, and walking with his God, will be published. His title for the book, *Order Restored*, suggests a review, or history, of what the Old and New Testament writers said about health. The book is much more than that. Garth sounds a clear call for Christians, Christian churches, and ministers to return to the healing ministries of the early church. He traces his fascinating story of the views of disease and health in the Old Testament, where no healers are described, to the healing ministries of Jesus, the disciples, and elders in the New Testament. He continues to follow this healing ministry up to about A.D. 300, at which time a great change took place and the healing ministry began to fade. Garth explains that a platonic or gnostic view of the person at that time divided the body from the soul. The soul contained the divine spark. The body was perceived as a prison. In the Middle Ages sickness was glorified. The Renaissance studies of anatomy and science broke loose these beliefs. In the sixteenth century, Ambrose Paré said, "I dressed the wound; God healed it."

Garth describes disease as disorder so that healing requires restoration of order in one's life. Disease is "the result of sin, the separation of the creature from the creator." He also makes a distinction between disease as "an objective phenomenon characterized by an altered biological functioning of the body" and as an illness that "is a subjective, personal phenomenon in which the individual perceives himself as not feeling well." He describes sickness as a social phenomenon—"a person acts sick." In making these distinctions, he suggests that a person can be cured of their illness by restoring order through faith and belief, even while still having the disease. As Garth states, there is "a healthy way to live a disease." For example, one may accept and live positively with a chronic disease such as rheumatoid arthritis.

Modern medicine, with its emphasis on making a diagnosis and dispensing medicines or surgery, has on occasion lost sight of the patient as a person. Sir William Osler, a famous physician, once said, "It is more important for the doctor to know the patient rather than the disease which the patient has." Allopathic or traditional medicine is now returning to an emphasis on the person, on empathy, on humanity, and on humanities. Such ideologies, along with medical ethics and alternative medicine, are being taught in medical school. We in medicine believe that empathy with the patient—an intellectual and sometimes emotional identification with their feelings—is more important than merely feeling sorry for them.

Garth describes the scientific advances of neuropsychiatry and their relationship to our immune system. He explains that a positive attitude strengthens our immune systems and decreases our susceptibility to disease. As pointed out by Bernie Siegel, patients with cancer will do better if they remain positive and undiscouraged.

In his final chapter, Garth describes the ministry of healing, which includes "the congregation as a healing community," in which healing occurs through Christian worship, music, Baptism, Communion; and prayer. congregations for praying and with the sick and confession. He describes such rituals of healing as the laying on of hands, and anointing with oil. In the past, the body has been the domain of the doctor and the soul the domain of the minister. Now we know that both must work together.

As an appendix he provides a service of spiritual healing. It is interesting to note that some churches have such services on a regular basis. Garth closes with the hope that there will be a renaissance of the healing ministry to restore order in our lives. We are grateful to him for this encouragement.

> Arthur E. Baue, M.D.
> Professor of Surgery Emeritus
> Saint Louis University

Preface

Only a few years ago I learned an important lesson while doing medical work among the Jicaque Indians in Honduras. What these Indians taught me was how vulnerable humans are to the threat of disease. Without the luxury of sanitation and modern medical technology, and with barely sufficient food supplies, the Jicaque Indians lived in fear of even the common cold. I noted how so many of the children died. I observed how the adults took precautions against any stranger who might bear a killing disease. Long lines of mothers and children patiently waited their turns at our humble clinic day after day.

For most people, like the Jicaque, health is a major concern in their lives. Of all the desires that rank first on our list of priorities, living our lives free from pain and sickness must certainly stand near the top. Life has taught us to endure many things, but disease presents a challenge that renders us vulnerable. Disease is a sign that all is not well; it is the symbol of our human frailty. We yearn for the aliveness we feel when we are healthy.

My purpose in this book will be to address the topic of health, medicine, and healing from a different point of view. What I seek to explore is how human life, characterized by the disorder of disease and illness, can be restored to the order that we call health. For this reason, I have examined the Old and New Testament Scriptures for a more inclusive and spiritual understanding of health and healing. I ask the questions—how are health and disease perceived in the cultural context of the Scriptures? What truths about health emerge that could substantially change the nature of our own approach to health and well-being?

Another of my goals in this book is to apply these truths to our current understanding of health, namely, the beliefs and practices of modern medical science. I believe it is essential, in any dialogue of healing, to discuss medical concepts against the backdrop of the health system in which most of us were raised and believe. The anticipated result will be a synthesis in which spiritual bridges will have been built from the biblical world to the world of today. Because modern medicine is presently undergoing changes in many areas of application, the ideas and insights of this book may be helpful to a wide range of people.

I am a medical anthropologist who has also been trained in theology; thus, I am comfortable writing about health both as a medical scientist and as a churchman. My experiences in anthropological field research include a health study for the U.S. government in Central Africa and numerous field studies among Indian tribes in Latin America. For many years it has been my aim to sensitize the Christian church to an awareness of and an appreciation for its healing potential. In numerous conferences, seminars, and workshops throughout America, it has been gratifying for me to see the interest demonstrated by pastors, laypersons, and medical professionals in bringing the world of health into the life of the church. To a large extent, the material in this book is the result of preparing for those conferences.

All across the face of America a new and vital interest in health and healing is emerging. For many good health is ranked second only to a happy family life as a desired goal in life. Never before in our history has there been so much health-oriented information made available to the general public. Because of the wellness movement, every form of preventive medicine, from nutrition to exercise to meditation, is offered in the marketplace of modern America. Alternative forms of healing, especially of the self-help variety, are freely discussed in magazines and books. Orthomolecular medicine, which includes megavitamin therapy and herbology, has become popularized as have medicinal approaches from traditional China and India. On the part of some, health has become such a faddish subject that it involves an almost "religious devotion" to bodily perfection.

Even the traditional, and somewhat conservative, medical institutions of this country are responding to changes in procedure that reflect the tastes of a more health-conscious society. Modern medical science, for example, has discovered that the pursuit of biophysical healing in and of itself is a futile goal. Research in the study of disease-causation reveals that the dimensions of the mind and spirit are crucial factors in the disease process. Recent studies in psychoneuro-immunology have shown that unhealthy emotions and negative moods are associated with the body's immunological system, What we think and feel seems to be as vital to the state of our health as the food we eat or the exercise we engage in. Among some medical scientists, including Herbert Benson of Harvard's Mind-Body Institute, the 'faith factor' in healing is no longer a wishful dream but a medical reality.

This interest in health and well-being has captivated not only the general public but the American church as well. After centuries of benign neglect, the Christian church is again becoming attentive to one of its historical legacies, the ministry of healing. We are witnessing a revived spirit of inquiry into matters of healing and its relationship to Christian theology. Pastors and laypersons are beginning to challenge the old ways, searching for new models more in tune with the biblical mandate of healing. The figure of Jesus the Healer, whose healing ministry has been "over-spiritualized" in countless sermons or conveniently overlooked, is now being discussed with serious intentions. Healing prayers and services of healing are becoming popular, no longer perceived as avant-garde expressions of Christian ministry. Surely we are at the vanguard of a powerful trend that is bringing about a different, more wholesome shape to the modern church.

One of the major reasons for this renewed interest in healing has been the emergence of the wholistic model of the person.[1] Wholism has always been the biblical view of the person: the human being is a total person, an individual with social, mental, emotional, and spiritual needs as well as obvious physical needs. In the context of modernity, however, wholism has forced us to revise our attitudes toward health care. Essential to the doctrine of wholism is the argument of interdependence. Changes in one dimension of the person will trigger changes in other dimensions of his or her personhood. What emerges from this unified understanding of the person is the conclusion that the health of the spirit is the vital dynamic in the health of the whole person. Medical studies are helping us appreciate that the spiritual life of a person is a primal factor in the healing process.

This new holistic or wholistic emphasis, incidentally, is making profound inroads in modern medical science and is bringing about some radical restructuring in contemporary health care. Many medical doctors are widening their purview of the etiologies that bring about disease as well as the therapies that both prevent and cure it. Alter-

---

[1]The terms "holistic" and "wholistic" are used in this book as synonyms. "Holistic" is the term of choice in scientific circles, ever since it was coined by Jan Smuts in 1927. The term "wholistic" is preferred by some because of its obvious relationship with "wholeness."

native forms of healing are emerging as commonplace both within and without the institution of medicine.

In effect, the doctrine of wholism represents a shift in worldview. The materialistic orientation toward life, so long the dominant worldview of the Western world, seems to be somewhat on the wane. Even within the medical community, a more humanitarian emphasis is moving to center stage. Translated into concrete behavioral patterns, this means a more sensitive treatment of individuals as persons of worth and meaning. Spiritual values, because they enhance the meaning of being human, are an important part of most wholistic systems.

The emergence of wholism as a competing worldview, expressed also as the biblical worldview, provides the contextual explanation for the foundation of this book. In addition, it provides the interpretive background that explains how health and healing are addressed in the Scriptures. My purpose will be to bring together both of these approaches to health, the ancient and the modern, in a unified framework of meaning and application.

Unlike most books which discuss biblical healing, the methodology used in this book will be unique. I employ the methodology of medical anthropology. Medical anthropologists consider it essential to examine the cultural setting in which disease and illness are being studied. As a correlative point, this also means a careful analysis of the religious beliefs that undergird the theory of disease and its cure. In brief, the health or medical systems operative in both the Old and New Testaments need to be deciphered if the reader is to comprehend the fullest meaning of these narratives.

Because this book is about the analysis of health and medicine in the Scriptures, it is essentially a book of biblical interpretation. Interpreting the Scripture is always a challenging process whether the purpose is to extract the meaning of a particular passage or to make a suitable application to a modern situation. The foremost challenge, of course, is a clear understanding of the hermeneutical process, the principles by which the Scripture is correctly interpreted. If the original meaning of the biblical passage is to be preserved, the interpreter must carefully use all the appropriate tools at his disposal, among them a knowledge of linguistics, a knowledge of history, and a knowledge of culture.

It is unfortunate that the last-mentioned of these—a knowledge of *culture*—is the least understood by most interpreters of the Bible. The result is often an Americanized or ethnocentric understanding of the

Hebrew and Greek cultures whose worldviews provide the infra-structure for the Old and New Testaments. Frequently we encounter cultural distortion when we seek insights about the Scripture's teaching of health and disease.

The conclusions to be drawn from this anthropological approach to the biblical narratives will be rich and enlightening. These conclusions will yield a clear understanding of what it meant to be sick in an age far different from our own. The reader will be asked to think about disease and health in a manner that will challenge some of his or her own presuppositions. But the greatest advantage of this anthropo-logical approach is the ease by which health and healing can be discussed in a "language" common to both the biblical world and the world of modern medicine.

The introductory chapter of this book, "Culture, Disease, and Health," introduces the reader to the topics of disease and health as these are studied by medical anthropologists. Apprehending the nature of medical systems, especially the varied cultural approaches to disease theory and health care, helps us gain a much deeper insight into the subject of health and well-being. It is a necessary foundation for the study of the biblical narratives.

In chapters 2 and 3, "Health and Illness in the Old Testament" and "Health and Healing in the New Testament," the Old and New Testaments are comprehensively examined and explained from the perspective of disease and health. Because these documents reflect different cultural settings, obvious differences in medical systems and health behavior will appear. However, a unity links the two testaments together. A dominant motif about health in the Old Testament, *shalom*, emerges as a reality in the New Testament in which the figure of Jesus the Healer is the focus of our study. Primary attention is given to the scope and purpose of Jesus' healing ministry.

"The Biblical Model of Health" is the subject of chapter 4 in which those timeless truths of health and healing, set forth in the Scriptures, are presented as a model for our current practice of health. In addition, we discuss the concept of "wholeness" which is the foundation of the biblical teaching about health and well-being.

Chapters 5 and 6 integrate the biblical system of healing and modern medicine. The topics of "The Healing of Persons" and "Faith and Healing" provide an understanding of whole person health care as well as the nature and place of faith in the healing process. Because these topics are currently the subject of much discussion within the medical community, it is appropriate that they be examined from the biblical perspective. The theme of "faith" is especially a sensitive topic, both within and outside the Church, and we argue that biblical faith must be differentiated from modern versions of suggestibility.

In chapter 7 we turn our attention to the subject of "Sickness and Suffering." No discussion about healing can ever be complete unless the prominent biblical theme of suffering is also addressed. Important issues of chronic suffering are addressed both apart from and in the context of the subject of death and the resurrection. It is significant that both the Scripture and medical science acknowledge the limitation of healing.

"The Ministry of Healing" is the title of chapter 8, in which we offer suggestions for a congregational approach to the healing ministry. Healing by means of Word and sacraments in Christian worship is presented in a new perspective. In addition, we have included a comprehensive discussion of other congregational rituals such as prayer for the sick with the laying on of hands, the anointing with oil, and a healing service. A key element in any approach to a ministry of healing is that the congregation perceives itself to be a healing community.

Throughout the process of writing this book, I have benefited greatly from the positive comments and constructive criticism of the many conferences at which many of these materials were first presented. I want to especially express my appreciation to Dr. Andrew Bartelt of Concordia Seminary, St. Louis, and Dr. David Lumpp of Concordia College, St. Paul, Minnesota, who read portions of this manuscript, as well as Micheal J. Chehval, M.D., of St. Louis who checked the draft from a medical perspective. Dr. Bruce Hartung, St. Louis, read the manuscript critically and suggested specific additions from recent literature. My students at Concordia University Irvine, many of whom have become skilled in medical anthropology and have accompanied me into the jungles of Central America, have provided me with the inspiration to see this manuscript through to its completion.

This project was made possible in large part by the University Committee of Concordia Academic Press, chaired by Dr. Joel Heck. I also want to thank Dr. Dale Griffin of Concordia Academic Press for his editorial assistance and for steering this book into its present form. Last, but not least, I express deep appreciation to Dr. Earl Gaulke of

Concordia Publishing House who long ago encouraged me to write and whose steady hand helped make this book a possibility.

Garth D. Ludwig

In reality, if medicine is the science of the healthy as well as of the ill human being, what other science is better suited to propose laws as the basis of the social structure . . . as *anthropology*? . . . Medicine is a *social science* in its very marrow and bone.

Rudolph Virchow, 1849

Chapter One

Culture, Disease, and Health

Never will I forget the remark of a woman whom I visited at her sickbed in one of our modern hospitals. Hooked up to a network of tubes and life-support apparatus, she said to me, "Being sick is no fun." The woman was in great pain, despite being given the best of medical care, and certainly was not enjoying the experience.

I also remember the remark of an ailing African chief at whose village I was doing field work years ago. He likewise was in great pain, his chest wrapped tight with native medicines, and his four wives hovering over him in anxiety. "Do you have any medicine for me?" he asked, almost as if I were his last hope.

Sickness is the common experience of all humanity. It is no fun for anyone. All members of the human species struggle against this persistent intruder who seeks to do them in. Deep within the human spirit there stirs a hope that the disease will be banished and health will be restored to its rightful place. It has been this way since the beginning of our history.

My purpose in this chapter will be to introduce the topic of disease and health care from the perspective of human culture. We who call medical anthropology our discipline study human societies in every area of the globe. Our objective is to understand how they work out solutions to the problem of disease through the use of medical systems. Medical anthropologists are as much at home with tribal peoples of the Amazon—for whom there is no division between magic, religion, and medicine—as they are with medical personnel in a contemporary hospital setting.

This book will focus on a biblical exposition of health and healing. For this reason the holistic orientation of medical anthropology will prove valuable in interpreting accounts of disease and healing in the Old and New Testaments. A knowledge of how cultures go about the task of treating their ill—in particular, the philosophies, medications, and health practitioners that subsume medical systems—is a necessary first step in approaching the biblical accounts of illness and health.

Some medical concepts have also been included to assist the reader to probe more deeply into the topics that will be discussed.

But first we need to focus on the nature and process of disease. Health has long been a dominant cultural pattern in human social life, but always in juxtaposition to the presence of disease. I agree with Paul Tillich who wrote that health is a meaningful term only when it is compared to its opposite—*disease*.[1] He pointed out that health is not a part of human nature, certainly not in the sense of an individual's functions, such as blood circulation, metabolism, or breathing. According to Tillich, we understand the meaning of health only after we comprehend how disease has *distorted* the nature of the human being.

This distortion by disease of our humanity—the entrance of disorder into the created world of order—will be a major theme in this book. It sets the stage for a discussion of the biblical solutions of that distortion, the restoration of order that we will call health. For that reason, disease as "disorder" bears a closer look. Any discussion of health must first be prefaced with an understanding of the nature of disease and the destructive trends it brings to the processes of life.

Disease and Disorder

People commonly refer to disease as "dis-ease." Usually what they mean is that an individual is not "at ease" with the circumstances that have befallen him. This is a purely individualistic description of disease, centering on an individual's discomfort. But it does not come close to capturing the symbolic power of disease in human life. I believe it is more accurate to think of disease as *disorder*.

Anyone who has experienced a serious physical or mental illness will admit that disease is a wrecker of human order. Disease comes at us as an unwelcome attacker on our personhood and brings to naught all our well-ordered plans. It snuffs out our dreams and hopes. But it does more than that. It extends the boundaries of chaos to our entire universe. When disease strikes, everything that is meaningful to us— health, vocation, family and relationships, the life of the spirit—is placed into a state of disorder.

---

[1] Paul Tillich, "The Meaning of Health," in *Religion and Medicine*, ed. David Belgum (Ames, Iowa: Iowa State University Press, 1967), 4.

There are few evidences of human frailty that are more frightening than the presence of disease. There is something savage about this intruder that makes us cringe. Who can bear to watch a small child die of leukemia or a loved one wasting away in the grip of Alzheimer's? We ought not glorify disease or romanticize its deadly intentions. Disease is not good. As Tillich reminds us, disease is a distortion of the created order.

Consider for a moment the effects of disorder that disease brings to our lives. Within our *bodies* disease produces massive disorder. Cancer cells are maverick cells out of order and create tumorous growths that metastasize throughout the body. Diabetes is essentially a pancreatic disorder because the insulin necessary to process sugar is not available. Psoriasis is a metabolic disorder of the skin, speeding up the process of skin replacement from 28 days to 8 days. Autoimmune disease is simply a disorder that tricks the immune system to attack the body rather than to protect it. Surely one of the purposes of medicine is to try to establish order out of disorder.

Within the *psyché* or mind, disease creates disorder with images of pain and anxiety. When we are ill, we feel out of control. It's almost as if another entity is managing our lives. Because psychological stability is related to being in control, disease cripples our capacity to make decisions and to build relationships. Disease also attacks our self-esteem and our sense of inner peace. We need not ponder too long why disease is usually accompanied by pain.

Within the dimension of the *human spirit* disease is especially lethal. Here it threatens the meaning of our human existence; indeed, it casts doubt about the sovereignty of God and His promise of grace. The orderliness of our relationship with the Almighty and the cosmos becomes strained at the onset of a serious illness. The theodical question—"Why me, God?"—is shouted to the heavens. In any episode of illness, anger and guilt are signals that disorder has invaded our spiritual life.

In the *social world*, disease inhibits normal functioning. Normally our lives are lived out in a more-or-less predictable regimen of order. Tedious though this may seem, at least it means that we are able to function. Yet feelings of resentment and frustration arise when we cannot manage the demands of an ordinary day, when family life and work must be cast aside for the unwelcome sickbed, or even worse, the hospital bed. Invalidism, the product of disease, has the potential to saddle its victims with a deep sense of shame. And what that shame symbolizes is the face of disorder.

The disease that is disorder is multidimensional in its effects on human life. It presents challenges to life's ideals and realities as nothing else. We need to understand the deeper meanings of disease and the mystery of its power. In a word, we need a theology of disease.

The Many Faces of Disease

In the Genesis account of creation, a figuration of order emanated throughout the universe. "God saw all that He had made, and it was very good" (Gen. 1:31). It is difficult to speculate on the conditions of Paradise in contrast to our current understanding of the processes of life. But with the Fall of humankind into sin, we know that confusion and disorder made their appearance in God's world of order. It appears that the processes of life underwent a change in their modes of expression.[2]

Here is where we must begin our analysis of disease in the cosmos. Several clues in the biblical account of the Fall attest to this topic of disease and sickness. One of the key passages in the Genesis narrative is God's declaration about the consequences of Adam's rebellion. God says, *"Cursed is the ground because of you; through painful toil you will eat of it all the days of your life. It will produce thorns and thistles for you"*(Gen. 3:17-18). Although disease is not specifically mentioned in this passage, the faces of disease are powerfully symbolized in at least three ways.

The Face of Cosmic Disorder

First, one aspect of disease is that it points to the *cosmic disorder* produced by the Fall. "Cursed is the ground. . . . It will produce thorns and thistles for you" (Gen. 3:17-18). According to the biblical account, a brokenness now pervades the created order. *The ground is cursed.* Instead of working on behalf of human enjoyment, the creative processes cause toil, hardship, and frustration. Even nature itself—

---

[2]Ibid., 5. Tillich speculates that the root causes of disease have their common cause in what he calls the "ambiguity of life." "Ambiguity means that in every creative process of life, a destructive trend is implied; in every integrating process of life, a disintegrating trend; in every process toward the sublime, a profanizing trend. Generally speaking, disease is a symptom of the universal ambiguity of life."

including the ecological arrangements of plants, animals, and inorganic life—presents challenges that may at times be sinister. It is not difficult to conclude that we have here the ideal condition in which disease thrives. Tillich's commentary on this possibility is penetrating:

> A symptom of the cosmic disorder is the enmity between the different parts of nature and between man and nature. The order of nature, called "covenant" between God and "the beasts of the field" (Hos. 2:18), is broken, and the result is chaos and self-destruction. . . . *The land itself fell sick*, and produces weeds under the curse of God, which results in enmity between man and animals (represented by the serpent), extreme pain in childbirth, fratricide, and above all, the loss of the food of the gods (the fruits of the tree of life) which in paradise continually overcame the natural mortality of man (emphasis added).[3]

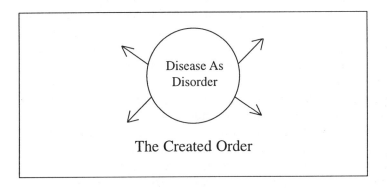

There are many ways we can understand the cosmic disorder that disease brings to the created world. From a literal point of view, it is accurate to say that the "ground is cursed" in respect to disease. In many instances, the locality of disease is found in the ground or in specific breeding sites in nature or again in animal reservoirs. If we use the language of medical science, disease is caused by *microorganisms* which are parasites, invisible to the eye, and which subsist by living on hosts such as humans or animals. William McNeill describes the process:

---

[3]Paul Tillich, "The Relation of Religion and Health: Historical Considerations and Theoretical Questions," *Review of Religion* (May, 1946), 349-50.

Microparasites are tiny organisms—viruses, bacteria, or multicelled creatures as the case may be—that find a source of food in human tissues suitable for sustaining their own vital processes. Some microparasites provoke acute disease and either kill their host after only a brief period of time, or provoke immune reactions inside his body that kill him off instead. . . . There are, however, other microparasites that regularly achieve more stable relations with their human hosts. Such infections no doubt take something away from their host's bodily energies, but their presence does not prevent normal functioning.[4]

We pause to mention that the Creator has not left humankind without protection against these deadly microparasites. The *potential* for healing exists within each of us. The human body possesses a marvelous defense system (the immune system) once characterized by Albert Schweitzer as "the healer within." White blood cells, produced in bone marrow and the lymphatic system, actually "ingest" disease parasites and constantly survey the body for signs of disease. Animals are equipped with a similar immune system. Many plants contain antibiotic elements to ward off disease and for that reason have become a source of medicine for both animals and humans.

Physical health, if it is to be restored, depends on the efficient functioning of the immune system. All healing systems "work" in the sense that they tap into the powerful healing resources of the immune system, whether they realize this fact or not. It is significant that belief systems can have a positive effect on this defense system and, as a result, actually stimulate the process of healing. The *placebo* is a prime example of how the power of suggestion can affect healing in the body. On the other hand, negative thoughts and emotions (the *nocebo*) can have a deleterious effect on the immune system and pave the way for the onset of disease.[5]

But there is another sense in which disease pervades the cosmos in which we live. Metaphorically, the entire world can appear "diseased"

---

[4]William H. McNeill, *Plagues and Peoples* (Garden City, NY: Anchor Press, 1976), 7.

[5]The term "placebo" means "I will please" whereas "nocebo" means "I will hurt." Some of the most exciting research in medicine is being made in the relationships between beliefs and sickness/health. See, for example, Robert Hahn and Arthur Kleinman, "Belief as Pathogen, Belief as Medicine: 'Voodoo Death and the Placebo Phenomenon' in Anthropological Perspective," *Medical Anthropology Quarterly* 14, no. 4 (August 1983): 3ff.

and out of sorts with its created potential for health and harmony. Human relationships can become alienated and can result in hostility, as the story of Cain and Abel so tragically demonstrates. Frequently, we speak of society itself being "broken" and in need of healing. We remember the "sickness of Nazi Germany" and its genocidal policy against the Jews or modern day race riots in which ethnic group strives against ethnic group. The United Nations building in New York stands as a constant reminder that healthy, cooperative relations between modern nation states is a better alternative than the "disease" of war.

Disease is so pervasive in the affairs of human life that "when one suffers, we all suffer." One day when I was doing field work in an African village, a woman of the village berated me for taking photographs and doing survey research, typical activities of any anthropologist. I knew that the chief was ill but saw no reason why that should deter me in my work. I then asked my interpreter why this woman was so angry and what she was saying to me. Never will I forget the answer I received: *"When the chief is sick, the whole village is sick!"* Traditional cultures have always understood sickness from the perspective of cosmic disorder and are much closer to the biblical sense than we in the Western world who insist that disease is something that only individuals suffer.

The Face of Sin

A second aspect of disease is that it is a result of *sin*, the alienation of the creature from the Creator. In the biblical account, God expresses his anger at Adam's rebellion and says to him: "Cursed is the ground *because of you*" (Gen. 3:17). These are hard words to hear because they relate sin and sickness in a way that almost suggests a cause and effect relationship. It is certainly not easy to suggest to individuals who are suffering debilitating diseases that they themselves are the responsible parties: to say—*"because of you."*

Throughout the history of medicine, sin and sickness have been closely related, not always in terms of cause and effect, but in the sense that each is an integral part of the brokenness of humankind. When an outbreak of cholera in India results in the deaths of many thousands of people, the cause cannot be blamed on any specific person or persons. Epidemiologists would rather point the finger at poor sanitation procedures, especially the handling of contaminated food and water. In a sense, then, all members of the human race share in the distortion of life that disease produces. Because "the land is sick," we ourselves become sick.

This does not mean, however, that we can easily dispense with the "because of you" aspect of disease causation as the biblical account suggests. We cannot because it is often *true*. In much of the current medical literature being published, there are many references to "because of you" accounts of how people are ruining their health by foolish and irresponsible behavior. The constant warnings about cigarette smoking and alcohol consumption are illustrations of these correlations between "because of you" behavior and the onset of disease. Psychosomatic disease, in which anxiety and worry are linked with disease, provide further evidence of what we have suspected all along: unhealthy (read "because of you") emotions are producing states of ill-health in a large part of our population.

We will have opportunity to examine this theme of sin/sickness in the following chapters when we survey the Old and New Testaments' accounts of disease. While the biblical narratives never separate these terms of "sin/sickness," they also discuss them in terms of their opposites: "wholeness/healing." We need to keep in mind that the biblical approach to sickness is utterly realistic about humankind's alienation from God. But at the same time it provides a realistic solution for the restoration of that relationship. Nothing is gained by separating sin and sickness as was the case when modern medical science began its quest a couple of hundred years ago. There is now a growing admission among many in medicine that human behavior and attitudes are strongly linked to the incidence of sickness.

Why is this factor of "sin and sickness" or its corollary, "wholeness and healing," such an important topic in health care today? Because it introduces into the medical dialogue the element of the *spiritual*. It raises the possibility of spiritual wholeness as a desired goal in healing. As long as disease is reduced to a mere bodily concern, there is no pressing need to address the deeper, spiritual concerns of the person. But if disease is perceived as being multidimensional in its character, then the focus of healing must change as well. Indeed, many in the field of medicine are discovering that the domain of the spirit is the focal point at which all health care must ultimately be directed. Martin Scharlemann spoke of this need in the following way:

> Men may be sound in body and agile in mind, and yet be devoid of wholeness. . . . Any really effective ministry of healing must begin with a

full appreciation of the nature of sin and the scope of its devastation. . . .
Advocates of healing recognize man's frustrations, his loneliness, his
feeling of a great void in life; but they rarely sound the depths of man's
basic ailment, which is the disruption and distortion of the very
relationship in which he was created to live.[6]

The Face of Pain

A third aspect of disease is the *pain* that usually accompanies
illness. "Through *painful toil* you will eat of it all the days of your life.
. . . I will greatly increase your *pains* in childbearing" (Gen. 3:16, 17).
The history of medicine is a history of dealing with the painful
symptoms produced by disease. In one sense the symptoms of pain can
be life-saving; they are signals that something may be seriously wrong
within the body. On the other hand, the intensity of bodily pain can be
maddening for the one who must bear it alone.

Alexander Alland, Jr., writes about the "noise" that disease
produces.[7] A major problem of medical diagnosis is to sort through the
"noise" of bodily pain in order to locate its cause, namely, the disease
or physical disorder. We can appreciate this fact when the physician
asks us "where" it hurts and "how severely" it hurts. According to
Alland, purely physical diseases produce more "noise" than do
psychosomatic diseases because the latter are more susceptible to the
suggestion and therapy of a health practitioner. An obvious goal of
medical therapy is to reduce or eliminate the noise of disease.

But the sensation of pain involves more than bodily processes.
Perhaps the suffering endured by the psyche and spirit is even worse—
the existential pain of the human spirit struggling for meaning in the
face of a world turned upside-down. It is during a serious bout of
illness that many raise the question of *theodicy*—"If God is good, why
does He allow me to suffer?" Thus, the God of the universe or another
cosmic power may be called in by the sufferer to answer the problem of
pain. It is significant that sickness, more than any other of life's
misfortunes, stimulates people to seek spiritual solutions for their
suffering. Yet even for secularists and others who no longer believe in

---

[6]Martin Scharlemann, *Healing and Redemption* (St. Louis: Concordia, 1965), 76-
77.

[7]Alexander Alland, Jr. *Adaptation in Cultural Evolution: An Approach to
Medical Anthropology* (New York: Columbia University Press, 1970), 177.

divine intervention, sickness may raise the question of *anthropodicy*. According to philosopher Stanley Hauerwas:

> Natural disasters, such as an automobile accident or hurricanes, tornadoes, earthquakes, we think that is bad luck. Such an evil requires no general explanation since there is nothing that anyone could do to prevent it. Once we no longer believe in the God of creation, there is no god that such disasters call into question. But sickness is another matter. Sickness should not exist because we think of it as something in which we can intervene and which we can ultimately eliminate. Sickness challenges our most cherished presumption that we are in control of our existence. Sickness creates the problem of anthropodicy because it challenges our most precious belief that humanity has in fact become god.[8]

The pain we endure in sickness implies a profound truth about the human being that needs to be mentioned at this time. Because pain is such a *total experience*, it demonstrates beyond any doubt that the person is a total unity as well. The processes of the body cannot really be separated from the processes of mind and spirit. Each dimension of the person exists in a union with the others. As Tillich has pointed out, the processes of the body, mind, and spirit "do not lay alongside or above each other but are present within each other."[9] What one dimension of the person experiences, the other dimensions experience as well.

Consider, for example, how our own language illustrates the close link between mind and body or "mind-body." We might have occasion to say about another person, "He is a pain in the neck," and actually feel a sensation in that part of the body. Again, if we were to describe a woman as "choking with rage," the experience is as literal as it is metaphorical. Faced with a disagreeable situation, any one of us might say, "I could not stomach that," and feel the disgust within our bodies. Modern studies of the emotions make quite clear that our feelings cannot be kept categorically distinct. They are as much experienced by the human spirit and body as they are an expression of the psyché.

The realization that we are not souls living in bodies but rather that we are "soul-bodies" or "spirit-bodies" is what is known as the *holistic*

---

[8]Stanley Hauerwas, *Naming the Silences: God, Medicine, and the Problem of Suffering* (Grand Rapids, MI: Eerdmans Publishing, 1990).

[9]Paul Tillich, "The Meaning of Health," in *Religion and Medicine*, ed. David Belgum (Ames, IA: Iowa University Press, 1967), 6.

perspective of the human being. We will have opportunity later to illustrate this biblical perspective of the person in greater depth. But we want to mention at this time that the holistic perspective is increasingly becoming a medical perspective. Since the emergence of psycho-somatic medicine and a great deal of medical research on the disease process, medical science is turning more to a systems model of the person.

This discussion of the theology of disease lays out the general problem area of health and healing that this book addresses. Much like "Paradise Lost"/"Paradise Regained," disease has created a distortion in human nature that can only be corrected if that order is restored. In order to gain a better perspective on how this order must be initiated, we need to examine more carefully the various dimensions of ill-health.

Disease, Illness, and Sickness

Another way of examining the reality that disease brings to human life is to use terms that behavioral scientists frequently use in their analysis of ill-health. These terms are, namely, *disease, illness,* and *sickness.* None of these terms means exactly the same thing; each refers to a different dimension of ill-health:[10]

Disease—Disease as an *objective* phenomenon characterized by an altered biological functioning of the body due to an attack of pathogens or other malfunctions which result in damage to its tissues or organs. Disease is a pathological concept. Diabetes, for example, is a disease. Of disease we usually say: "a person *has* a disease."

Illness—Illness is a *subjective, personal* phenomenon in which the individual perceives himself as not feeling well. When an individual feels ill, he senses pain, frustration, and upsetment. The pain is experienced psychologically and spiritually as well as in bodily symptoms. The concept of suffering is connected to the word "illness." Of illness we usually say: "a person *feels* ill."

Sickness—Sickness occurs when illness becomes a *social* phenomenon. Other members of society observe an individual's discomfort and encourage him to adopt the sick role. When a person

---

[10]See the general discussion of these terms in Andrew Twaddle, "Sickness and the Sickness Career: Some Implications" in *The Relevance of Social Science for Medicine,* eds. Leon Eisenberg and Arthur Kleinman (Dordrecht, Holland: D. Reidel Publishing Co., 1981), 111-112.

becomes sick, it is no longer personal. A physician and/or medications become part of the scene. Society recognizes this as a changed social status and excuses the individual from his normal duties. Of sickness we may say: " a person *acts* sick."

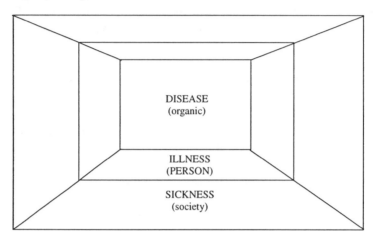

Model of Non-Health

There are advantages in making these distinctions about ill-health because each expresses itself in a different manner and each demands a different solution. For example, a biological malady in the intestinal tract will be dealt with much differently than psychological pain. Yet both can be aspects of the same experience of ill-health.

But there is a larger concern that these specific terms address. The disorder of ill-health attacks the person in such a total manner that the needs of the *whole person* must be considered. As will be made clear, health care cannot merely concentrate on the problems of the body and overlook the maladies of the psyché or spirit. Conversely, we cannot call effective any treatment whose object is solely to bring comfort to a patient while a raging malignancy is left untended. Whole person health care means precisely this: caring and curing are aimed at restoring the unity of the whole person. We will recognize the truth of that statement if we examine the concepts of disease, illness, and sickness in greater detail.

The Concept of Disease

There are occasions when we can say that an individual is suffering the effects of disease, illness, and sickness at the same time. For example, take the case of a person in the last stages of terminal cancer. The disease (a tumor) has been diagnosed by an objective, physiological process. Illness is involved because the sufferer feels pain and is given comfort by means of medication and spiritual support. Sickness is also included because the victim is obliged to take on the sick role and is ministered to as a patient.

However, consider a more common example, such as hypertension, when an individual has a *disease* but does not necessarily feel ill. In addition to not feeling ill, he may certainly not act "sick." People with hypertension may continue to function rather normally even though they have a serious disease.

The same is true of other diseases which do not express themselves with any overt symptomology, especially in their early stages. Some viruses have this quality, residing benignly for years within a person before erupting with a vengeance. A person may test positive for HIV virus, for example, and feel absolutely no ill effects. Furthermore, in some societies, a particular disease may be so common that people bear it without complaint or hint of suffering. Among the Mano of Liberia, yaws (a suppurating sore on the legs) is so frequently encountered that the people say: "Oh, that is not sickness. Everybody has that."[11]

In appraising the distinction between disease and illness, Cecil Helman refers to "disease" as the doctor's perspective and "illness" as the patient's perspective.[12] Although there is much truth to that equation, it is probably more accurate to refer to disease as the medical perspective. According to Foster and Anderson, disease connotes a pathological condition that can be verified by laboratory tests or other forms of clinical examination:

> We must distinguish between *disease,* a pathological concept, and
> *illness,* a cultural concept. We speak, for example, of plant and animal
> diseases, quite divorced from culture. But man's diseases become socially

---

[11]Quoted in George Foster and Barbara Anderson, *Medical Anthropology* (New York: John Wiley and Sons, 1978), 41.

[12]Cecil Helman, *Culture, Health, and Illness* (Bristol, England: John Wright and Sons, 1985), 65, 68.

significant only when they are identified as illness, a physiological malfunctioning that is seen to threaten the individual and his society.[13]

Modern medical science proceeds according to a methodology known as the medical model of disease. This model considers matters relating to sickness only "real" when they can be objectively observed and measured. To a modern physician, trained in scientific rationalism, disease is an abnormality within the body, a "clinical fact," the cause and effect of which must be discovered. For example, a change in the color of a patient's tongue or an elevation in his blood count are clinical facts to a physician, much more "real" than the patient's beliefs about what caused him to be ill.[14] The patient's tongue and blood count can be measured but not his beliefs.

Among medical scientists, diseases are abnormal changes in the body and are referred to as "entities." Each disease has its own specific personality, symptoms, and signs. This perspective also assumes that diseases are universal in their identities. For example, typhoid fever will be the same disease in whatever cultural context it may appear. Its causes, clinical picture, and treatment will always be the same.

There can be no doubt that medical science has advanced our understanding of diseases by isolating them as "entities." We have much to be thankful for about discoveries in pathology and antibiotics because of such scrutinizing procedures; no one desires to return to the past. But the irony of this medical advance is that the patient as a person is often lost in the process. That is to say, the patient's *disease* is being treated but the patient's *illness* may be left untended. When medical personnel talk among themselves about "the colostomy in room 412," we have reason to wonder whether the disease is of greater interest than the person in whom it resides. According to Coe, "it may be proper to say that, as a medical scientist, he does not deal with the sick man at all, but with the physiological processes that occur within the organism."[15] Perhaps the most trenchant criticism of the Western medical model is that it has made great progress in the science of treating disease, but in doing so, it has lost the art of attending to illness.

---

[13]Foster and Anderson, op. cit., 40.

[14]Helman, op. cit., 66.

[15]Rodney M. Coe, *Sociology of Medicine* (New York: McGraw-Hill Book Co., 1970), 95.

We ordinarily do not see "medical shortfalls" of this type in traditional or native cultures. Possessing neither antibiotics nor a thorough understanding of the human physiology of disease, traditional curers offer a wholistic approach to curing that partly compensates for these deficiencies. In their healing therapy, they make no distinction between disease, symptoms, or personal pain. Their singular goal is to heal the person. According to Ackerknecht:

> That old dichotomy between mental and bodily disease, which we seem largely unable to overcome even with psychosomatic medicine, just does not exist among primitives, either in pathology or in therapy. The whole individual is sick and the *whole individual is treated* (emphasis added).[16]

The Concept of Illness

Illness is a much more inclusive term than disease and refers to the personal response of the patient to his feeling unwell. Illness rather focuses on how the *person* interprets the symptoms that one feels, how they affect one's behavior, and what one intends to do about them. E. J. Cassell states the matter quite simply: "'Illness' stands for what the patient feels when he goes to the doctor, and 'disease' for what he has on his way home from the doctor's office. Disease, then, is something an organ has; illness is something a man has."[17]

Another way to say this is that disease becomes an *illness* when "personal suffering" is involved. If a woman has a common cold—in which all the symptoms of sneezing, coughing, and personal distress are present—she may admit that she is ill. But she may not act sick. In fact, she may carry out the affairs of her daily life and avoid the sick bed at all costs.

Illness is such a personal experience that it will vary tremendously from individual to individual, from the hypochondriac to the stoic denier of pain. The *meaning* given to the experience will also vary from person to person and from culture to culture. For example, two people may experience the same disease (such as viral pneumonia) but may

---

[16]Edwin Ackerknecht, *Medicine and Ethnology: Selected Essays* (Baltimore: The Johns Hopkins Press, 1971), 25.

[17]E. J. Cassell, *The Healer's Art: A New Approach to the Doctor-Patient Relationship* (New York: Lippencott, 1985), 47 ff.

interpret the meaning of the experience quite distinctly. One person might focus her attention on the feeling of discomfort and self-pity whereas another might spiritualize the experience and believe that she is receiving spiritual benefits from her illness. According to Renee Fox, the meanings that are given to a patient's episode of ill-health are "profoundly influenced by his social and cultural background as well as by his personality traits."[18]

On the other hand, illness may exist when no disease is present. If an individual suffers mental and emotional distress, whether from the stresses of life or from an addiction that has gained mastery over the person, we can justifiably call this an "illness." Such a phenomenon happens much more frequently than we care to admit. Physicians are often called upon to treat people who complain of an illness but have *no* disease.

When people become ill, they seek explanations for the impairment of their well-being. They try as best they can to organize their illness into a meaningful experience that they can make sense of. One way of looking at this process is provided by Helman. He suggests that the following questions are typical that people ask themselves in their illness.[19] (1) *What has happened?* (2) *Why has it happened?* (3) *Why has it happened to me?* (4) *Why now?* (5) *What would happen if nothing were done about it?* (6) *What should I do about it?* In other words, illness forces a person to develop some kind of response to the disease or to the emotional upsetment that he now faces. A plan or medical strategy must be devised if the person is to cope with the illness.

This is why a person is very vulnerable during an illness; in some situations we might even say "critical." Depending on the personal situation of the individual, illness may open her up to an even worse scenario if she cannot deal with her distress satisfactorily. Consider a woman who has recently divorced. Because she may feel a deep sense of emotional pain as well as fear about her future, she is experiencing illness. If she cannot adequately cope with her situation, her illness will worsen and she may become a prime candidate for a psycho-somatic disease.[20]

---

[18]Quoted in Helman, op. cit., 69.

[19]Ibid., 72.

[20]Christopher Peterson and Martin Seligman, "Explanatory Style and Illness," *Journal of Personality* 55, no. 2 (June 1987). *"We tentatively conclude that passivity,*

We should not be surprised that *religion* plays a dominant role in illness. For it is during "illness" that the total needs of the person are most apparent. Not only does religion provide meaning for the sufferer but it may very well influence the outcome of the illness itself. Unlike science, religion offers explanations that personalize the illness experience and relate the person to the larger cosmos. The extraordinary success of Rabbi Harold Kushner's book, *When Bad Things Happen to Good People*, gives credence to the fact that the domain of the spirit is very important to people in illness episodes. Until recently, the Western medical tradition has tended to de-emphasize the relationship of illness, healing, and the spiritual life. However, in traditional societies, this relationship has always been a primary concern.

The Concept of Sickness

Sickness is very much like illness in that it involves the personal behavior of the patient and many of the meanings that illness brings. The key distinction is that sickness also involves a change in social status. Sickness means that the individual is perceived by others as being ill and that provisions are being made to restore that person to health. Usually this refers to the adoption of the "sick role."

The onset of disease and illness does not necessarily mean that a person will progress into what we call sickness or the sick role. During the course of an illness, a person may adjust his activities, take medications, and present his distress in manifold ways. Medical sociologists describe these sequential actions as *illness behavior*, the way a person perceives and acts upon the symptoms which he recognizes as causing pain and malfunction. For example, a man might awaken with a sore throat and take some aspirin or even call for a doctor. But we do not refer to this as sick role behavior. It is only when illness is defined as sufficiently serious to remove a person from his normal roles and alter the role behavior of those around him that a person assumes the sick role.

As Talcott Parsons describes it, the *sick role* is a social role in which a patient has certain rights and obligations:

---

pessimism, and low morale foreshadow disease and death, although the process by which this occurs is unclear."

One of the rights accorded to him is to be excused from normal duties. . . . Moreover, the sick person is not expected to recover without help; that is, it is appropriate in this situation that one has a claim upon others for assistance and care. . . . The sick role also imposes certain obligations on the sick person. . . . The normal state of being well means that being ill is undesirable, and, therefore, one is obliged to want to get well as soon as possible. Related to this is the obligation to seek competent technical help and cooperate in the process of getting well.[21]

Having said this, we need to recognize that not all people who "act sick" actually have a disease or even feel ill. Hypochondria can become a purposeful strategy that people use to avoid participation in the realities of life. Because sickness excuses a person from social responsibility, sickness may actually be enjoyed by some. There are situations in which people may say they "feel ill" but evince no demonstrable disease, a malady known as "medical students' disease." This is a form of hypochondria believed to afflict 70% of medical students who, because they learn about various diseases, frequently imagine that they have them and develop typical symptoms and signs.[22]

On the other hand, the sick role can produce a stigma of *shame* in certain cultural contexts. In the Old Testament, for example, lepers had to announce their presence by crying out, "Unclean! Unclean!" American culture, as do other societies, tends to look down on those who are victims of "shame diseases" which may include alcoholism, AIDS, syphilis, and gonorrhea. Among certain American Indian tribes, cultural sanctions regarding disease are so strong that an individual may not admit that he is sick. Instances can be cited in which a person has so disguised his pain by denying the sick role that he is literally at death's door before treatment is allowed.

What is important in adopting the sick role is how the illness is presented to the social group and how they respond to it. It appears that each culture has its own "language of distress" and this can vary widely from culture to culture.

Research by anthropologists among various ethnic groups reveals the wide variety of illness behavior that is shaped by culture. Mark Zborowski studied patients in a veteran's hospital in New York City

[21]Coe, op. cit., 101-102. This discussion of the sick role was adapted from Talcott Parsons, *The Social System* (New York: Free Press, 1951), chapter 10.

[22]Helman, op. cit., 87.

and found that Italians and Jews were much more emotional in their responses to pain than were Irish and Old Americans.[23] He concluded that Italian and Jewish cultures "allow for free expression of feelings and emotions by words, sounds, and gestures; both the Italians and Jews feel free to talk about their pain, complain about it, and manifest their sufferings by groaning, moaning, crying, etc. . . ." In contrast, the Old Americans and Irish adopted a behavior pattern in which they virtually denied the pain or responded to it with a stiff upper lip.

This discussion of the concepts of disease, illness, and sickness has really been a discussion of the multidimensional aspects of disease. Perhaps more than we care to admit, these remarks illustrate the profound sense of disorder that disease has provoked in the human condition, not to mention the challenges that face health caregivers who must deal with disease. Certainly it should be clear that at the heart of every illness experience there exists a *person* who is in pain and whose primary need is to have that pain treated wholistically.

We are at the point in the development of this theme that we need to look at the topic of health care. In their struggles with disease and its many faces, human societies have devised cultural solutions that are designed to cure and care for the sick. Medical anthropologists refer to these solutions as medical systems.

Culture and Medical Systems

Healing or *medical systems* have existed from antiquity and are found in every cultural group throughout the world. Although they are as distinct as the cultures that bear them, they do share some common features. Medical systems may seem to consist of the social interaction of the curer and the sick person, but they are more complex than this. Some medical systems involve the whole panorama of the forces of the universe in their approach to healing.

What characterizes all healing systems, however, is their common concern to meet the threat of disease and to promote health and well-being. It is how healing systems seek the restoration of order in human life that provides us with insights into the biblical approach to disease and health.

---

[23]Mark Zborowski, "Cultural Components in Response to Pain," *Journal of Social Issues* 8 (1952): 16-30.

The following definition of a wholistic medical system may be offered: *A medical system is a culture's practices, methods, and substances taken together with its beliefs, values, and traditions that enable it to deal with disease, illness, and sickness.*

A close look at this definition reveals that medical systems include more than medications, drugs, or physicians. They focus especially on an understanding of the nature of disease, how it was caused, who is assigned to care for the ill person, how the ill person is to act, the treatment that is to be followed, and what it means to be healthy.

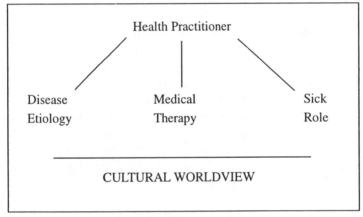

Medical System

Medical System

This definition also implies the fact that every medical system needs to be examined in the light of its own cultural context. Medical systems are products of the cultures that bear them; they make little sense without an understanding of the worldviews and belief systems that are intrinsically a part of them. Ann McElroy and Patricia Townsend put it this way:

> Anthropology has usually emphasized that health and healing are best understood in terms of a given society's system of ethnomedicine, and the "insider's view" is necessary to understand how a society defines and diagnoses disease. Western medicine, on the other hand, usually considers

disease as a clinical entity that can be diagnosed and treated while ignoring the cultural context.[24]

It is this "insider's view" that equips anthropologists, because of their unique training in cultural worldviews and patterns, to analyze every medical system on the globe. By virtue of this ethnomedical perspective, the medical systems of the Old and New Testaments can also be examined to enrich our own understanding of the timeless lessons they teach.

Medical Pluralism

Another advantage of the "insider's view" is understanding *medical pluralism*, a cultural pattern in which people participate in more than one medical system at the same time. It may surprise the reader to learn that there are many medical systems operative in the United States. Because we are a society with many subcultures and religious orientations, a profusion of healing systems make up the fabric of our diverse society. We might list a few of these systems which exist apart from modern medicine: chiropractic, homeopathy, naturopathy, folk medicine, faith healing, and various ethnic approaches to healing. Each of these healing systems has its own philosophy and its own approach to health and well-being. Some are so different from the allopathic medical model as to resist any useful comparison. But to the followers of these alternative forms of healing, these medical systems are valid purveyors of health and legitimate ways in which healing can be obtained.

World Views and Medical Systems

According to W. H. R. Rivers, who pioneered the study of medical systems cross-culturally, every medical system is based on a definite, patterned, underlying *belief* system.[25] These beliefs about disease and health, fashioned in their cultural contexts, shape the philosophy and

---

[24]Ann McElroy and Patricia Townsend, *Medical Anthropology in Ecological Perspective* (Boulder, CO: Westview Press, 1985), xvii-xviii.

[25]See the discussion of Rivers's approach in Lorna Moore, Peter Van Arsdale, JoAnn Glittenberg, and Robert Aldrich, *The Biocultural Basis of Health: Expanding Views of Medical Anthropology* (Prospect Heights, IL: Waveland Press, 1980), 194.

practice of health care in every human society. Lorna Moore and her colleagues make this point clear:

> Cultural beliefs about health and sickness serve as the foundations of all medical care. To understand why one population treats an open wound with a wad of cow dung while another uses merthiolate requires a deep understanding of the belief systems of each society. Incantations and rituals have different meanings for different groups. The diversity of cultural beliefs clearly illustrates the tremendous capabilities and adaptations of human beings . . . ecologically.[26]

But how are beliefs about sickness and health derived and why do we see such a wide variety of beliefs cross-culturally? It was Rivers's conclusion that the group's worldview was at the heart of their belief system. Rivers conceptually broke down all cultural worldviews into three variables: magical, religious, and naturalistic.

Magical Worldviews

Magical worldviews relate to beliefs about disease, illness, and sickness that result from human manipulation of the forces of the universe. Wherever magic is found, we find people using formulas and other forms of mechanical control to bring about the desired goal. Typical of magic are such phenomena as imitative and contagious magic, which describe the practice of sorcery, as well as witchcraft. The paraphernalia of magic include amulets, talismans, fetishes, images, incantations, and the like.

Magic has a long history in matters of disease and the quest for health. As an illustration of how someone could get sick through imitative magic, the Ojibwa Indians believed they could cause intense pain in a distant enemy if they made a small image of their victim and ran a needle through it. Imitative magic operates on the "law of similarity" because the image made of the victim is "similar" to the victim himself. Conversely, if a Solomon Islander wanted to get rid of fatigue, he would throw a stick or a stone over a mound where the path was steep and difficult. Throwing away the stick was a magical way of

---

[26]Ibid., 200.

"invoking the mystical connection between the small objects and human tiredness."[27]

Contagious magic relates to the "law of contagion," the belief that any part of the human body such as hair, teeth, placenta, or nail parings was magically united with the person forever. For this reason, tribal peoples in traditional societies often hide the placenta of a newborn baby for fear that an enemy might place a spell upon the baby. While in Africa I was introduced to a "twin ceremony" in which eggs were rubbed on the bodies of women who had delivered twins. Because the birth of twins was believed to be a dangerous omen that attracted evil spirits, touching the eggs to the mothers was a magical way of transferring evil from the mothers to the eggs.

It should be remembered that among magically-oriented peoples *all* misfortunes, including crop failure and famine, as well as sickness, are considered to be caused by sorcery, witchcraft, or other uses of magic. Among such tribal peoples, health practitioners are usually shamans or sorcerers who manipulate the powers of the universe for their own ends and are viewed as "doctors" with extraordinary, mystical powers.

Religious Worldviews

Religious worldviews, in contrast, suggest that the events of life, including disease, illness, and sickness, are controlled by spiritual beings or powers. Disease may be perceived to be a punishment or chastisement in which the ill person has offended the gods or spirits who inhabit the universe. Healing can only be achieved when supplication or rectified conduct have restored the imbalance of nature. Robert Anderson describes the relation between religion and sickness in this manner:

> One many speak of religion when natural events are believed to be influenced by the intervention of some higher power. The will of this high power cannot be controlled directly as with magic, but can be influenced by supplication and propitiation. In the practice of religion . . . essentially capricious deities possess the power to do as they wish. In anger, a god or a spirit may smite an offender. Conversely, the sick can hope to be cured by means of prayer and offerings. In this way, priests, rather than

---

[27]Robert Anderson, *Magic, Science, and Religion: The Aims and Achievements of Medical Anthropology* (Fort Worth, TX: Harcourt Brace College Publishers, 1996), 48.

magicians and sorcerers, serve as the society's practitioners of the sacred.[28]

Many healing systems of the world possess religious worldviews and may include spiritual powers as far ranging as a singular God, such as in the Christian worldview, to multiple gods, spirits, demons, and ghosts. Intervention by the gods in the world of humans is a major theme of religion in matters dealing with sickness and health. For example, in Africa it was believed that "the spirit" of smallpox brought epidemics to certain tribal peoples. Among the Dyaks of Borneo, an epidemic of plague was believed to be caused by evil demons. Medieval Christians in the fourteenth century were certain that the ravaging effects of the bubonic plague were a punishment for their disobedience to the Word of God.

Curing ceremonies among people with religious worldviews usually involve the whole community and center on prayers, rituals, fastings, and other supplications to restore the broken relationship between the sick person and the deity. Indeed, it has often been the case that these curing ceremonies were believed to have an wholistic effect. Healing the sick individual brought healing to the entire community as well.

Naturalistic Worldviews

In the *naturalistic worldview*, disease is viewed as being subject to natural law. People become sick because they have either voluntarily or involuntarily violated an obvious law of nature such as suffering a wound from a fall. The naturalistic view is characteristic of modern, Western medicine in that the cause of disease is believed to be the result of some pathogen—a virus, bacteria, or tumor—which has overcome the body's defenses. But naturalistic disease causation is also recognized to a certain extent in all human societies.

Rivers's conceptual approach to medical systems helps us understand how religion, disease, and health interact within a unified system. We may question Rivers's division of worldviews into neat categories—often these are blends—but we can certainly agree that medical systems are belief systems. Frequently it may be the case that magic and religion are combined within a single worldview, such as

---

[28]Ibid., 52.

with the ancient Egyptians, which we term *magico-religious*. On the other hand, religious and naturalistic beliefs may be combined together, a worldview held by the Greeks of Hippocrates' age and, to some degree, by modern-day Americans. The appropriate label for this worldview blend would be *religio-scientific*.

The concept of "naturalistic" beliefs raises the question whether native peoples actually perceive the world in terms of *supernatural* in contrast to *natural* as if these were two separate worlds (dualism) rather than a single, undivided universe. The term "supernatural" is a western, analytical concept that is used to differentiate the secular world as distinct from the spiritual world. But native peoples have no such notions of a dualistic universe; they make no distinction between the world of the spirits and the world of everyday life. Both are living realities and are dealt with as realities. For this reason George Foster has suggested the use of the term "personalistic medical systems" to refer to medical systems that focus on religio-magical causes of disease. In contrast he suggests using the term "naturalistic medical systems" to refer to medical systems that explain illness in impersonal, systemic terms. Foster goes on to say:

> Personalistic and naturalistic etiological systems are, of course, not mutually exclusive. Peoples who invoke personalistic causes to explain most illnesses usually recognize some natural, or chance, causes. And peoples for whom naturalistic causes predominate almost invariably explain some illness as due to witchcraft or the evil eyes. Yet in spite of much overlap, most people seem committed to one or the other of these explanatory principles to account for most illness.[29]

Ecological Models

More recently, medical anthropologists have been using an *ecological* model in which cultural beliefs about disease are examined in relation to its environment and social system. This approach has added a lot of useful information to our understanding of disease, illness, and sickness. By means of this model, the investigator can focus on the particular misfortunes or diseases of a society and observe how these people are coping in their situation. In other words, the beliefs about disease that a particular culture possesses are shaped by the environment in which they live—whether the tropics, urban, rural

---

[29]Foster and Anderson, op. cit., 54.

or otherwise—as well as by social sanctions that inform members how to cope in their culture.

According to some scholars, each type of society throughout history has had distinctive forms of sickness.[30] As we will observe in chapter two, "skin diseases" are frequently mentioned in the Old Testament. Literature from the Middle Ages dwells to a large extent on the plagues and epidemics that cast such a dark shadow on these societies. During the early modern period, infectious diseases, including smallpox, measles, and influenza, were the dreaded killers of human life; they appear prominently in the novels and stories of the age. It does not surprise us that in contemporary America, heart disease and cancer inspire the greatest fear. Movie actor John Wayne, before he finally succumbed to cancer, once said to the American public: "I beat the big C." In sum, disease patterns in themselves can shape how a culture defines sickness as well as the beliefs they hold about well-being and health.

The Functions of Medical Systems

All medical systems have a single, overriding function as their goal: to *restore the sick person to health*. Whether you or I would find ourselves in the emergency ward at a large hospital in Philadelphia or being treated by a folk doctor in the Appalachian mountains, the objective would be the same. The test of any medical system is that the sick person is made well, if at all possible.

Nevertheless, medical systems provide a number of other functions which may not be so obvious but which are essential for the well-being of the patient as well as for the culture of which he is a part. Many of these functions could be described at length, but we will limit our discussion to the most important ones.

Medical Systems Offer a Theory of Disease

A major function of any medical system is to provide an explanation for how an illness or disease came to exist. It also supplies a reason why a particular patient fell ill, and it often speaks to the social phenomenon of illness, or sickness. In other words, disease theories are *explanatory models* that deal with causality (sometimes called etiology)

---

[30]Ibid., 199-200.

and include the explanations given by people to account for the loss of health. All disease theories are rational and logical even though there may be disagreement about the assumptions of the theory. According to Margaret Clarke:

> They are broadly gauged systems of concepts about nature of illness and its place in human existence. For example, they explain what disease is, how it comes about, why it exists, what can prevent it or control it or cure it, and why it attacks some people and not others. Human beings seem to have a need to provide explanations for themselves of various kinds of good and ill that befall them.[31]

Western people are familiar with a scientific understanding of disease causation in which disease is explained naturalistically—for example, as a failure of the body's immunological defenses against pathogenic agents. In other cultures, by contrast, causality of disease may be explained as due to the intervention of a spiritual being who brings punishment to the victim. In much of Africa disease causation is attributed to ancestor spirits who, because they have been neglected or offended, take out their vengeance on tribal clan members.

We mention in passing that disease theories in the ancient world, and in many traditional societies today, focused heavily on religio-magical explanations of which the following are the most common: (1) soul loss; (2) breach of taboo; (3) spirit possession; (4) disease-object intrusion; and (5) sorcery.[32] Thus, among the Navaho of Arizona, witchcraft is cited as the major cause of an illness. The assumptive world of the Navaho is far different from the scientific world of the West. But we cannot argue with the rationality or logic of their beliefs. If the assumptive world includes magical powers that bring evil, then it is logical, given such a worldview, that witchcraft can cause disease.

It is sometimes helpful to understand disease theory in terms of multiple levels of causation. The two principal levels of causality that are addressed by explanatory models are:

---

[31]M. Margaret Clark, "Cultural Context of Medical Practice," *The Western Journal of Medicine* vol. 139, no. 6 (December 1983): 4.

[32]See the discussion in Moore et al., op. cit., pp. 194-95 and 201-11. These five disease causation concepts, which have worldwide distribution, were identified by Forrest Clements in his pioneering work in 1932.

(1) immediate causes: refers to the immediate, observable reason for the disease. Examples of such causes are pathogens, malignancies, and wounds. Immediate causes explain *how* a person becomes ill.

(2) ultimate causes: refers to the meaning and purpose behind the illness. Examples of such causes are genetic susceptibility, stress, "bad luck," magic, spirit beings, or "God's will." Ultimate causes explain *why* a person becomes ill.[33]

The distinction between these two levels of causation is often the difference between a doctor's explanation for a disease and a patient's explanation. Usually when a patient asks a doctor *why* he is ill, he receives an answer about *how* he became ill or the explanation of the disease. Modern medicine is uncomfortable with ultimate causes and almost always will skirt the question or seek to persuade the patient that the question cannot be answered. In the Western world, ultimate causes are often turned over to religion and philosophy because they are perceived as being nonscientific issues.

A friend of mine, suffering from glaucoma, knew all the medical reasons for his disease and how the condition was slowly deteriorating his vision. Nevertheless, in his conversation with me, he voiced a need to know "why" he was suffering from this eye disease since he neither smoked nor drank, and as he reminded me—he was a deeply spiritual person who took his faith seriously.

Members of most non-Western societies are usually not satisfied with explanations of disease that focus only on immediate causes. "They want to know *why* in one child in the same family as another child—eating the same food, sleeping in the same room—leukemia developed, and did not in the sibling."[34] It is this area of ultimate causes for which most of the so-called folk systems of medicine or ethnomedicine provide explanations.

Because different medical systems are directed to different levels of causality, we are not surprised to see the phenomenon of "medical pluralism." A family may bring a sick member to the doctor's office for treatment of the "immediate cause" and at the same time will consult a spiritual healer to deal with the "ultimate cause." Situations such as these happen frequently on the mission field where natives attend the

---

[33]Clark, op. cit., 4.

[34]Ibid., 4.

missionary clinic for care of the immediate symptoms but turn to their old native religion for answers to the ultimate cause.[35]

The importance of disease theory as one of the major functions of healing systems cannot be minimized. Disease theory provides meaning to the person who suffers, putting the person's illness into perspective. It answers the major questions that always seem to surface when illness strikes. Such questions as—"what did I do to deserve this malady?" or "why am I in such pain?"—are common to people of all cultures. The desire to know the cause or reason of the suffering is not so much for intellectual information as it is for emotional catharsis.

Dealing with a serious disease is almost always a heart-wrenching, existential drama. The more meaning that can be provided to the sufferer at such a vulnerable time can literally be life-saving. People deal much better with the known than the unknown. Disease theory fulfills this basic function within medical systems. It offers a logical and rational explanation for the presence of disease, and enhances knowledge about sickness and illness also.

Medical Systems Provide Health Care

A second major function of medical systems involves specific beliefs about how to organize care for sick people and use the knowledge of disease to assist patients who are ill. The delivery of health care usually includes a number of people in order to mobilize all the possible resources of the culture for healing. At the very minimum this will consist of the curer and the patient.

We need to understand that disease threatens not only the life of the sufferer but it also affects the social and economic life of the group of which he is a part. As much as we would like to believe that all health care is done for altruistic or humanitarian reasons, the survival of the community is also an important part of the equation. In addition to reasons of human compassion, it makes sense to save the victim in order to insure the continuation of the community. The most frequent human response to disease has been to treat the ill person with whatever medications have been found to be effective. The only other

---

[35]Scharlemann, op. cit., 79-80. Scharlemann takes issue with medical mission work that separates religion and medicine. Medical systems that form an undivided whole in regard to religion and medicine usually do not have problems with medical pluralism because they handle both immediate and ultimate causes of illness.

alternative—to abandon the sick person for the safety of the group—has only been utilized during outbreaks of epidemics, famine, or war.

The health care provided by a culture is logically related to the disease theory. There will always be a strong concordance between the explanation for the disease and the set of beliefs about how the disease should be treated. For example, it is commonly believed by American Indians that sickness is a consequence of breaking a cultural taboo. The therapy follows logically: the victim must confess his sin before the tribal community in addition to a purification ceremony. This is why patients of a native health practitioner usually accept the diagnosis of their ailments and will voluntarily take the medications he advises.

Health care in all cultures involves an interaction between the health practitioner and the patient. In most cultures, certain persons are set aside as having expertise in the "healing arts" and have received training from another health practitioner. Indeed, the image of the "doctor" is often characterized as a position of power because he or she is the socially legitimated person to whom decisions in illness and disease are sanctioned. The difference in non-Western societies is that the health practitioner usually assumes more roles than the doctor in Western countries. Frequently the health practitioner is a "priest" figure as well as a dispenser of medications, the focus of his treatment aimed at the whole person rather than simply the medical symptoms of the disease.

Arthur Kleinman has suggested that in complex societies, there are three overlapping sectors of health care: (1) the *popular* sector, (2) the *folk* sector, and (3) the *professional* sector.[36] Each of these sectors of health care has its own explanation for treating ill-health as well as defining who the healer is and how healer and patient should interact in their therapeutic encounter.

The *popular* sector of health care is where ill-health is first recognized and where health activities on behalf of the ill person are initiated. Within this sector, the main area in which primary health care is applied is the "family" and within the family, the main providers of health care are *women*, usually mothers or grandmothers.[37] In addition to the family, medical advice is solicited by ill people from a whole host of other sources including paramedical professions (nurses,

[36]Arthur Kleinman, *Patients and Healers in the Context of Culture* (Berkeley: University of California Press, 1980), chapters 2 and 3.

[37]Helman, op. cit., 43-44.

pharmacists), spouses of doctors, self-help groups, and even hairdressers. It is estimated that 70-90% of health care takes place within the popular sector, in both Western and non-Western societies.

The *folk* sector involves healers who participate in either sacred or secular healing activities and depend on their own reputations to attract clients. While members of neither the professional nor popular sectors, they occupy an intermediate position in complex societies. In American culture, folk healers include spiritual healers, Christian Science readers, "faith healers," root doctors, Granny women, herb doctors, spiritualists, acupuncturists, and the like. The *shaman*, a traditional healer who enters trances and masters spirits, is a major folk healer in many cultures. Obviously, the relationship between folk and professional healers tends to be marked by mutual suspicion and, at times, open hostility.

In the *professional* sector, we refer to those health practitioners who are legitimated by their own societies and are regarded as members of an approved profession. In the United States, professional health care that is legally sanctioned is modern scientific medicine or allopathic medicine. This includes not only physicians of various specialties but also other recognized paramedical professions such as nurses, physiotherapists, occupational therapists, and medical social workers. The dominant symbol of the professional sector is the hospital, which has a social structure all its own and in which the power of the profession is at its greatest; to a lesser degree this also includes clinics and the offices of private practitioners.

Health care in all human societies involves both caring and curing. It is not enough to simply dispense medications or to organize treatments for the patient. The sick person must also be *cared for*. That is, the needs of the individual in the sick role require the care and energy of others who are concerned about the patient. In any discussion of human illness, we need to give more attention to the crucial roles of those who perform "morale" and support services for the sick. In Western culture, these services are often the contribution of clergy, family, friends, and self-help groups. In non-Western cultures, the caring and curing roles are frequently combined and involve a healing community who participate with the sick person in the healing ceremonies. This provides a powerful affirmation of the sick person as Jerome Frank makes clear:

> Many rituals have an altruistic quality. All the participants try to help the patient by performing parts of the ritual, interceding for him with the powers he has presumably offended, or defending the patient to them. . . . The performance of services to others may help to counteract the patient's morbid self-absorption and enhance his sense of self-worth by demonstrating that he can still be of use to them.[38]

Medical Systems Provide Preventive and Curative Modalities

Medicine, no matter what the culture, will always be a two-sided phenomenon. It is necessary to examine health care from the point of view of *preventive medicine* as well as from the perspective of *curative medicine*. Preventive medicine is those health activities and strategies that are designed to ward off and prevent the onset of disease. Conversely, medications and therapies designed to cure persons of those diseases they currently are suffering are known as curative medicine. Medical systems in all cultures include aspects of both; however, it is more frequently the case that one of these two modalities will be more emphasized in a cultural group than the other.

Non-Western societies lack a formal institution known as public health, which may lead some to conclude that such cultural groups lack preventive medicine. But among such traditional peoples, preventive medicine consists of personal acts and culturally sanctioned behavior that are designed to avoid illness.[39] If people believe that disease is sent by angry gods or resentful ancestors, the proper procedure is to observe the social taboos and ceremonies that placate these spiritual beings.

The Middle East has long favored preventive medicine at the expense of curative medicine, a phenomenon that is at the heart of the Old Testament narratives. Even today visitors to Arab countries will immediately notice the assortment of amulets and talismans worn as protection against the presence of evil powers. Those who fear that babies will become ill because of the envious glance of a barren woman will place amulets around the infant's neck, wrist, or waist to ward off the "evil eye." Wherever there is a strong belief in sorcery, witchcraft, or spirit-possession, we can reliably predict an emphasis on prevention. Beliefs of this nature have wide distribution, especially in Latin America. The hex signs painted on Pennsylvania Dutch barns or the use

---

[38]Jerome Frank, *Persuasion and Healing* (New York: Schocken Books, 1969), 51.

[39]Foster and Anderson, op. cit., 41.

of the Christian cross as a symbol of protection are other examples of preventive medicine.

Curative medicine is illustrated by the use of medications and prescribed therapy known as *materia medica*. Most often these medications are herbs, taken from roots and plants, that are believed to be effective cures of certain diseases or symptoms of illness. In Africa and South America we encounter a rich tradition of herbal medicine, many of these herbs having become, over time, some of the basic medications now popularly used in modern medicine. The health practitioner of the Mbaki tribe in Africa personally escorted the author through the jungle, collecting a variety of plants designed to cure particular maladies including one for snakebite and another for measles. I was also introduced to the herbal medicines of the Cuna Indians of Panama by a venerable folk doctor of the tribe who informed me that the medicines he had collected had no power until "sung over" with a healing prayer.

Common wisdom may draw the conclusion that curative medicine is the mainstay of modern American health care. But curative medicine, no matter how effective the "magic bullets" against infectious diseases, cannot adequately explain the relatively high standard of health in America. Since the beginning of this century, preventive medicine has probably contributed far more than curative medicine toward optimum health care in the United States. The sanitary disposal of sewage and waste, minimum standards for potable water, quarantines, food and drug restrictions, and immunizations of children have all spared the United States the ravage of disease that afflicts developing countries. And the emphasis on preventive medicine has grown even stronger with the success of the wellness movement in encouraging people to exercise more, to restrain from smoking, and to be more selective in their diets. The economic motive also looms large in any discussion of preventive medicine. As so many have discovered, it is a lot less expensive to prevent a disease than to endure the cost of curing it.

Medical Systems Shape and Control Human Behavior

Little appreciated by most people is the fact that health, disease, and illness can have a profound effect that goes far beyond an individual's discomfort. There are sociocultural correlates that are involved in most illness episodes, all of which demonstrates that sickness is essentially a *social event*.

For example, the woman who always comes down with an illness during a family crisis is perhaps calling attention to her own insecurities; in such a manner she can manipulate members in her family to behave in appropriate ways. As we are all aware, the alcoholic's disease is far-reaching. It touches numerous people and actually generates the spread of the disease and its consequences to a multitude of victims.

More specifically, medical systems themselves have the power to shape the behavior of people in that they express the moral norms of society. Among the Ojibwa Indians of central Canada, food is scarce and there are strong cultural norms to share one's food with others. Those who refuse to share their food know the consequences: they are threatened with illness by means of witchcraft. In many traditional societies, fear of sickness from angry gods or tutelary spirits is enough to insure that most people hue the line in regard to the mores of their cultural group.

Among peoples of Latin America a folk disease known as *bilis*, represented by a jaundiced condition, is believed to result from the expression of anger; thus, cultural beliefs can have an inhibiting influence on how people behave. There are some who are convinced that the growing incidence of AIDS has already begun to shape the sexual practices of many Americans in a more conservative manner. In this case, the fear of the disease itself can intensify cultural norms about appropriate sexual behavior.

One of the values of healing rituals, as these are observed in non-Western cultures, is that they illustrate the recognition that illness is a public affair, not simply a private interaction between doctor and patient. Foster and Anderson raise a provocative issue about the practice of medicine that merits our attention:

> In many non-Western societies. . . . illness is marked by social dimensions not normally felt to be a part of scientific etiologies. Patients may have fallen out of harmony with their natural and social environments, and their illnesses are often interpreted as reflecting stress or tears in the social fabric. The purpose of curing therefore goes well beyond the limited goal of restoring the sick person to health; it *constitutes social therapy for the entire group*, reassuring all onlookers that the interpersonal stresses that have led to illness are being healed (emphasis added).[40]

---

[40]Ibid., 116.

Toward the Restoration of Order

Disease personifies a profound disorder in the world and in the life of humans who live in this world. Throughout this chapter we have attempted to describe the pervasive ways in which disease has distorted our human nature. There is no sphere of life—including human relationships, cultural patterns, ecological relationships, and social institutions—in which disease has not brought confusion and deformity.

If health is to be achieved, it is obvious that order must be restored. The meaning of health implies an orderliness to the processes of life and a purposiveness within the created order. As we have seen, cultural medical systems have provided a partial answer to this quest for order. In many ways, healing systems have been successful in dealing with the challenge of disease. Curing and caring have been a dominant feature of human social life from the beginning of time.

But these successes can only be characterized as partial. At their best they represent a renewal of order; they are certainly not a complete restoration. The question can be asked: Is there one medical system that can even supply most of the needs of the sick person, a healing system designed to bring the optimum of health and wholeness to human sufferers?

Many thought that modern medical science was such a medical system. Its technological success over previously lethal pathogens seemed to announce a new age in which disease would be conquered forever. But then disappointment after disappointment ensued. Not only was medical science unsuccessful against diseases that originated in the human spirit, the chronic diseases that defied biochemistry. It also displayed vulnerability to new diseases for which there seemed to be no solution. Even medical optimist and essayist Lewis Thomas had to admit that AIDS was a grim challenge:

> It comes as something of a surprise, even a shock, to realize that we are faced by a brand-new infectious disease about which we understand so little and can therefore *do* so little. Modern medicine has left in the public mind the conviction that we know almost everything about everything. This is as good a time as any to amend the impression.[41]

---

[41]Lewis Thomas, *The Fragile Species* (New York: Macmillan, 1992), 44.

Other members of the medical establishment went much further than Thomas and believed that the root problem of medical science was that it offered only a partial answer. Unlike non-Western medical systems that treated the whole person, modern medicine seemed ill-equipped to deal with the deeper problem of "illness" and meaning. Patients were unhappy that their personhood was so often violated in the treatment of the disease while the core causes of their illness were left untended. Many doctors felt that medicine needed a new approach, an approach that dealt seriously with the individual's *religious* needs. Typical of books written by Christian doctors is this statement:

> I believe that the curative, health-giving power of wholesome religion is being sadly neglected. My medical studies and practice, and my religious experience, both confirm me in the conviction of the importance of religion for healthy living, for the cure of the sick, and for the prevention of much suffering.[42]

There is a flurry of activity today to extend the model of medicine to include the domain of the mind as well as the spirit. Because of research in the field of psychosomatic medicine, psychology and psychotherapy are joining hands with medical science in the battle against disease. The popularity of the holistic health model has made it possible to talk seriously about the spiritual health needs of the person. Complementary medicine is pushing the boundaries even further into a deeper understanding of the unitary needs of the person.

Nevertheless, we need to return to the theme of disease as disorder. According to the Scriptures, there is another solution that should be explored. If the emergence of disease, illness, and sickness as disorder began because of human rebellion against the God of creation, then it will be necessary to examine the biblical solution of that disorder.

That is essentially the quest of this book. It is our task now to look closely at the biblical materials and to examine how the Old and New Testaments propose a restoration of order.

---

[42]James Van Buskirk, M.D., *Religion, Healing & Health* (New York: Macmillan, 1952), 1.

Chapter Two

Health and Illness in the Old Testament

No Doctors in Israel

F ew of us would have been happy with the medical services in ancient Israel. Personalized medical care, as we currently understand that term, was almost nonexistent among the Hebrews. No doctors or professional health care workers would have been available to assist us with our medical needs.[1] At the best there would have been only local folk healers or home remedies to call upon at the onset of illness.

If professional doctors were available in ancient Israel, the Old Testament makes scant mention of this fact.[2] Nor do doctors appear to be legitimated sources of healing. This comes much later in Israel's history. The physician is described favorably as a "creation" of God in the apocryphal book of Ecclesiasticus. But this occurs long after Israel had been thoroughly influenced by Hellenistic culture and Greek medicine.[3]

In almost every culture, certain designated persons are selected to fulfill the role of the healing practitioner. Such a practitioner might be represented as a shaman, a folk doctor, a *curandéro*, a member of a medicine society, or a licensed physician as is the case in the United States. Only on the rarest of occasions do anthropologists locate a

---

[1]Hans Walter Wolff, *Anthropology of the Old Testament* (Philadelphia: Fortress Press, 1974), 146. *"There is no clear evidence in the Old Testament for the existence of an actual professional group of doctors in Israel."*

[2]The Hebrew word for physician is *ropé*, a reference to "one who sews together or repairs." We almost never see this term in the context of healing activity in the Old Testament. One of the exceptions is Jeremiah's plaintive cry, *"Is there no balm in Gilead? Is there no physician there?"* (Jeremiah 8:22)

[3]Ecclesiasticus was written in the second century B.C. In chapter 38:1-15, the physician is described in favorable terms, e.g., *"Honour the physician with the honour due him, according to your need of him, for God has given to him, too, his lot; for healing comes from the Most High"* (v. 1).

culture in which no practitioner of the healing arts resides. The Old Testament surprises us in that no distinct healer is set apart for this task. Priests are mentioned in regard to skin diseases, but their professional relationship to the sick person was to determine his cleanliness according to Levitical law, not to engage in any healing activity (Lev. 13:1-46).

If the lack of professional healers in Israel is distressing, we discover very little healing activity or *materia medica* cited in the Old Testament. Some notations of healing are referred to in the later prophets such as applying oil to wounds or wrapping wounds with bandages (Isa. 1:6, Ezek. 30:21; 34:4; Hos. 6:1). Perhaps the only true prescription worthy of mention is the advice of Isaiah to King Hezekiah to wrap his boil in a poultice of figs (Isa. 38:21). There are no references to herbs or prescription drugs for internal pathologies throughout the corpus of the Old Testament. Surgery as a medical art is noticeably absent in all the narratives. One reasonable explanation for this is that the Hebrews were ignorant of the anatomy of the body because they were forbidden to touch corpses.[4]

An anthropological survey of the Old Testament Hebrews suggests the following conclusion. Here is a culture in which little emphasis on medical healing is to be found, at least from the viewpoint of comparative medical systems. But we should not presume that this indicates a lack of interest in health. On the contrary, abundant evidences of the virtues of health and well-being are demonstrated throughout the Old Testament. However, the importance of healing as an art, or even as a science, among the Hebrews is certainly not a cultural priority. The absence of legitimated health practitioners and the few accounts of medications seem to describe a society that approached health and healing in other ways than is traditionally the norm.

A major purpose of this chapter will be to describe how Israel approached the problem of disease, illness, and sickness and, in doing so, to reveal the unique nature of their health system. That Israel was distinctive among all the nations of the Near East in its approach to health—Yahweh Himself was a Healer without peer—will emerge as a dominant theme in the Old Testament. Before engaging in this inquiry, however, we need to understand how other cultures in the ancient Near East practiced the art and science of medicine.

---

[4]Wolff, op. cit., 147

The Egyptian and Mesopotamian Health Systems

In contrast to Israel, Egypt and Mesopotamia had thriving medical systems and were world leaders in their medical approach to the problem of disease. As early as 1500 B.C. both of these neighbors of Israel possessed legitimated physicians and surgeons whose medical practices encompassed diagnostic as well as prescriptive dimensions of treatment.

The Egyptian and Mesopotamian medical systems can be described as "personalistic medical systems," using Foster's terminology, because of their heavy reliance on magico-religious techniques. But there was also a strong emphasis on empirical and rational medical treatment in their medical systems. Modern historical research reveals that more than a few of their therapeutic techniques were sound and medically effective. In the interest of objectivity, we need to examine some of the positive contributions of Egyptian and Mesopotamian medicine.

Egyptian therapy, for example, included the ability to repair fractures, set dislocations, and to cauterize wounds.[5] Their doctors had learned the effective use of myrrh and other resins as a healing balm for sores and wounds of the skin. Egyptian ingenuity had even created a bandage that adhered to the skin, a prototype of our modern Band-Aids. We might also mention that Egyptian physicians were superior diagnosticians. They would carefully observe the patient's face, eyes, and general body condition. It was standard procedure to inspect all wounds and to probe with the finger. The Egyptian physician, in fact, would question the sufferer as to his symptoms and pains much as a modern doctor would proceed.[6]

Dr. Guido Majno has done extensive research on the ancient medications of the Egyptians and Mesopotamians and has concluded that many of their therapies for wounds were effective then and would be effective today.[7] In laboratory tests of herbs used in Egyptian ointments, he has verified the presence of anti-bacterial agents. A

---

[5]Guido Majno, *The Healing Hand: Man and Wound in the Ancient World* (Cambridge, MA: Harvard University Press, 1975), 92 ff.

[6]Henry Sigerist, *A History of Medicine I: Primitive and Archaic Medicine* (New York: Oxford University Press, 1967), 326-27. A typical examination also included smelling the patient and observing the fluids and other material that came out of the body.

[7]Majno, op. cit., 113.

grease-honey mixture that inhibits the growth of bacteria was popularly used as a salve. The medical practitioners of ancient Egypt even made use of copper on infectious wounds, now known to be effective against streptococci bacteria.

Mesopotamian physicians were also skilled in their approach to medical therapy, although they were probably not as advanced in certain areas of medicine as the Egyptians. One of their standard treatments was the use of sesame oil as a dressing on wounds which, according to modern tests, rapidly kills staphylococci bacteria. Its counterpart among the Hebrews was olive oil. Indeed, in the ancient Near East olive and sesame oil constituted a basic need of life; besides its medicinal qualities, oil was the major source of light and was a spiritual symbol in anointing ceremonies, a fact widely reported in the Old Testament. Following is a description of a surgical dressing procedure in ancient Mesopotamia:

> Wash a fine linen in water, soak it in oil, and put it on the wound. Bray powder of acacia and ammonia salt, and put it on the wound; let the dressing stand for three days . . . and knot a bandage over it. Leave the dressing three more days. . . . Thus continue until healing ensues.[8]

In passing, we should mention that Egyptian physicians were skilled in surgery and displayed an extensive knowledge of human anatomy, most likely due to their mastery of embalming techniques. We remember that Egyptian doctors embalmed Joseph at his death (Gen. 50:26). Of all the legacies that Egypt has passed down to modern medicine, the physician's *prescription* is probably the best known. We still write prescriptions in the style and form developed millennia ago in ancient Egypt.[9]

It is worth noting that Egyptian physicians were world famous and other nations coveted their services. Cyrus and Darius, kings of Persia, surrounded themselves with Egyptian doctors. Even the *Odyssey* speaks of their renowned reputation in the ancient world: "In medical knowledge the Egyptian leaves the rest of the world behind."[10]

A word of clarification is necessary here as we introduce the subject of doctors and health practitioners. A variety of healers

---

[8]Ibid., 52.

[9]Sigerist, op. cit., 337.

[10]Ibid., 325.

abounded in these two nations of Egypt and Mesopotamia, not all being doctors in the sense of the empirical medicine we have been describing thus far. Whereas some healers represented a more empirical approach to healing, other healers were more involved with religio-magical elements of the universe. But *all* healers were products of the magico-religious worldview that was imbedded deep within these ancient cultures. In Egypt, for example, physician/healers were separated from priest/healers and also from magician/healers although each of these systems overlapped with each other. A patient would proceed from one healer to another depending upon the nature, severity, and cause of the disease. In contrast, Mesopotamia presented a more unitary system. All healers were members of the priesthood, including physicians and surgeons. One order of priests were exorcists/magicians whereas another order of priests were physicians who dispensed drugs and performed operations. In both Egypt and Mesopotamia, physicians were ranked in hierarchical order according to their craft and were rewarded for their services.

The *materia medica* of both the Egyptian and Mesopotamian medical systems included medications for internal and external ailments. Drugs were the major therapeutic agents in their respective medical kits and, in Egypt, were doled out in exact measurements even as in modern pharmacology. The composition of these drugs included substances taken from plants, animals, and minerals, and grinding them into a potion of beer or wine; sometimes they fashioned them into the form of a pill made of bread dough. The Egyptian pharmacy alone could boast an inventory of almost 700 drugs.[11] There is also evidence that Egyptian doctors experimented with rectal and vaginal suppositories and practiced dentistry by means of a pharmacological treatment of the gums.

In assessing the general effectiveness of Egyptian and Mesopotamian medicine, we need to be cautious about drawing enthusiastic conclusions. Not all the therapies they offered, especially their drugs for internal maladies, were as medically valid as their sheer quantity seems to suggest. The eminent medical historian Henry Sigerist states the matter well:

> Many, perhaps the majority, of Egyptian drugs used had no perceptible effect according to modern pharmacological standards. They

---

[11]Majno, op. cit., 108.

became a part of the *materia medica* and remained part of it for thousands of years for magic reasons. In many instances this is readily apparent . . . (for example) a recipe in which blood from a raven was used to prevent hair from becoming grey too soon. This was a simple case of sympathetic magic. Such a system, however, was able to include a great amount of sound empirical knowledge.[12]

In both Egypt and Mesopotamia, the use of drugs was as much for symbolic religio-magical purposes as for medicinal purposes. Thus, in Egypt, to protect a child from threatening demons, the physician would prescribe a drug mixed with herbs, garlic, and honey which the child would then consume. In ancient Akkadia doctors would prescribe boiling cow dung in water as a plaster to be placed on a head filled with sores. The logic was to cause the demons, who had brought the sores, to be so revolted by the dung they would leave.

What is significant about these medical systems is that, however advanced they may appear in some of their empirical-rational techniques, they were laced with *magico-religious assumptions*. We need to examine this worldview of magic and religion if we are to objectively evaluate the total medical orientation of Egypt and Mesopotamia.

Magico-Religious Medical Practices

To properly assess the medical systems of the ancient Near East, an introduction into their worldview is necessary. This was a cosmology in which people believed that the universe was filled with gods, demons, and ghosts, some benevolent and some malevolent. Because humans were vulnerable to their powers, they tried, as best possible, to maneuver themselves through life while keeping on good terms with these supernatural beings. From the viewpoint of religion, they sought to supplicate the gods to be favorable and to grant them health and prosperity. From the viewpoint of magic, they sought to manipulate and control the sinister powers of demons and ghosts.

In such a worldview, diseases were believed to be caused by various evil spirits, demons, or ghosts who were offended in some manner by an individual's behavior. Disease might also be sent by a

---

[12]Ibid., 284. Compare also the remarks of Majno (ibid., 108) who says: "*Next to nothing is known about the effectiveness of ancient drugs; and even when the drug is known, experimental studies are almost nil.*"

god or goddess or even by sorcery from another person. Whatever the source of this malady, however, the result in the mind of the sufferer was that no healing could begin unless the god was reconciled or the demon was cast out.

Basically the magico-religious approach of the Egyptians and Mesopotamian medical systems was focused on handling two problems. First, they sought to deal with the physical symptoms of the disease by using naturalistic medical treatments. Secondly, they sought to solve the ultimate cause of the disease by using magic and/or religion. Frequently divination was employed to locate the ultimate cause. If magical power was considered to have caused the disease, then it was reasoned that magical power must remove it. For this reason their medical books prescribed incantations, magical charms, and invocations to healing deities as the necessary means to drive out the demons of disease. The conventional belief of the times dictated that, unless the incantation was said perfectly, none of the medical treatments would be effective.

In Egypt, for example, it was commonly believed that an evil spirit or ghost could be discharged from the sick person through certain prescribed incantations. The magician would purify the patient, speak some magic words, perform a rite, and the therapy was complete. Sometimes this included a magic spell being placed on a linen or bead or on one of their drugs. The art of medicine consisted of selecting the right drugs, preparing them in the magically correct way, and speaking the appropriate words over them.

Egyptian religion in medicine focused on the gods associated with healing. It is apparent that Thoth was the major god of healing, considered by the Egyptians to be a physician himself. According to Egyptian beliefs, it was Thoth who cured Horus when he was bitten by a scorpion. By protecting Horus he protected every sick man. The Greeks identified Thoth with their Hermes.

Mesopotamia shared many of the magic and religious beliefs of Egypt; in fact, magic was even more integrated in their approach to religion. The Babylonians used magic to exercise control over the world of the gods, not only for purposes of healing but whenever they felt in distress. This was a medical system in which doctors did not work on the 7th, 14th, 19th, 21st, and 28th days of the month because these days were considered unlucky.

In distinguishing the Egyptian and Mesopotamian approach to disease causation, two differences might be mentioned. First, the

Mesopotamians were much more conscious of demons being the source of disease. Magical methods of dealing with demons by such means as rattlesnake oil, lizard's blood, urine, feces, and swine's teeth fill their medical lore. Second, the Mesopotamians had a more rigorous understanding of disease as a retribution for sin than the Egyptians.

> Sickness sent by the gods directly or through the medium of demons was the chief form of punishment, for the individual's own sin, for that of his parents or his clan. But sickness could also befall man because he had not been cautious and the evil spirits took hold of him although he had not committed any offense. Sin, sickness, and possession by demons, however, were so intimately connected that the terms became synonymous.[13]

In evaluating the effectiveness of the Egyptian and Mesopotamian medical systems, encumbered as they were with a magico-religious approach to healing, the reader might well be tempted to dismiss much of their medicine as sheer superstition. But what must not be forgotten is that the power of suggestion in the mind of the patient is a very effective means of healing, even if the medium is a magical incantation. It is not impossible that these magic ceremonies had some degree of effectiveness from a psychosomatic perspective. Says Sigerist approvingly:

> The oral rite was all important. The correct choice of words to frighten a spirit, to enlist the help of the gods, the intonation probably also in which a spell was recited or sung, this all must have had a profound effect upon the patient. We know the power of suggestion and know how highly responsive religious individuals are to such rites. I should not be astonished if the sorcerer with his spells had had better results in many cases than the physician with his drugs.[14]

---

[13]Sigerist, op. cit., 411.

[14]Ibid., 280.

Israel's Rejection of These Health Systems

We can assume that Israel knew of the quasi-sophisticated medical systems practiced by their neighbors. Because of the trade network that typified relations between nations of the ancient Near East, it would be surprising if Israel was not acquainted with Egyptian and Mesopotamian medicine; cultural borrowing was a common feature in the Old World.

Perhaps the Hebrews even used some of these medicinal elements as part and parcel of their own folk remedies. The biblical record is not clear on these matters. Nevertheless, Israel deliberately chose not to establish these foreign medical systems as "systems" in their own midst. We need not ponder too deeply to discover the reason. The fact that the therapies of the Egyptians and Mesopotamians were contaminated with the practice of magic as well as idolatrous worship is ample cause for their prohibition among the Hebrews (Deut. 18:9-13). How could the God of Israel share His throne with the healing powers of Isis, Horus, and Thoth, the healing gods of Egypt?[15] What collaboration could Yahweh have with any of the manipulative devices of magic as practiced by Babylonia?

It is not stretching our argument too far to suggest that Israel rejected not only the pagan incantations of their neighbors but their professional medical systems as well. So integrated were these medical systems that to partake of one aspect was to partake of them all. One of the vignettes that reveals much about the Hebrew attitude toward these alien medical systems is the judgment pronounced on King Asa, grandson of Solomon. He probably made use of Egyptian doctors:

> A disease attacked Asa from head to foot in the 39th year of his reign, and what is more, he turned in his sickness, not to Yahweh, but to *doctors* (2 Chron. 16:12, author's translation).

The rejection of the world's finest medical systems meant that Israel had a different agenda in its approach to health and well-being. Obviously this agenda focused on their own relationship to Yahweh and the instructions about sickness and health that he himself had laid

---

[15]Wolff, op. cit., 147. *"Israel dealing with sickness is Yahweh's exclusive prerogative. He himself never falls sick and is never wounded, unlike gods such as the Egyptian Horus, whom Thoth has to cure after he has been stung by a scorpion."*

down. As we turn to this topic, we also need to inquire more deeply into the nature of sickness and what it meant to the Hebrews.

Sickness and Disease in Ancient Israel

Sickness is described in the Old Testament by the term "hillah" which refers to a state of *weakness*.[16] The entire 38th psalm is a snapshot of a person who is so weak, he hardly has any strength left. His physical functions have all but ceased. He is filled with mental apprehension because of his worsening condition. He especially feels concern about his spiritual relationship to the Lord.

> Because of Your wrath there is no health in my body; my bones have no soundness because of my sin. My guilt has overwhelmed me like a burden too heavy to bear. My wounds fester and are loathsome because of my sinful folly. . . . My back is filled with searing pain; there is no health in my body. I am feeble and utterly crushed; I groan in anguish of heart. . . . For I am about to fall, and my pain is ever with me. I confess my inequity; I am troubled by my sin. (Ps. 38:3-8, 17-18)

This psalm of David reveals the profound depths of the experience of illness. We are given no indication of the particular disease that burdened him, but it is instructive to note the holistic nature by which illness was perceived by the Hebrews. All dimensions of human personhood are mentioned in this episode of illness: the processes of the body as well as those of the mind and spirit. We note also the close correspondence of sin and sickness. This is a theme that occurs time and again in many of the biblical narratives.

We should also examine the conditions that contributed to and made sickness a dreaded reality in Hebrew life. Disease was endemic in ancient Israel. We can assume from the environmental stressors of this tropical region, especially the abundance of parasites, that the sickbed was a common experience. Diseases of an infectious nature were rampant, and at times epidemic, due to the close quarters in which these people lived. But they were only a part of the total package of pain and distress that the peoples of the Old Testament experienced. Slow chronic infections (which include malaria, schistosomiasis, filiarisis), functional disorders, mental disorders, injuries, and the infirmities that

---

[16]Ibid., 143. *"This term almost always designates a state of weakness—of slackness and exhaustion; that is to say, vital power has been sapped."*

come with aging complement this "background noise" against which human life has always been lived.

The biblical writers were well acquainted with *epidemics* caused by contagious diseases and numerous accounts are to be found in the Scriptures. When skin diseases become infectious and spread to larger, intact groups of peoples, they can result in epidemics or plagues. Indeed, plagues represent one of the three great pestilences of the Old Testament, ranking just behind the sword and famine (cf. Jer. 14:12). Zechariah with terrifying words announces a fearful plague to come (14:12): "Their flesh will rot while they are still standing on their feet, their eyes will rot in their sockets, and their tongues will rot in their mouths."

A deadly plague, accompanied by tumors, attacked the Philistines as punishment for their seizure of the ark of the covenant. This plague apparently was borne by rats because of their representation on the guilt offering of gold symbols (1 Sam. 6:4-5). We read also of the pestilence that was the result of David's sin of numbering the people and which killed 70,000 out of 1,300,000 able-bodied men of Israel and Judah (2 Sam. 24). Some people believe that the chilling account recorded by Isaiah (Isa. 37:36) in which "an angel of the LORD went out and put to death a hundred and eighty-five thousand men in the Assyrian camp" overnight, and which led Sennacherib to withdraw from Judah without capturing Jerusalem, was a dreadful epidemic.

We do not know with precision the exact parasite that caused these epidemic outbreaks. William McNeill states that bubonic plague was not always the cause of these epidemics:

> There is no good reason for supposing these ancient epidemics were outbreaks of bubonic plague. Any of the familiar civilized infections—whether propagated via the respiratory tract, like measles, smallpox, and influenza, or via the alimentary canal, like typhoid and dysentery—could have produced the sort of sudden outbreak of mortality recorded in the Bible.[17]

What is sobering for the reader to consider is how pervasive disease was in the daily life of the Hebrews. Perhaps there existed the same percentage of morbidity and mortality as are reported in modern, underdeveloped nations. Children particularly were victims in this

---

[17]William McNeill, *Plagues and People* (Garden City, NY: Anchor Press, 1976), 80.

environment, perhaps as many as 50% succumbing fatally to disease before the age of five. It is not an overstatement to conjecture that every household knew personally the tragedy of sickness and death. Any interpretation of health and illness in biblical times should reflect the ecological context in which these people lived.

Diseases of the Old Testament

Many diseases are described in the Old Testament, but what is significant is the distinctive pattern by which they occur. We note that almost all diseases that are described are *external* diseases, not internal pathologies.[18] Disease for the Hebrews seems to be characterized as a visible malady that made the person "different" and which clearly marked an individual as not being whole. This is not an unimportant discovery as will later be made clear in our interpretation of the Old Testament. Following is a classification of diseases that are referred to in the Old Testament:

Skin diseases are especially described and include an assortment of ailments.[19] *Boils* are frequently mentioned and reported in various grades of morbidity (Exod. 9:9-10). Job seems to have suffered from simple boils (2:7) whereas King Hezekiah was probably afflicted with gangrenous carbuncles (2 Kings 20:7). Other maladies that affected the skin are *tinea*, a general term for skin eruption or eczema (Lev. 13:30); *scab*, a crusty eruption caused by a fungus or ringworm (Lev. 13:2); *scurvy*, probably a skin disease from a parasitic insect (Deut. 28:27); *inflammation*, a generalized reference to any skin ailment such as a burn or wound (Lev. 13:28; 28:22); and *rash*, most likely vitiligo, a skin disorder in which loss of pigmentation resulted in white patches of skin (Lev. 13:39).

The disease referred to as *leprosy*, which covers in detail the entire 13th and 14th chapters of Leviticus, presents a problem of interpretation. Because it is described as curable and self-limiting, it was

---

[18]This does not mean that the Hebrews knew no diseases of an internal nature; they simply had no labels for such symptomologies.

[19]See the variety of diseases that are discussed in M. and J. L. Miller, *Encyclopedia of Bible Life* (New York: Harper & Row, 1955), as well as in Hans Walter Wolff, *Anthropology of the Old Testament* (Philadelphia: Fortress Press, 1974), 143-44.

probably not Hansen's disease.[20] Most, but not all, of the descriptions of biblical leprosy appear to be various skin disorders such as psoriasis, ringworm, eczema, or vitiligo. Such disorders disfigured the victim but did not disable him. What seems to be objected to as far as biblical leprosy is concerned was the "blotched appearance" of the victim. It was a visible reminder that the person was not whole.

Blindness is frequently mentioned in the Old Testament and was probably one of the most common ailments suffered in the ancient Near East (Lev. 26:16; Deut. 28:28). Whether the condition was congenital or the result of disease is not always made clear. Epidemiologists report that eye disease still occurs in high incidence in this area of the world.

Lameness and other crippling infirmities are mentioned. Such maladies include clubfeet, vertebrae disorders, and broken hands or feet (Lev. 21:18-20). We can conjecture that a sizable number of people suffered from disabilities of this sort.

Paralysis is not referred to in the Old Testament but evidences of paralysis due to strokes or spinal cord diseases are hinted at (1 Kings 13:4; Prov. 26:7). 1 Sam. 25:37 seems to describe a stroke and Jer. 4:19ff. a heart attack.

Fevers were a common phenomenon in ancient times and are reported on numerous occasions (Lev. 26:16; Deut. 28:22). Most of these febrile conditions seem to be of the malarial, typhoid, and typhus types; fevers are also known to have accompanied the disease states of bubonic plague and smallpox.

Mental illness is referred to as "confusion of the mind" (Deut. 28:28-29). There are very few references to mental illness in the Old Testament although it does report the delusions of Nebuchadnezzar (Dan. 4:19ff) and David's feigning madness (1 Sam. 21:12-15). We can assume that mental illness was known and probably occurred with some frequency.

---

[20]Hansen's disease is the medical term for the morbid condition of true leprosy, caused by a bacteria that attacks the nervous system of the victim. The extremities of lepers are worn away because the victim has lost a sensation of pain; in some instances the extremities are eaten by rats. It is significant that the Leviticus narrative refers to fungus growths on walls and mildew on clothes as "leprosy" (13:47-59; 14:35-57). According to Levitical law, the leprous victim was considered unclean. If the condition seemed to be contained, he was quarantined for a stipulated period of time; but if the condition was perceived as chronic, he was isolated from the community.

What is significant about the pattern of external diseases is that they are especially noted in the list of prohibitions from the priesthood (Lev. 21:18-20, author's translation):

> No one . . . blind or lame, or one who has a limb too short or too long, or a man who has an injured foot or an injured hand, or a hunchback, or a consumptive, or a man with a defect in his sight, or an itching disease, or scabs, or crushed testicles, may approach the sacrificial service of the sanctuary.

As we evaluate the Hebrew perception of disease, it is important to note this emphasis on the *external* appearance of the person. The disease and its symptoms marked the person off as being *non-whole*. Any disfigurement that came as a result of sickness was a signal that the victim was out of order with the wholeness that God intended. This emerges as a crucial datum in understanding sickness and health in the Old Testament. It was tragic enough that disfigurement would mar a person's status in Hebrew culture; for a priest it simply was not allowed.

The Sick Role in Israel

Descriptions of illness in the Old Testament emphasize the groaning and suffering of victims as disease saps their energy or as they prepare themselves for their final days (Pss.6:6; 31:10). The sick man in Ps. 88 complains of a lifelong disease that he has suffered since his youth and which now has brought him to the brink of the grave. When Hezekiah is told to put his house in order because of impending death, he laments: "In the prime of my life must I go through the gates of death and be robbed of the rest of my years?" (Isa. 38:10) In all of these narratives of illness, the sick person appears to be suffering his disease *alone*. There are no doctors, no friends or companions, not anyone to share the depth of his pain.

Perhaps the most palpable reason for this alienation is that sickness conferred on the person a stigma of "shame." No wonder disease was so dreaded in Israel. It seems to have brought with it the added distress of estrangement from human comfort. The diseased person was made to feel, by cultural tradition and religious sanctions, repulsive to his friends and family (Ps. 88:8; Isa. 54:12). This became part of the experience of illness and the implications of sickness. Listen again to the cry of the sick man in Psalm 38:

My heart pounds, my strength fails me; even the light has gone from my eyes. My friends and companions avoid me because of my wounds. my neighbors stay far away. (vv. 10-11)

When Job's three friends saw him covered with sores, they wept aloud and shared his shame by not speaking with him for seven days (Job 2:11-13). Lepers were especially treated as outcasts and, according to Levitical law, were made to cry out their shameful presence to all who approached them (Lev. 13:45-46).

It is clear from the Old Testament narratives that sickness was a tragic burden to bear, essentially because it symbolized the deepest kind of pain. Not simply the pain of the disease, but the deeper psychological and spiritual pain of being cut off from the fellowship of the community, i.e., the sickness. The reader needs to be alerted to this condition in order to comprehend the fullness of the compassion of Jesus when He encountered these "alienated sufferers" of His day.

The Healer of Israel

To whom did the Israelite believer turn when sickness invaded his life and what were his resources for healing? Here the Old Testament is very clear. Yahweh Himself was considered to be the "Healer of Israel." No more important a statement about sickness and health exists in the Old Testament than this covenant promise of Yahweh to His people:

> If you listen carefully to the voice of the LORD your God and do what is right in His eyes, if you pay attention to His commands and keep all His decrees, I will not bring on you any of the diseases I brought on the Egyptians, for *I am the LORD, who heals you.* (Exod. 15:26)

According to the Old Testament, Yahweh stands as the central actor who alone holds in His hands the ultimate authority of both disease and healing. The God of Israel has no rivals who can either command the processes of disease to commence or the processes of healing to begin. No other spirit, whether the gods of Egypt or the demons of Babylonia, can challenge this authority of God. Even Satan, who torments righteous Job with a fearsome disease, does so only by God's permission (Job 2:1-7).

There are two significant clues from this passage in Exod. 15:26 that help us to understand the foundation of Israel's medical system.

First, the explanation of disease is associated with the God of Israel; and second, the source of health and healing is found only in the God of Israel.

Disease Theory in the Old Testament

Perhaps the most illuminating passage to describe disease causation is the proclamation of Deut. 32:39 in which God says, "There is no god besides Me. I put to death and I bring to life, *I have wounded and I will heal*, and no one can deliver out of My hand." Such a statement does not suggest that God is an arbitrary God, one who sends disease to those whom He wills or heals those whom He wills. The statement is rather a polemic against any rival or cosmic power who seeks to challenge God's supremacy as the source of anything. What it means is that only Yahweh has ultimate power over the processes of life and death. Only Yahweh can bring diseases such as He did upon the Egyptians; this is not the work of Isis nor any other deity. And it is only Yahweh who can bring health and healing, not Thoth or Horus or even Asclepius or Apollo.

We need to probe further to discover the explanation for the reason why God sends disease. Two dominant themes seem to stand out in accounting for the incidence of disease and illness in the Old Testament.

First, *Yahweh sends disease to individuals and nations but He also heals individuals and nations*. In the close relationship between sin and disease in the Old Testament, we have an ample explanation why God could send disease. The original disorder that sin brought to the cosmos has already been described in chapter 1. We are not surprised that this process continues in the Old Testament because people continued in their rebellious behavior. Many narratives describe how individuals and nations brought upon themselves the calamity of sickness because of their pride and disobedience.

For example, Miriam was struck down with leprosy because she expressed jealousy of Moses (Num. 12:1-16). David and Bathsheba's child became sick and died after one week because of David's sin of adultery and murder (2 Sam. 12:15-18). Elisha's servant Gehazi illegally accepted a reward from Naaman with the result that he and his descendants were smitten with leprosy (2 Kings 5:25-27).

On a national level, God punished the Philistines with a plague after they captured the ark of the covenant (1 Sam. 5:6-12). This punishment of the Philistines can be cited as a fulfillment of the promise of God to inflict diseases on those who hate the children of Israel (Deut. 7:15). When David held a census against God's will, his sin brought the wrath of God upon Israel in the form of a devastating plague (2 Sam. 24:10-25). The prophets also speak of God sending disease to the children of Israel for their disobedience (Jer. 24:10; Hab. 3:5). Hosea shouts to the people to repent, "Come, let us return to the LORD; for He has torn us to pieces, but He may heal us; He has injured us but He will bind up our wounds" (6:1).

The explanation of disease as *punishment* for sin is understandable, and to a certain extent, meaningful in that the purpose of sickness is clearly perceived. If an individual understands *why* he has become ill, at least this removes the mystery of the illness. This explanation also provides a strategy for healing: "Cleanse me with hyssop and I will be clean. . . . Let the bones You have crushed rejoice" (Ps. 51:7-8). There is a strong element of hope even for those who have brought their sickness upon themselves as the above passage from Hosea indicates.

In discussing the explanation of disease as punishment, it should be made clear that there is little evidence in the Old Testament that specific sins brought forth the consequence of sickness. What we read from those who are sick is rather a general confession of sins, an acknowledgment that they belonged to the state of fallen humanity. Unfortunately, later Judaism took this explanation of disease as punishment and turned it into a rigid retribution theory of sickness—the belief that any instance of sickness was the particular consequence of some specific sin. Such a theory of disease branded the person as a "sinner" and provided no hope or comfort to the sick person. Jesus addressed this distorted reasoning in the case of the man born blind (John 9:2).

A second explanation for disease and sickness in the Old Testament is that *Yahweh chastises His people in order to bring them the full measure of His love.* According to Darrel Amundsen and Gary Ferngren, "Suffering in general and sickness in particular were seen not simply as punishment but rather as chastisement that was not vindictive but corrective."[21] Many passages in the Old Testament support this view. "Blessed is the man You discipline, O LORD," says the psalmist

[21]Darrel W. Amundsen and Gary B. Ferngren, "Medicine and Religion: Pre-Christian Antiquity," in *Health/Medicine and the Faith Traditions: An Inquiry into Religion and Medicine,* eds. Martin E. Marty and Kenneth L. Vaux (Philadelphia: Fortress Press, 1982), 63.

(94:12). Proverbs 3:11-12 presents a similar notion: "My son, do not despise the LORD's discipline and do not resent His rebuke, because the LORD disciplines those He loves, as a father the son He delights in."

Here we come face to face with one of the deepest mysteries of the purpose of sickness. Disease sent as *discipline* offers an explanation but it provides little comfort. When one is told that God's ways are mysterious and beyond human comprehension, it is sometimes difficult to comprehend the meaning behind the suffering or to rejoice in it. It was not easy for Job to hear the advice of a friend, "Blessed is the man whom God corrects so, do not despise the discipline of the Almighty. For He wounds, but He also binds up; He injures, but His hands also heal" (Job 5:17-18). This assessment by Eliphaz is certainly in harmony with Old Testament thought, but it was of no comfort to Job.

Nevertheless, the Old Testament makes clear the truth that God's mercy and goodness are never far away, no matter what the explanation for sickness. When God seemed to be "silent" and when all other explanations failed, the righteous sufferer in ancient Israel could find comfort in God's grace and the promise of His goodness. Indeed, he could do more. He could throw himself on the mercy of the Healer of Israel and pray for healing.

Healing through Confession and Prayer

When disease struck the life of a believer, the sick person was expected to dialogue with Yahweh as did Job and many others. King Hezekiah prayed fervently to the Lord as he wept about his morbid condition (Isa. 38:2-3). This coming face to face with Yahweh begins with a prayer for mercy, a prayer we commonly observe in the psalms:

> Be merciful to me, O LORD, for I am faint. O LORD, heal me, for my bones are in agony. My soul is in anguish. How long, O LORD, how long? (Ps. 6:2)

This pattern of pleading and dialoguing with the Lord is common in the Old Testament and indicates the spiritual nature of the sickness. It seemed proper to the Hebrew mind that if a disease were to be healed, there first needed to take place a revitalization of the relationship between the individual and the Lord (cf. Ps. 38:1-8). Perhaps this is also the lesson behind the narrative of the fiery serpents in which Moses set up a bronze serpent as a visual symbol of trust in the healing power of Yahweh (Num. 21:4-9).

For this reason, sickness was a time of spiritual reflection during which the ill person discovered acts of commission or omission that related to his illness. David made confession of his sins in his sickness with a prayer that seems to be echoed in the New Testament book of James 5:16:

> The LORD will sustain him on his sickbed and restore him from his bed of illness. I said, "O LORD, have mercy on me; heal me, for I have sinned against You." (Ps. 41:3, 4)

The first step in recovery from sickness was to receive Yahweh's forgiveness, a precondition for the gift of health and the assurance of salvation that would follow (Ps. 32:1-5; Ps. 103:3-5). In fact, forgiveness of sins and healing are all of a piece. "No one living in Zion will say, 'I am ill'; and the sins of those who dwell there will be forgiven" (Isa. 33:24). This prophecy prefigures a dominant motif in the healing ministry of Jesus (Mark 2:5-12).

When finally the cessation of sickness occurred, the illness relieved, and the disease cured, the joyous person sang praises to Yahweh who delivered him from sickness and the grave. "O LORD my God, I called to You for help and You healed me." (Ps. 30:2) Even the pagan, Naaman, healed by God of his leprosy, praises the God of Israel and vows to serve Him all of his life (2 Kings 5:15-17).

It should be apparent that the narratives of the Old Testament illustrate a wholistic understanding of sickness, disease, illness, and health that we referenced earlier. Physical maladies can never be separated from the domain of the spirit. It then follows that spiritual activities such as confession and forgiveness are indispensable in effectuating a physical cure. "[He] forgives all your sins and heals all your diseases; He redeems your life from the pit and crowns you with love and compassion" (Ps. 103:3). Old Testament theology leads us to recognize that fallen humanity is susceptible to the diseases that are the common lot of people. The way back to health is through the Lord who alone has the power to heal and to grant salvation. To seek "other" healers rather than the Lord, especially those who represent false gods, betrays a hopeless understanding of the real needs of the person.

The Old Testament Approach to Health

In the Old Testament, health is related to the word *shalom*.[22]
Throughout the Old Testament *shalom* has the meaning of "well-being"
in the widest sense of that word and encompasses prosperity (Ps. 73:3),
bodily health (Isa. 57:18; Ps. 38:3), and also salvation (Isa. 43:7). The
giver of *shalom* is Yahweh Himself whose providence touches all areas
of life.

Shalom is perhaps best translated as "peace" or "wholeness." A
person was said to have *shalom* when an individual's life demonstrated
a harmony with God, with his neighbors, with the environment and
with himself. In brief, a "healthy person" was one whose life
relationships were centered in the peace and wholeness of God
Himself. The concept of *shalom* as "peace" is the climax of the blessing
in Numbers 6:26 in which this well-known statement appears: "The
LORD turn His face toward you and give you *peace*."

Health for the Hebrews was more than a state of physical and
psychological wellness as the Western world usually defines that term.
Health was rather perceived as a state of "wholeness" that assumed the
unity of all things under the rule of God. In the Hebrew worldview,
health included a person's relationship to God as well as his
relationship to his family, community, livestock, and even his property.
It assumes an integration of all dimensions of life as well as the
universe in which one lives; an imbalance in one part adversely affects
the other parts. Westerners often have difficulty comprehending this
concept of wholeness because the Western worldview emphasizes
separation and individuation.[23] But it is essential to capture in our
minds the concept of wholeness if we seek to unlock the deeper
meanings of the Old Testament.

---

[22]See the discussion of this term in Colin Brown ed., *The New International
Dictionary of New Testament Theology*, vol. 2 (Grand Rapids, MI: Zondervan, 1986).
The appropriate Greek word that corresponds to *shalom* is *eirene*, also translated as
"peace" or "wholeness."

[23]A provocative discussion about the social conflicts that banish the solidarity of
shalom is raised by Martin Scharlemann in *Healing and Redemption* (St. Louis:
Concordia, 1965), 22-25. Scharlemann describes the contemporary Western world as
"excessive individualism, cosmic detachment, and social and cultural fragmen-
tization."

Holiness and Health

A key word that sheds light on the meaning of wholeness, and by extension, the Hebrew approach to health, is the word *holiness*. When we look at the injunction in Leviticus 19:2—*"Be holy because I, the LORD, your God, am holy"*—we note that every facet of Hebrew life revolved around the concept of holiness. Holiness was established by God to be the lifestyle of His people. In living holy lives, they were, in fact, reflecting the nature of Yahweh Himself.

The word "holy" (*qadosh*) means at its root "to be set apart" or to "be separate." Traditionally theologians have applied this term to moral categories so that holiness is usually translated as "separate from sin." But it is difficult to understand how a woman menstruating or giving birth to a child is considered unholy (Lev. 12:4-8; 15:25-30) in the sense that these are morally reprehensible activities. When one examines the length and breadth of the Levitical laws, the prohibitions mark every area of life as being "holy/unholy" or "clean/unclean." Surely all of this must relate to health in some way because many of the diseases of the Old Testament are said to make a person "unclean" or "unholy" (cf. Lev. 13-15). It seems obvious that health is very much related to this word "holy" and sickness with the word "unholy."

Mary Douglas, an anthropologist, has done a brilliant study of the laws of Leviticus and has applied the skill of linguistic analysis to the context of these laws.[24] Her observation is that the basic idea of holiness is the "order, the completeness, and the wholeness of God." What the Levitical laws represent is how God imposes order on the world of the Hebrews for the purpose of making them aware of the order, unity, and completeness of Himself.

It is Douglas's explication that the dietary laws of Leviticus 11 make sense only when seen as a design from God to bring order to the categories of creation. Observe the reading of Leviticus 11:43-44, *"Do not defile yourselves by any of these creatures. Do not make yourselves unclean by means of them or be made unclean by them. I am the LORD your God; consecrate yourselves and be holy, because I am holy."*[25]

---

[24]Mary Douglas, "The Abominations of Leviticus," in *Purity and Danger* (London: Routledge and Kegan Paul Ltd., 1993), 41-58.

[25]Ibid., 41-42. Douglas makes a convincing case that hygiene is not the compelling reason for the prohibition against eating unclean foods. There are too many inconsistencies in the list of unclean foods to lend credence to this *post hoc facto* interpretation.

We might ask the question, "Why should eating a crawling insect or an animal make a person unholy?" However, if we keep in mind that the vital idea behind holiness is the *discrimination of order*, there is a lot of sense to this command. Yahweh is not a God of confusion. Yahweh is whole, complete, and one. Therefore, Israel must be whole, complete, and one.

We can now gain an insight in what health meant to the Hebrew people. Health meant to be holy and complete, just as God was holy and complete. By contrast, sickness connoted the concept of being unholy or unclean. The Levitical laws are truly rational and understandable. They are the imposition of God's order and they create for His people a style of life that reflects the Giver of life.

If a person got out of order, he was considered polluted and was mandated by the purification ceremonies to become ceremonially clean again. This was one of the functions of the priesthood: to certify that a person's disease was sufficiently removed from his body in order to pronounce the person clean (see Lev. 13:1-45). At every turn of life, the Hebrew believer was made to see what was holy and what was not. The laws turned his thoughts constantly to the oneness and holiness of Yahweh, the Holy One Himself.

Preventive Medicine

This analysis of holiness makes clear how Israel applied their understanding of health. To say it in terms of modern medicine, the medical system of ancient Israel was *preventive medicine*. The focus by which the Hebrew believer lived was "not to become sick." Hypothetically, if a person kept the order that God had imposed—that is, obedience to the holiness laws—he would be spared the ravages of sickness.

This is precisely what Exodus 15:26 says: *"If you listen carefully to the voice of the LORD your God and do what is right in His eyes, if you pay attention to His commands and keep all His decrees, I will not bring on you any of the diseases brought on the Egyptians, for I the LORD who heals you."*

Prevention, not curation, is the dominant theme of the Old Testament. This in itself is certainly not bad medical strategy. A strong argument can be made for isolating people with infectious diseases. When we carefully examine many of the holiness laws, we discover that they promote effective sanitation procedures. Consider the example of burying one's excrement in the ground (Deut. 23:10-14) or protecting food and water from pollution of unclean objects (Lev. 11:31-38). Although these sanctions predate our scientific understanding of the danger of parasites and micro-organisms, the principle of contagion (uncleanness pollutes cleanness) is similar. Moses, in fact, has been called by some "the father of modern prophylactic medicine."

The holiness laws can be considered a basic foundation for a holistic model of health. Their purpose was to bring *order* to Israel's life under God and to demonstrate how health could be achieved and sustained. The principle that "holiness equals health" pervaded every dimension of their existence: the physical, the social, and the spiritual. The key to this ordered life, of course, was the personal relation between the believer and Yahweh.

But, as we are well aware, the laws of God are no guarantee of human success. In point of fact, the "failures" of the holiness laws crowded the streets of their cities and towns and were embodied in the blind, the leprous, and the lame. The sick were everywhere! Surely it is true that the law of God can only point to righteousness; it cannot make a person righteous. The same is true for health. The law can prescribe but it cannot heal.

A Typology of the Healer Who Is to Come

The Old Testament turns our eyes forward to the New Testament era when a new approach to health and healing shall emerge in the form of a healing Messiah. Rather than focusing on prevention, the Messiah will usher in the kingdom of God in which the free gifts of wholeness and healing are dominant markers. He Himself will be THE HEALER whom the world seeks and who will bring an added dimension to the phrase *"I am the LORD who heals you"* (Exod. 15:26). This new strategy, however, builds on the foundation of the old. The Healer who is to come is the "Holy One," because only a Holy One can give health and holiness as a free gift to those who cannot keep the law.

It is significant that the prophets describe the coming Messiah as being engaged in a healing ministry. Isaiah, in a seminal passage, speaks quite specifically about the ministry of the Servant of God who will proclaim the "year of the Lord's favor."

The Spirit of the Sovereign LORD is on me because the LORD has anointed me to preach good news to the poor. He has sent me to bind up the brokenhearted, to proclaim freedom for the captives and release for the blind. (Isa. 61:1, author's translation)

Indeed, the Messianic Age will introduce the reign of the Prince of Peace who will bring to this earth a new reign of justice and righteousness. A new age will appear. The description of this new age (Isa. 11:1-9) is nothing less than a description of *shalom*, the order restored by God to the people of Israel and to the world. Walter Roehrs comments on the meaning of these important verses:

A dramatic change takes place in their lives. It is a transformation no less radical than the reversal of prevailing hostile instincts in the animal world to the harmony which prevailed in the Garden of Eden before man's sin turned all of creation into an arena of conflict. . . . The Messianic King is capable of making all things new and of calling into being a "new creation."[26]

Yet even in the Old Testament there are glimpses of this new age to come. Very few miraculous healings occur in the Old Testament but when they do, they can be considered a typology of the promised Messiah's ministry.[27] The charismatic prophets, Elijah and Elisha, both are channels through whom God's healing power is manifested. Elijah stretched himself over the son of the widow of Zarephath and his prayers for the restoration of the boy who had succumbed to illness were answered (1 Kings 17:17-24). This account is reminiscent of Jesus' restoration of the widow's son at Nain (Luke 7:11-16). Elisha, as well, was involved in a dramatic healing with the leprous Aramaean general Naaman whom he ordered to bathe in the river Jordan seven times (2 Kings 5:1-14). The biblical narrative reports that "his flesh was restored and became clean like that of a young boy."

These accounts of God's healing power are signs of the kingdom of God to come, that new age when God would reveal Himself in the person of His own Son, the Deliverer whom Malachi prophesied would "rise with *healing* in [His] wings" (4:2).

---

[26]Walter R. Roehrs, *Concordia Self-Study Commentary* (St. Louis: Concordia, 1971), 453.

[27]Wolff, op. cit., 145. *"Medical treatment was apparently only applied in exceptional cases, by charismatics."*

Chapter Three

Health and Healing in the New Testament

Even for the casual reader, the Gospel accounts of Jesus the Healer are stirring to both heart and mind. It seems as if a "new age" has appeared! The coming of Jesus Christ is accompanied with dramatic healings that are as gripping as they are extraordinary. Disorder and pain give way to health and healing in a remarkable manner.

In the first chapter of Mark more healings are reported than in the entire Old Testament put together. That chapter records the healing of Peter's mother-in-law, the demoniac in the synagogue, a leper who begs for mercy, and multitudes of others who camp at his doorstep. The healing activity of Jesus was fervent and intense.

Nearly one-fifth of the Gospels are devoted to Jesus' healing. All told, we count forty-one distinct instances of physical and mental healings in the Four Gospels. This does not include the 16 cases of healing in the book of Acts. Clearly, the New Testament does not hide the fact that this is a chronicle about health and healing.

It is readily apparent that the accounts of health and healing in the New Testament are far different from those in the Old Testament. The towering center of these accounts is the figure of Jesus, the Healer. For the writers of the New Testament, Jesus the Messiah is at the heart of all their explanations about disease and sickness and about healing and wholeness.

But there are other differences in the New Testament to be encountered as well. In these narratives we discover a new rational approach toward healing, the Greek medical system, which blends itself successfully within Jewish culture. Doctors now appear with sophisticated medications and therapies. In addition, what stands out so dynamically in the New Testament narratives is the change in focus: the change *from prevention to curation,* from prophylaxis to healing.

A major objective of this chapter will be to describe as well as to explain the purpose and scope of Jesus' healing ministry. As we go about this task, we need to take seriously what Jesus said about his healing activity. But it is also necessary that we interpret the healing ministry of Jesus in the light of the medical context in which he lived. The times were different from the days of the Old Testament.

Doctors in the New Testament

The careful reader of the New Testament narratives is immediately impressed by the frequent occurrence of *doctors.* Apparently physicians are practicing medicine openly without any interdiction from Jewish law. Their presence is so common that we can assume a general acceptance of doctors among the Jews in the first century A.D.

For example, we read about a woman suffering from a hemorrhage who had spent her entire savings on doctors (Luke 8:43-48). Jesus also notes the popularity of doctors when he said: "It is not the healthy who need the doctor but the sick," a statement reported by all three synoptic writers (Matthew 9:12; Mark 2:17; Luke 5:31). There is also the laconic saying of Jesus at Nazareth: "Physician, heal yourself" (Luke 4:23).

Indeed, professional medical activity is so pervasive that we even locate a member of the profession within the inner circles of believers. Paul refers to Luke, one of the evangelists, as the "beloved physician" (Colossians 4:14). The presence of a medical man so close to the healing ministry of Christ is an important datum as we apply the New Testament to modern life.

A question emerges at this point of our inquiry. Why are doctors allowed as legitimate sources of healing in the New Testament whereas in the Old Testament this was perceived as unacceptable? What has changed? We need to look more closely at the ecology of the New Testament.

The world of Jesus of Nazareth was a world dominated by the aegis of the Roman Empire, perhaps the most competent and well-organized empire in human history. According to Wayne Meeks, this was primarily an urban world: the power of ancient Rome was to be found in the cities.[1] This urbanization process began much earlier

---

[1] Wayne Meeks, *The First Urban Christians: The Social World of the Apostle Paul* (New York: Harper & Row, 1983), 9-15.

when the Greeks, under Alexander the Great, created a world of cities. Greek became the language of the Mediterranean world and the prosperity of trade drew this world together. When the Roman armies made this world their empire, much of the Greek influence remained, especially the Greek language.

But the Greeks influenced the lives of people far beyond the scope of language. Perhaps their most lasting contribution was in the field of medicine. Because of the genius of Hippocrates, and his Roman successor, Galen, Greco-Roman doctors were the toast of the ancient world.

Hippocratic Medicine

In the New Testament we are introduced to this new health system, known popularly as the Hippocratic or Greek medical system. Hippocrates (380 B.C.) is so esteemed by modern physicians that he is called the "founder of modern medicine." By means of his efforts a center of medical instruction was established on the island of Cos to which apprentices from all parts of the world came to be trained.

Hippocrates brought to the study of medicine a spirit of inquiry, based on rational thought, and a naturalistic understanding of disease. By despiritualizing the treatments of former times, especially eliminating magic from the practice of medicine, he was able to understand healing as a natural system unto itself. His approach to medicine can be summed up by the phrase *vis medicatrix naturae*, namely, the healing power of nature.

Hippocrates had a rather sophisticated knowledge of the human body. He understood the positioning of the nerves, the muscles, and bones and their functions within the structure of the body. This advancement in anatomy paved the way for much greater precision in terms of diagnosis and applied therapy. In addition, Hippocrates was a competent surgeon (for the Greeks medicine and surgery were one and the same) and advanced this procedure to the point of operating on "fallen lungs."

The distinct advantage in the Greek approach to healing was the attention given to *cleanliness* and the orderliness of their clinical procedures. The Greeks possessed superior antiseptics, especially the use of wine on wounds, and understood to some degree the process of gangrene. Greek medicine was well-known for the beautiful white bandages which were tied according to specific instructions and which have since become a dominant symbol of modern medical practice. In describing the treatment of a carpenter whose axe had slipped and cut his foot, Guido Majno relates how the Greek doctor applies cold water to inhibit the flow of blood:

> Then–surprise–a beautiful white bandage, rolled from both ends, is soaked in red wine and applied dripping, with an adroit play of both hands.[2]

Incidentally, Dr. Majno conducted experiments with both red and white wines, the major antiseptics of the Greeks, and discovered that "the effect of wine is truly bactericidal," that is, that wine effectively kills bacteria.[3] Rather than attributing this effect to the alcohol in the wine, the active agents are the presence of *polyphenols* in the wine. Polyphenols have since become the basis of modern antiseptics, the discovery of Lord Lister who demonstrated their mastery over bacteria.

The Greeks were quite skilled at suturing wounds with a bronze needle and thread and then covering the suture with a mixture of copper oxide and honey, along with the ubiquitous heavy white bandage. Hippocrates devotes considerable attention in one of his books to the suturing and bandaging of the faces of boxers whose sharp, cutting gloves often left the faces of their opponents sliced to ribbons.

Typical procedure of a practicing physician at the time of Jesus was to place one's ear to the patient's back and listen for evidence of fluid in the lungs. If the doctor felt that pus within the lungs needed to be drained, he would make an incision and allow the pus to drain out of a piece of tin pipe.

> When the pus becomes as thin as water, slippery to the finger, and scanty, put into the wound a hollow tin drain . . . Signs that the patient

---

[2]Guido Majno, *The Healing Hand: Man and Wound in the Ancient World* (Cambridge: Harvard University Press, 1975), 150. Perhaps the meaning of the color "white" to refer to health comes to us from the Greeks. However, many cultures of the world consider the color "red" to be the color of health.

[3]Ibid., 186-188.

will escape death: if the pus is white and pure and contains streaks of blood, there are good chances of healing. But if the pus . . . on the next day flows thick, greenish and fetid the patients die after the pus has run out.[4]

Hippocratic Medical Theory

The guiding principle in Hippocratic medical theory was the concept of harmony with the forces of nature, especially as these forces operated within the human body. Hippocrates devised the system of four humors—blood, phlegm, black bile, yellow bile—fluids of the body which he believed were related to the health of the individual. Health represented that state of the body when these substances were in correct proportion to each other. Conversely, illness resulted when any of these humors reached a stage of excess or declination.

Hippocrates further believed that these humors varied in quantity throughout the year, depending on the climate and weather. Because phlegm increases in the cold and moist days of the winter, its season is in the winter. Inasmuch as blood increases during the warm and rainy days of spring, its proper season is spring. The hot and dry days of the summer was the season for yellow bile whereas the cool and dry season of autumn was the time when black bile predominated. All Greek physicians were instructed to keep in mind that every disease was most prominent during that season most in keeping with its nature.

Proper medical treatment consisted in bringing the particular humor back into balance, a process that involved such therapies as bleeding, starving, purging, or feeding the patient. It is apparent that this "naturalistic" approach recognized that the healing power within the body became operative when a balance was achieved. In Hippocrates' words:

> Disease caused by over-eating are cured by fasting; those caused by starvation are cured by feeding up.
> Disease caused by exertion are cured by rest; those caused by indolence are cured by exertion. To put it briefly, the physician should treat disease *by the principle of opposition* to the cause of the disease

---

[4]Ibid., 157.

according to its form, its seasonal and age incidence, countering tenseness by relaxation and vice versa. This will bring the patient most relief and seems to me to be the principle of healing (italics added).[5]

The Good and the Bad of Hippocratic Medicine

This principle of balance sometimes worked in the interest of the patient. But almost as frequently it produced more harm than good, especially if the treatment of choice was to "bleed" the patient, a procedure that was to be standard medical treatment up to the nineteenth century. The New Testament's account of a woman whose medical condition worsened under such treatment illustrates the point: "She had suffered a great deal under the care of many doctors and had spent all she had, yet instead of getting better she grew worse" (Mark 5:26). Majno's words echo the worst of Greek medicine:

> All in all, Greek care for the wound itself probably did little harm and some good. It is quite another story when one comes to the general treatments. . . . They range from bad to hair-raising. Imagine cutting the veins of a patient who was already half bled to death through his wound, plus the combined effects of enemas, purges, vomiting, plus the side effects of poisoning with hellebore, and all of this on a starvation diet.[6]

To Hippocrates' credit, he began a system of medicine that was an improvement over anything else at the time. Through his efforts, scientific medicine had its beginnings and the healing arts were advanced considerably. The more apt genius of Hippocrates, however, was his wholistic orientation to health and healing. Even though he had a critical eye for a naturalistic cause of disease, he never divorced this fact from the patient's own lifestyle and other intervening factors in the environment. Modern doctors who take the Hippocratic Oath should also remember that Hippocrates remained a firm believer in the need for religious therapy as well. Although this was not an integral aspect of his treatments, Hippocrates was a believer in Greek divinities

---

[5]Quoted in Foster and Anderson, *Medical Anthropology*, (New York: John Wiley and Sons, 1978), 77.

[6]Majno, op. cit., 188.

and was a member of the cult of Asclepius, the major healing god of the Greeks.

Knowing what we do about the Hippocratic focus upon naturalistic medicine, it seems clear why the Jews in the New Testament made use of Greek doctors and this medical system. They did so because the system can be used without attendant religious beliefs even as modern medicine can so be used. Since it was naturalistic in its approach, Jewish law could find no reason to bar it from use. Further, there were obvious medical benefits in Hippocratic medicine, a fact that a suffering populace would quickly notice.

There is much to commend as we evaluate the Greek medical system against the backdrop of the New Testament. We need to recognize that sick people were being healed and cared for in a relatively efficient manner before the coming of Christ to this world. The Greek medical system has evolved, through the contributions of Galen, Arab physicians and others, into our modern health care system. Few will debate the truth that God healed by means of this system even as he heals today through the ministry of modern medical science.

Nevertheless, it is at this moment of history that God brings healing of a much larger scope to the world. In terms of the restoration of order and specifically, the distortion of human nature, we need to understand what this healing encompasses. With this background before us, we turn our attention to the ministry of Jesus the Healer.

Jesus the Healer

Seldom does a Man on a mission begin his ministry in such an spectacular manner as does Jesus of Nazareth. He erupts upon the scene in Israel as the Healer par excellence. The crowds who followed him in large numbers had never seen anyone like him before.

Mark gives some insight as to the pace by which he worked: "For He had healed so many, so that those with diseases were pushing forward to touch Him" (Mark 3:10). In the villages and towns where He preached, the sick emerged in droves that they might brush against His garment and be healed. His reputation as a prophet/healer circulated far beyond the boundaries of Galilee. Matthew tells us that people came as far away as Syria (Matthew 4:24):

News about Him spread all over Syria and people brought to Him all who were ill with various diseases, those suffering severe pain, the demon-possessed, the epileptics, and the paralytics, and He healed them all.

Time and again the Gospels report that the people marveled at this man who, as He announced the coming of the kingdom of God, cured the incurable. The masses of people were awe-struck by His authority over the powers of the cosmos. As the amazed crowd said—after watching Jesus heal a demon-possessed man who previously could not speak: "Nothing like this has ever been seen in Israel" (Matthew 9:33).

The Method of His Healing

We gain an insight into Christ's healing ministry, and the power at His command, by taking careful note of the method by which He healed. In almost every instance the healing is instantaneous. One case is recorded in which a blind man receives his sight gradually (Mark 8:22). By and large, however, the cessation of disease is rapid when Jesus issues the command for it to loosen its grip. It is this rapidity of the curing process that provoked wonder in the eyewitnesses who observed Jesus at work.

Jesus used many different techniques in His healing activity. He healed by command; He healed by touch; He healed by using physical elements. There seems to be no clear-cut pattern in His approach except that in most instances He *touched* the person He healed. Touching the sick person is obviously a symbol in itself, a signification of human compassion and concern. We will have opportunity to explore some of the modern research on touching in another chapter. Most often Jesus seems to have touched the ill person at the location of the malady itself. When He healed the two blind men near Jericho, He touched them on their eyes (Matt. 20:34).

His most common technique was to speak some words of consolation and to lay His hands upon the sick person (Mark 6:5). On the other hand, there were occasions when the sick touched Jesus or His garment (Mark 5:25-34) or even the fringes of His cloak (Mark 6:56). On one occasion when a woman suffering from a hemorrhage touched the edge of Jesus' cloak, He said to the crowd, "Who touched Me? . . . Someone touched Me; I know that power has gone out from

Me" (Luke 8:45-47). It was then that the woman came forward and in the presence of all the people, told why she had touched Him and how she had been instantly healed.

Sometimes Jesus healed by making a verbal command such as when He healed the ten lepers (Luke 17:14) or the nobleman's son at a distance (John 4:50). It is significant that the healings took place at the moment of the command. There are three instances in which He used saliva, alone or mixed with earth, two of these men being blind and the other deaf and dumb (Mark 7:33-34; Mark 8:23; John 9:6-7). The use of saliva was believed to have curative powers in Jesus' time.[7]

The Gospels do not mention that Jesus used oil in His ministry to the sick. However, it is of more than a little interest to us that Jesus instructs His own disciples to anoint the sick with oil (Mark 6:13). The use of oil on wounds was a familiar medical therapy at the time. Nonetheless, it appears to have a symbolic meaning in this context and in the context of James 5:14-16. Anointing guests with oil, especially on the head, was a common procedure in that age and signified that the person was included in all the blessings of the household (see Luke 7:44-47). Anointing with oil could have been interpreted by the sick as being the recipient of the blessing of a loving God.

In the New Testament there are two different Greek words for the word we translate as "anoint." The word *aleipho* is used for anointing with oil such as we have it in James. To denote a sacred or symbolic act through which a person is "anointed" for a holy mission, the writer uses *chrio*.

Aside from healing multitudes of the sick, the Gospels report that Jesus raised three persons from the dead, namely, the daughter of Jairus (Matt. 9:18ff.), the widow's son of Nain (Luke 7:11-15), and Lazarus, the friend of Jesus (John 11).

The Manner of His Healing

Jesus dealt with the sick in a manner that can truly be described as compassionate. His approach to the sick person was far removed from

---

[7]Leslie Weatherhead, *Psychology, Religion, and Healing* (New York: Abingdon-Cokesbury Press, 1951), 59. The use of saliva as a "popular medical measure . . . (was) recommended by Galen, the physician of Marcus Aurelius."

the cold, clinical procedure that concentrates on disease states rather than on the person. Some healers have empathy for what the ill person feels, but Jesus goes further. He identifies with the sufferer and the bondage of his disease.

We are moved by his sensitivity to those who were in pain, the gentleness of his demeanor to the outcasts of society. Once a man with leprosy approached Jesus with the plea, "Lord, if you are willing, you can make me clean" (Matt. 8:2-4). According to Levitical law (Lev. 13:46), Jesus ought not to have gone near him, let alone touch him. Yet Matthew underscores the love by which Jesus dealt with the sick: "Jesus reached out His hand and touched the man. 'I am willing,' He said. 'Be clean!'"

As we have already referenced, sickness in the Old Testament bore with it the stigma of shame. Yet Jesus broke through this barrier of shame in order to reach out to the rejected masses of His day. It was especially those who were labeled "unclean" by the church authorities and refused entrance into the temple that galvanize His attention. Jesus seems to have gone out of His way to heal the lame, the blind, and the dumb.

What etches itself on the modern reader's mind is that Jesus demanded no spiritual pre-condition of those He healed. He accepted all who came to him for healing and turned no one away for reason of station in life, moral failure, or spiritual immaturity. Paul Tournier comments:

> Think of all those sick people who flocked to Jesus. He never repulsed them; he never told them that they must first repent. His calls to repentance were directed to everybody, and especially to the healthy and the self-satisfied. But with the sick his first care was to afford consolation, relief and healing.[8]

Jesus appears to have dealt with every ill person in a unique way. Sometimes He would ask a question as He did in the case of the demoniac's father when He inquired as to the boy's condition (Mark 9:21). On another occasion He asked a lame man a question that might be asked by a modern physician, "Do you want to get well?" (John 5:6)

---

[8]Paul Tournier, *A Doctor's Casebook in the Light of the Bible* (San Francisco: Harper & Row, 1960), 195.

In the case of the Syro-Phoenician mother whose daughter was possessed by a demon, Jesus purposely provokes this woman in order to extract from her a fervent expression of faith (Mark 7:25-30). He then proceeded to heal the young girl.

In every case Jesus expressed Himself as the wise and compassionate physician, probing deeply into the human spirit wherein lie those unresolvable conflicts that provoke disease. He challenged the spirit to release its toxic poisons, to receive the gift of forgiveness, so that the fullness of healing could proceed. When He healed the Capernaum paralytic (Mark 2:1-12), the compassion of the Healer's heart touched the illness of this man's spirit—"your sins are forgiven"—as well as the paralysis of his legs—"get up, take your mat, and go home."

In a manner exemplary for those who practice healing as an art, Jesus directed His compassion to the whole person, reaching intently into the source of the sufferer's malady. Referencing our comments about disease and illness in chapter one, Jesus not only healed the disease, but He especially treated the person's illness. Here was not simply a wonder worker. Here was a Healer whose ministry was a demonstration of divine love in action

The Authority of the Healer

What was the source of Jesus' healing power? This has been a matter of much debate over the years by those who seek other than a theological explanation for His ability to cure physical disease. Some have believed that Jesus possessed shamanistic powers while others have asserted that Jesus healed by the power of suggestion.[9] Even His own declared enemies were convinced that Jesus healed by the power of Beelzebub, the prince of demons (Matt. 12:24).

The record of the Gospels, however, affirms that the source of Jesus' healing power from a human perspective was that He was anointed by *the Spirit of God*. On that occasion when He proclaimed

---

[9] Wade Boggs, Jr., *Faith Healing and the Christian Faith* (Richmond, VA: John Knox Press, 1956), 66 ff. Boggs states that Jesus could have used the power of suggestion but with the qualification that He did so by directing the thoughts of the patient Godward. The use of suggestion was a mechanism to arouse in the patient an attitude of eager expectancy.

His messianic mission to the home folks at Nazareth, Jesus made this announcement: "The Spirit of the Lord is on me because He has anointed me . . . "(Luke 4:18). The relationship between Jesus' healing and the Spirit is made more definite in His response to the Pharisees who questioned the source of His power. In this response Jesus said: "But if I drive out demons by *the Spirit of God*, then the kingdom of God has come upon you (Matt. 12:28). The Lukan version of this account is slightly different: "But if I drive out demons by *the finger of God*, then the kingdom of God has come to you" (Luke 11:20). Thus, in Jesus own words, His authority to heal the sick rests in the power of the Spirit of God.

Any attempt to link Jesus with the art of magic or with psychic slight of hand is intellectually dishonest. Jesus was not a magician and throughout His ministry eschewed all manner of magical practices or ritualistic formulas. Nor did He even desire the reputation of being a "miracle worker." On many occasions He told the sick person He had healed to keep the matter quiet (Matthew 8:4). The New Testament presents the healing ministry of Jesus as an demonstration of His messianic mission to redeem the world from the power of sin and Satan. His healing power was an expression of that mission.

In passing, we need to point out that Jesus' healing the sick is in no way a condemnation of other healers or medical systems, as limited as these approaches might be. On the contrary, He seems to affirm the doctors of His day and implies that God's healing power can work through their ministrations and medications. How else do we understand His comment, "It is not the healthy who need the doctor but the sick" (Luke 5:31)? However, as we shall soon discover, the scope of Jesus' healing ministry goes far beyond a focus on physical health and healing.

Jesus prepared Himself for the ministry of healing by communion with His Father. He felt the need for *prayer*, particularly as He stood against the hostile forces of disease and the power of evil. It is important for our understanding of His healing work to appreciate the outpouring of energy and concentration that the task of healing required of Jesus. The phrase in Luke 6:19 is revealing—"And the people all tried to touch Him because *power was coming out of Him and healing them all.*" No wonder that previous to this experience of healing the crowds, Luke reports that Jesus "went out into the hills to pray, and spent the night praying to God" (6:12).

The Wounded Healer

There is another picture of Jesus the Healer that brings us closer to the cross and His mission to reconcile to God a world broken in sin and disorder. Jesus is the "wounded healer" because He suffers as He heals.

Henri Nouwen has written some provocative words about healing in his book, *The Wounded Healer*, in which he states that every healer must look after his own wounds in order to be prepared to heal the wounds of other. In a previous book he describes the art of a genuine healer:

> When we honestly ask ourselves which persons in our lives mean the most to us, we often find that it is those who, instead of giving much advice, solutions, or cures, have chosen rather to share our pain and touch our wounds with a gentle and tender hand.[10]

The ministry of Jesus more than aptly fulfills this description of the suffering healer. It is noteworthy that Matthew authenticates the healing ministry of Jesus as a fulfillment of the Old Testament prophecy of the Suffering Servant (Is. 53:4). Matthew says that Jesus, as He healed the sick, fulfilled the words of Isaiah's prophecy (8:16-17):

> When evening came, many who were demon-possessed were brought to Him, and He drove out the spirits with a word and healed all the sick. This was to fulfill what was spoken through the prophet Isaiah: *"He took up our infirmities and carried our diseases."*

According to Roland Miller, there are two possible ways to interpret this passage.[11] First, it can have the meaning that Jesus bore our physical diseases in the sense of bearing them away. That is, Jesus

---

[10]Henri Nouwen, *Out of Solitude* (Notre Dame, IN: Ave Maria Press, 1974), 32.

[11]Roland E. Miller, "Christ the Healer," in Henry Letterman (ed.), *Health and Healing: Ministry of the Church*, (Chicago: Wheat Ridge Foundation, 1980), 36-37.

bore away our sicknesses by destroying the power of sin by His suffering and death. Golgotha thus illustrates how Jesus rescues humankind from *both* sin and sickness.

However, this verse can also mean that Jesus actually bore our sicknesses in His person. This seems to be the literal sense of the passage. As He went about healing the sick and dealing with human infirmities, Jesus felt and bore the weight and sorrow of our illness just as He bore the weight and punishment of our sins. The lesson here is that healing of any kind, physical, mental or spiritual, is costly to the Healer. Jesus pays a price in terms of His own humanity. As He "carries our diseases" in His person, He becomes for us a wounded healer.

We can illustrate this cost by noting that the exercise of compassion is emotionally hurtful to the Healer. Luke, for example, describes the response of Jesus when He saw the pain of the widow of Nain whose only son had just died: "When the Lord saw her, His *heart went out to her* and He said, 'Don't cry.'" (Luke 7:13)

The Greek word here—*splangnidzomai*—refers to being moved in one's intestines, considered to be the seat of compassion and affection. Today we might say in the vernacular, "guts." Thus, a paraphrase of this passage would make it to read, "When the Lord saw her, He *hurt in His guts for her*."[12]

Think also of the demands on His time and strength that healing the sick cost the humanity of Jesus. Mental and physical exhaustion were a daily corollary of His healing because of the crowds who clamored to see Him. The interaction was intense and time alone for communion with His Father was not readily available. Miller describes another cost the Healer faced, namely, loneliness:

> Jesus suffered in his loneliness. Healers know the feeling. It is profound and enervating. Who understood what he was doing as he healed? No one had a clear sense of what it was all about. His own brothers grappled with him and tried to drag him home. His disciples attempted to dissuade him from his insane course. Again and again he had to chide those nearest to him for their lack of understanding, not an easy thing to do. . . . Healers are lonely, and their true efforts are seldom

---

[12]William Hulme, "New Life through Caring Relationships in the Church," in *Word & World: Theology for Christian Ministry*. Vol. 11, No. 4, Fall, 1982, 342.

known. Will we ever know how lonely the Healer was and what this meant to him?[13]

In assessing the healing ministry of Jesus, we need to focus on a theology of the cross rather than on a theology of glory. Much of the modern distortion of Christ's healing ministry can be attributed to an overenthusiasm for the works of wonder He performed, incidentally, the same trap the Pharisees fell into when they asked Him to do a miracle. The response of Jesus to seekers after miracles was that He would give then no other sign than the sign of the prophet Jonah, the symbol of His forthcoming suffering and death (Matt. 12:38-40).

Those who follow Jesus must follow His healing path and really participate in the sorrows of the wounded. Healing exacts the price of pain to the person who is unafraid to touch both the inner and outer lives of the sick and ill. It should be obvious that Jesus the Healer is not magnified by modern "faith healers" who glibly scream out a magical aphorism—"claim the healing"—but who know nothing of what the sick person feels. The way of the Healer is to share the pain of others by entering into their world of shame and degradation. This is the theology of the cross!

Disease and Sickness in the New Testament

Disease and sickness in the New Testament need to be evaluated in the light of the culture of the times. Although the Jewish people possessed many of their same religious traditions, they had become a changed people. They now bore the influence of some new cultural traditions, principally the Hellenistic and Roman, which blended to some degree with Judaism. Disease in the New Testament divides itself somewhat along these lines.

We mention first how the New Testament narratives reveal the influence of the Greek medical system. There are new diseases described and new symptomologies referred to that never appear in the Old Testament. This is especially apparent when we read the Gospel of Luke and enjoy the benefits of his training as a physician. He uses the medical terminology of his day.

---

[13]Miller, op. cit., 35.

Jesus, for example, healed a man of dropsy or *edema* (Luke 14:2), a swelling of the limbs because of an internal functional disorder. The term *paralysis* is mentioned (Mark 2:3; Luke 5:18) as well as *dysentery* (Acts 28:8). Luke describes the healing of a man with a withered hand (Luke 6:6-10) which may have resulted from poliomyelitis in his youth as well as the healing of a woman who suffered *bleeding* for 12 years (Luke 8:42-48). The description of Herod Agrippa's death by worms is distinctly Greek (Acts 12:22-23).

While the New Testament is affected by Greek medicine, it is not completely given over to the Greek worldview. The Jews retained some of their former traditions. Thus, we are not surprised to see a blend of Hebrew and Greek medications as is reported in the Parable of the Good Samaritan (Luke 10:34). The stricken man's wounds are treated with oil (Hebrew) and wine (Greek) and then bandaged.

Many of the diseases reported in the Gospels are those we have already encountered in the Old Testament. These are diseases that may be characterized as "external" in nature and as a result, mark their victims as unclean according to Levitical Law.

Numerous instances of healing *lepers* are recorded (Matt. 8:1-3; Luke 17:12). Jesus adapted Himself to the Jewish cultural tradition by having these healed lepers show themselves to the priests in order to be officially certified as clean.

There are several examples of healing *lameness* which includes palsy and other crippling infirmities (Mark 2:1-12; John 5:16). There are two cases reported where permanent damage was evident. The healing of man who was *deaf and dumb* is mentioned in Mark 7:31-36. (See also Matt. 9:32-33.)

Blindness was a common malady in Jesus' day and it is no wonder so many examples are cited of this particular healing. One of these cases centers on a man born blind (John 9:1-41). The other instances may have been healings of those who lost their sight by means of disease; for example, blind Bartimaeus (Mark 10:46-52) or the two blind men in Jericho (Matt. 20:29-34) seem to evince the healing of those who once were able to see. This definitely is the case when Jesus healed the blind man of Bethsaida who, after Jesus spit on the man's eyes, he said, "I see people; they look like trees walking around." After Jesus' touched his eyes again, the man's sight was fully restored (Mark 8:22-26).

There are two accounts of sickness involving *fever*. One was the mother-in-law of Peter, perhaps malarial fever and more serious than imagined (Mark 1:30-31); and the other, the nobleman's son who suffers from a serious febrile condition (John 4:46-54).

One new phenomenon that the Gospels introduce is *demon possession*.[14] Jesus healed many of these tormented persons by casting out the spirit of torment. These were among His most dramatic healing episodes. A few examples that the New Testament reports are the healing of the chained man of the Gerasenes (Mark 5:1-17), the daughter of the Syro-Phoenician woman (Mark 7:25-30), and the boy with the deaf and dumb spirit (Mark 9:17-29). Some of those whom Jesus healed of demon-possession were victims of other maladies as well. What is significant is that the victim of demon-possession is said to be possessed with an *unclean spirit* (Mark 1:23). This suggests that the person is polluted according to Levitical law and required a certificate of cleansing.

There is no disease in the record of the Gospels that was impervious to the power of the healing Christ. Jesus heals *every type of disease* He encounters, even curing a woman whose back was bent over for 18 years (Luke 13:10), a disease that might be diagnosed by modern medicine as *spondylitis deformans*. The record of diseases in the New Testament appear to occur mainly in the organic categories although it seems apparent that Jesus could have and did heal diseases of a functional disorder, those especially susceptible to the power of suggestion. We might conclude by stating that the description of disease in the Gospels emphasize the types of diseases that are particularly resistant to medical knowledge, then and now. The blind receive their sight, the lame walk, the deaf hear.

---

[14]I am treating these narratives as bona fide examples of demon-possession rather than as some have interpreted them, as first century examples of mental illness. It has also been theorized that the particular symptom which enabled demon-possession to be differentiated from other afflictions was the evidence of suicidal impulses. The reader may pursue the discussion of this subject in Leslie Weatherhead, *Psychology, Religion, and Healing* (New York: Abingdon-Cokesbury Press, 1951), 89-101. What should not be lost in these remarks on demon-possession is that those whom Jesus healed are later described as in their right mind and in full possession of their faculties.

Disease Theory in the New Testament

The New Testament perception of the cause of disease is much more clearly elucidated than in the Old Testament. The origin of disease is linked with the activity of *Satan* and the bondage of his evil kingdom. Human sin is certainly involved in sickness but more in the sense that it is allied to Satanic activity who brings disorder to God's earth. In the mind of Jesus—those who were blind and lame, those who lived in the excruciating pain of febrile disease, those whose spirits were possessed by demons—were the victims of an *enemy* whose goal was to frustrate and destroy God's handiwork.

This enemy, who stands behind sin and disease, is Satan whom Jesus described as "the father of lies" (John 8:44). According to Scharlemann:

> Disease is not part of God's creative intent for man. . . . But men fell prey to another rule, the tyranny of the Evil One. Jesus came to destroy the works of this alien power, to bind the strong man, as He himself put it (Mark 3:27). The battle was joined also along the front of disease and suffering. To the task of overwhelming the kingdom of darkness belonged the job of restoring the whole man to a full relationship with God.[15]

From the first pages of the New Testament, we observe how *hostile* the attitude of Jesus was against sickness and how unrelenting his antagonism toward it. No wonder! He recognized the hand of the Evil One in the disorder of people's lives. He saw disease. illness, and sickness as the enemies of God's creation, as forces to be routed, as being against the creative purposes of God.

The evidence for this truth is massive. When Jesus healed Peter's mother-in-law, He strongly rebuked the sickness (Luke 4:39). He banished demons from an afflicted boy and commanded the tormentors to leave: "You deaf and dumb spirit, I command you. Come out of him and never enter him again" (Mark 9:25). The Pharisees were upset that Jesus healed a woman on the Sabbath Day whose spine was bent over. He responded sharply: "Then should not this woman, whom Satan has

---

[15]Martin Scharlemann, *Healing and Redemption* (St. Louis: Concordia, 1965), 84.

kept bound for eighteen long years, be set free on the Sabbath Day from what bound her" (Luke 13:16).

Perhaps the strongest illustration of Jesus' confronting Satan was when He cast out demons such as in the case of the man in the synagogue at Capernaum "'What do You want with us, Jesus of Nazareth? Have You come to destroy us? I know who You are, the Holy One of God!' 'Be quiet,' said Jesus sternly. 'Come out of him.' The evil spirit shook the man violently and came out of him with a shriek." (Mark 1:24-26)

Even the disciples of Jesus were to share in the loosening of Satan's grip upon the children of God. When the seventy disciples returned from their appointed mission to tell Jesus of their success, the Healer remarked, "I saw Satan fall like lightning from heaven" (Luke 10:18). The end of Satan's power was in sight even though the final consummation of this victory has been reserved until the Day of Judgment.

A second aspect of disease causation in the New Testament is the relationship between sin and disease, a theme much elaborated upon in the Old Testament. After He healed the man at the Pool of Bethesda, a man who had been an invalid for thirty-eight years, Jesus later spoke to him at the temple and told him not to sin anymore lest something worse happen to him (John 5:14). We need not draw the conclusion that the man had done some terrible sin for which reason he had originally become lame. Jesus was simply exhorting the man to mend his ways and to live a life of wholeness under God.

In Jesus' day there was a popular notion among the Jews that any instance of sickness was the direct consequence of some particular sin. A corollary belief of this *retribution theory of disease* was the assumption that those who were sick were greater sinners than those who were not. Jesus attacked this rigid dogma while at the same time recognizing that sin is the fundamental evil by which people are shackled and bound.

The most explicit New Testament example of this dogma was when Jesus' disciples asked him concerning a man who has been born blind: "Rabbi, who sinned, this man or his parents, that he was born blind?" "Neither this man nor his parents sinned," said Jesus, "but this happened so that the work of God might be displayed in his life" (John 9:2-3). Jesus categorically denied that the man's blindness was due to any specific sin or that he was a greater sinner than others. He also denied that those Galileans massacred by Pilate were sinners above all other Galileans because they suffered these things (Luke 13:2-5). On this last occasion he said to the crowd, "But unless *you* repent, you too will perish." The point Jesus was making was to turn people from the sins of others to a reflection of their *own* sins. Repentance of sins was not the special need of sick people. Repentance was everyone's problem, whether healthy or sick.

On many occasions Jesus forgave the sins of those whom He healed. Such was the case of the palsied man about whom the Healer responded to His adversaries: "Which is easier to say, 'Your sins are forgiven,' or to say, 'Get up and walk'? But so you may know that the Son of Man has authority on earth to forgive sins. . . . Then He said to the paralytic, 'Get up, take your mat and go home'" (Matt. 9:5-7). It is clear from this account that Jesus was not suggesting any causal link between the sins and the paralysis of the sick man. But He does underscore the fact that both are related to the fallen and distorted state of human nature; both need the healing touch of God. As so often is a pattern in the Bible, forgiveness and healing are all of a piece (cp. Psalm 103:3).

Perhaps no greater confusion has existed nor greater harm done in terms of disease and health than the retribution theory of disease. The essence of this theory is that God in His anger is punishing the victim for a particular sinful behavior. Dr. Tournier adds these provocative comments:

> How often do we find sins without disease, and diseases without sin! . . . Endless harm is done by this idea of a relationship of cause and effect between the two. Countless despairing people have had to undergo indescribable suffering and torture because their ills have been thought to be the result of their actual sins.[16]

Nevertheless, we do need to make clear that psychosomatic diseases do occur, and while these are not direct cause and effect consequences, they do illustrate the close correspondence of the spiritual domain and the processes of the body. Worry and fear, spiritual failures in their own right, often trigger disease states in the

---

[16]Tournier, op. cit., 194.

human body. The admission of such medical facts indicates that a relationship between sin and sickness does exist, not because God is punishing the person, but because all people are members of a *fallen and sinful humanity*.

Some evidence of naturalistic disease causation is found in the New Testament, the most notable example being Paul's advice to Timothy about his stomach problems: "Stop drinking only water, and use a little wine because of your stomach and your frequent illnesses" (I Tim. 5:23). On balance, however, disease theory in the New Testament is predominantly personalistic.

This discussion of disease theory unveils an attitude toward sickness that is helpful in understanding Christ's ministry of healing. It surely is not surprising, given the origins of disease in Satan's warfare against God's creation, why the Healer was not gentle with disease and why He sought to release people from its lethal grip.

But the hostile attitude of Jesus toward sickness helps us comprehend another truth as well. We begin, at last, to understand the purpose and mission of his coming to this earth. He came to bring to a fallen world a New Order. He came to bring the kingdom of God.

The Purpose and Mission of the Healer: The Kingdom of God

As we turn our attention to the grand *purpose* of Jesus' healing ministry, we need to begin where Jesus began. In His first sermon at Nazareth, He announced that the Messianic mission was not only to proclaim the good news but to deliver people from their sickness (Luke 4:18-19; Is. 61:1-2).

> The Spirit of the Lord is on Me because He has anointed Me to preach good news to the poor. He has sent Me to proclaim freedom for the prisoners and recovery of sight for the blind, to release the oppressed, to proclaim the year of God's favor.

In this passage our eyes become focused on the larger purpose of Christ's mission to the world. The Messiah has come to *restore order* to a world that was distorted by the power of sin and the lethal effects of disease. A new age appears and it is different from the past.

I am in agreement with Roland Miller who suggests that Jesus was initiating the *shalom* of God in His ministry as the Messiah.[17] The Day of the Messiah was to be a "recovery" of God's creation, to mend the broken relationship between God and humankind as well as to mend the distortion that disease had brought to human lives. In His mission to the world, Jesus was called to proclaim to all the peace of God and to share with all God's wholeness and health.

It is important to pay attention to Jesus' own words. He does not minimize the significance of His healing ministry, but always refers to it in terms of a mission He had to do. Before He healed the man born blind, He said to His disciples, "As long as it is day, we *must do the work* of Him who sent Me" (John 9:4). Jesus was conscious of the fact that His Father had commissioned Him to wage war on the kingdom of evil and disease. As He liberated victim after victim from the chains of disease, He was demonstrating the presence of *shalom* and the restoration of order within God's creation.

For example, when Jesus healed the woman with an issue of blood, He said to her: "Daughter, your faith has healed you. Go in *peace* and be freed from your suffering" (Mark 5:34). There is more here than a physical cure. Jesus was bringing to her the *shalom* of God. Miller explains this larger purpose of Jesus' healing:

> The word *shalom*, which carries the inclusive sense of total well-being, is translated in the New Testament by *eirene*, peace. Originally the Greek term *eirene* really meant the absence of conflict. It is used sometimes in that sense in the New Testament and is especially important in conveying the idea that the warfare between God and man has ended because of Christ, and a new relationship has come into being. But very often *eirene*, peace, is filled with the Old Testament meaning of *shalom*, the total restoration of the true state of humanity.[18]

Of course, Jesus did not use the word *shalom* to announce that He was bringing a new regime of wholeness to replace the old. He rather makes use of a term that describes the effects of *shalom* but which, in addition, emphasizes the rule of God in human hearts. This term is the *kingdom of God*. In Mark 1:15 Jesus says, "The time is fulfilled and

---

[17]Miller, op. cit., 22-23.

[18]Ibid., 22-23.

the kingdom of God is upon you." With this announcement He proceeds to heal one and all as He invites them into the Kingdom.

> (The kingdom of God) is an expression that signifies all the bother that God went to in order to undo the consequences of the Fall, including the presence of disease, with a view to re-creating the conditions of Paradise.[19]

Throughout His earthly ministry, Jesus pictures the kingdom of God as the personal entry of God into the lives of people, reconciling them to Himself in a manner in which there is a new order, a new community. It is the "treasure hidden in a field" that has been found (Matt. 13:44); it is the "pearl of great price" (13:45). In the kingdom of God, men and women discover the genuine purpose of their lives because they are at peace with God and with one another. And in this Kingdom they find health and wholeness.

Jesus consistently related His healing activity to the emergence of the kingdom of God. Who in particular did Jesus invite into the Kingdom? The very ones who had been the most hurt by the forces of dis-order and who needed wholeness in Christ, namely, the blind, the lame, the poor, those who lived in alleys and hedgerows (Luke 14:16-24). It should not surprise us that Jesus touches their bodies with healing because healing is part of the process whereby people become whole.

Healing and Faith

It is in the context of the kingdom of God that the New Testament introduces the topic of *faith* and healing. In account after account of His healing the sick, Jesus commends the faith of those whom He healed. Sometimes faith appears as a precondition of the healing; at other times it is a consequence of being healed. At times Jesus acclaims the faith of the sick person herself such as the woman with the issue of blood (Luke 8:48). But on other occasions it is the faith of others that was the critical factor. Of the faith of the centurion whose servant Jesus healed, the Healer said: "I tell you the truth, I have not

---

[19]Scharlemann, op. cit., 83.

found anyone in Israel with such great faith" (Matt. 8:10). In all of these accounts Jesus is the object of the person's faith, the Anointed One of God who alone has authority over disease and sickness.

Because of the importance of faith in any discussion of healing, especially in the light of the interest of medical science in the topic of faith, an entire chapter in this book has been set aside for such a task. Nevertheless, I feel it essential to point out the close correspondence between faith and the kingdom of God. It should be apparent that Jesus praises the faith of those who are healed because faith receives the blessings of the Kingdom. Immediately after Jesus commented on the great faith of the centurion, He spoke about those who would sit down with Abraham, Isaac, and Jacob in the kingdom of God (Matt. 8:11). We dare not remove faith in the Healer from the context of God's kingdom of grace.

Teaching and Healing Are Messianic Activities

One of the attitudes in times past that has aborted interest in Christ's healing ministry has been the assumption that the major activity of Jesus the Messiah was His preaching and teaching. The fact that He healed the sick was thought of as a secondary activity or, as some have believed, only a means to draw attention to His divinity. Martin Scharlemann, however, points out that Jesus' ministering to the sick was not "ancillary to His preaching and teaching, but were the signs which confirmed the presence of the redemptive power of God among men. . . . "[20]   Certainly, the internal evidence within the Gospels to support such a view is weighty.

The evangelist Matthew, for example, seems to structure his Gospel according to the twofold aspect of Jesus' messianic mission, namely, preaching and healing. In both Matthew 4:23 and 9:35, the *exact same passage* is repeated:

> Jesus went throughout Galilee, teaching in their synagogues, preaching the good news of the Kingdom, and healing every disease and sickness among the people.

---

[20]Ibid., 90-91.

It can be argued that Matthew deliberately set these passages as markers to make a strong theological point about Christ's coordinated ministry of preaching and healing. Thus, Matthew 4:23 accents the "preaching" activity of Jesus which covers chapters five, six, and seven whereas Matthew 9:35 accents His "healing" activity which predominates in chapters eight and nine.

One of the major questions in Jesus' day centered on whether He was the Messiah that God had promised. Some believed but many doubted. Even John the Baptist had his doubts and sent his disciples to inquire of Jesus if He were the One. How does Jesus confirm to John that He is the 'Anointed One' of God? It is significant that Jesus demonstrates the validity of His Messiahship by calling attention to His *healing* ministry (Matthew 11:2-6):

> Go back and report to John what you hear and see. The blind receive sight, the lame walk, those who have leprosy are cured, the deaf hear, the dead are raised, and the good news is preached to the poor.

Jesus also involved His own disciples in His healing ministry and gave them instructions in which healing was made a *coordinate responsibility* with preaching the Gospel. If, as some have argued, Jesus healed for the singular purpose of proving that He was the Son of God, then why does He instruct His own disciples to heal? Once again we find our answer in the foundation of the healing ministry, the kingdom of God (Luke 9:1-2).

> When Jesus had called the Twelve together, He gave them power and authority to drive out all demons and to cure diseases, and He sent them out to preach the kingdom of God and to heal the sick.

The training of the disciples in the healing ministry was an important part of their work as they accompanied Jesus in His journeys from city to city. On more than one occasion we read of their successes in the healing the sick (Mark 6:13; Luke 10:18) as well as their failures (Mark 9:28-29). Much later, after the outpouring of the Spirit at Pentecost, these same apostles, especially Peter and John, carry on the healing ministry in the manner they had been trained.

The Healing Miracles of Jesus

It is appropriate that we comment on the healing miracles of Jesus in the context of His ushering in the kingdom of God. For this is precisely what the healing miracles mean. They were signs of the Kingdom. Roland Miller makes this observation:

> They were the signal that the time has come for God to put in his hand, to enter into the fray, to personally and powerfully take on the forces of evil. They were not spectacles. They were rather the signs that a decisive attack was underway and that the age of salvation had now begun. Like all signs, they were meant to be read. They testified not simply that the Kingdom had come, but that it had come in Jesus.[21]

Miller is absolutely correct. The healing miracles were not spectacles. They were for the purpose of restoring God's order. Jesus shared His power with those who were in the greatest need of it, namely, the diseased, the handicapped, and the oppressed. From the perspective that the miracles overcame the power of disease, they can rightly be called signs of power. But from the point of view that they brought healing and wholeness, they are more appropriately called blessings of God's kingdom. When challenged by His opponents, Jesus openly responded that His healing miracles were a demonstration that the kingdom of God had come to the earth. He said: "But if I drive out demons by the Spirit of God, then the kingdom of God has come upon you." (Matt. 12:28).

Probably the weightiest problem that faces us as we attempt to apply Christian healing to the modern age is the problem of miraculous healing. Untold grief has been caused, not to mention irreparable harm to the cause of Christ, by those who claim that the standard of healing must be the same as that practiced by Jesus—"Take up your bed and walk." In the minds of many, there must be a dramatic, otherworldly aura in healing if it is to truly be a miracle of God.

For this reason, it is necessary that we interpret the word "miracle" with the meaning that it held in the minds of the writers of the New Testament. In the first century A.D., the universe was perceived by people as an open universe; that is, God was thought of as dealing

---

[21]Miller, op. cit., 24.

directly with the affairs of men in the natural order of life. They had no concept of observable laws by which the universe was sustained and ruled as we do today. Whenever such people saw an event not immediately explicable, they called it a "sign" of God and from them it elicited awe and wonder. For example, an eclipse of the sun or a catastrophe in nature would constitute such a sign.

> For Paul, as for his contemporaries, miracles occurred in the natural order of things, for they provided a glimpse into what was going on all the time throughout the universe. They were in no way intended to reveal the momentary suspension or even violation of natural laws. . . . Miracles, therefore, were reckoned with as occurrences which might be expected as providing evidence for the immanence of God.[22]

In our scientific culture, on the other hand, "miracles" are thought of as exceptional happenings in which the statistical odds of something occurring are improbable. Or else they are perceived of as events that stand in contradiction to general laws sustaining the universe. But this is not the Scriptural definition of miracles. In the New Testament, they are rather thought of as signs of the natural order pointing to the power of God.

The Greek terms used in the New Testament to refer to miracles make this point clear.[23] *Dynamis* means a mighty work that is a sign of divine power (Matt. 13:58). *Semeion* means a sign of divine intervention (John 4:54). *Teras* is used only with *semeion* such as in the phrase "signs and wonders" (John 4:48) and can also be translated "marvels." The common use of these terms in the New Testament points to a cosmology far different than the Newtonian universe perceived by modern people. We need to keep this word "miracle" unencumbered by our own epistemology and let it mean what the biblical writers say it means—a divine power of God.

Today many of the events of life inexplicable to the early church are made understandable by the application of laws that the scientific method has demonstrated. Such a development makes these events no less a "work of God" because we now understand some of the natural

---

[22]Scharlemann, op. cit., 35.

[23]Note the discussion of these terms in Morton Kelsey, *Healing and Christianity* (New York: Harper & Row, 1973), 106-108.

principles involved. As we grasp the deeper meaning behind the processes of healing, a subject we will pursue in greater detail in chapter five, we become all the more humbled by observing how God's power works in natural but comprehensible ways.

Yet even as we admit this, we must also acknowledge that there is much about healing we still do not understand. Inexplicable healing events occur daily which medical science cannot always explain; some doctors and others call these events "miracles."[24] I once spoke with a man who was operated on for an advanced case of throat cancer. He referred to his successful recuperation as a "miracle" and was convinced that his healing was due to the power of God. There is no doubt that God was responsible for his healing inasmuch as He is the source of all healing. Nevertheless, the man's use of the word "miracle"—he meant by it that he had survived the odds—is the modern use of the term.

Therefore, caution needs to be exercised in the use of the term "miracle" because it can mean different things to different people. From the viewpoint of the New Testament, the healing miracles of Jesus Christ and those performed in His name by the apostles were *signs* that the kingdom of God was breaking through into the world of men. Daniel Simundson adds this comment:

> We often trivialize the healing miracles by making them an end in themselves instead of seeing the larger meaning conveyed by them. We often turn an eschatological hope into a hope for the present world. Though Jesus has come, the final age has not yet emerged in all its glory.[25]

None of this is to say that God does not do "mighty works" in our midst today. He can and does perform prodigious healings, sometimes in a natural manner and sometimes in ways that are beyond the pale of human explanation. But in observing these signs of God's activity, it is

---

[24]Some books by medical professionals have appeared with the theme of miraculous healing, among them: Bernie Siegel, M.D., *Love, Medicine, & Miracles* (New York: Harper & Row, 1986).

[25]Daniel Simundson, "Health and Healing in the Bible," in *Word & World: Theology for Christian Ministry.* Vol. 11, No. 4, Fall, 1982, 339.

well to understand that they point to his grace now and also to the kingdom of glory to come.

Not Everyone is Healed

An important question that is often raised about the healing ministry of Christ centers on the fact that He did not heal everybody. Thousands of sick people inhabited Israel at the time of Jesus, yet He healed only a fraction of those people. To cite a specific situation, many ill and infirm were crowded at the pool of Bethesda, yet Jesus healed only one lame man at that place (John 5). Many other instances in the New Testament make clear the fact that, even though the restoration of order had begun, not everybody was physically healed.

We read that Paul had to leave Trophimus at Miletus because of his illness (2 Timothy 4:20). Paul himself suffered a debilitating handicap, a thorn in the flesh, that was not taken from him despite his many prayers (2 Corinthians 12:7-9). Even though divine healing was available, Christian believers continued to use their traditional medical systems. As we referenced earlier, Paul encouraged Timothy to drink a little wine for his stomach malady (1 Timothy 5:23).

One answer to this question is that while Christ ushered in the kingdom of God in His earthly ministry, the total consummation of this Kingdom has been reserved until the end time. It will be on the Day of Resurrection when God will complete the restoration of order, at which time "He will wipe away every tear from their eyes. There will be no more death or mourning or crying or pain, for the old order of things has passed away" (Rev. 21:4).

The New Testament points our eyes to the reality of the resurrection, not to an age of medical glory in the here and now. In our interpretation of the healing ministry of Christ, we need to put health in its rightful place and resist making it the end goal of our lives. Scharlemann correctly states that "health is only a *penultimate*, a next-to-the-last gift and not the ultimate reality."[26] He goes on to explain why Jesus did not fling out His word of power and heal every sick person as He did the centurion's son (Matt 8:15-17):

---

[26]Scharlemann, op. cit., 86.

Jesus did not engage in such universal healing by divine fiat for the same reason that He did not jump from the pinnacle of the temple. He did not come to gather followers in any other way than by asking them to see in His work a token of that full restoration which God had in mind for all his faithful ones at the end of history.[27]

What Jesus did accomplish was to begin the process by which people could be liberated from the powers hostile to God. In this interim period before He returns again, we share with all creation the eschatological hope—"The creation waits in eager expectation for the sons of God to be revealed" (Rom. 8:19). Yet even now, although disease and suffering remain, the blessings of wholeness in the kingdom of God are freely available to all.

As a reminder that the Day of Sabbath Rest is surely coming, there are victories over disease, sickness, and illness, and the power of evil. These victories are signs of the Spirit's presence in the church. The healing ministry of Jesus will continue until He comes again to make us whole even as He is whole.

Healing in the Apostolic Church

The healing ministry continues without abatement after the Holy Spirit appears at Pentecost. As the Spirit manifests His power through the small band of believers, and as the early church grows in numbers, one aspect of the Spirit's power is the blessing of healing. We should not be surprised that this is so. No fewer than 16 cases of healing are reported in the book of Acts. At the very beginning of their apostolic careers, Peter and John are channels of the healing power of Jesus. Peter said to the cripple who sat by the temple gate (Acts 3:6-8):

> "Silver and gold I do not have, but what I have I give you. In the name of Jesus Christ of Nazareth, walk." Taking him by the right hand, he helped him up, and instantly the man's ankles became strong. He jumped to his feet and began to walk. Then he went with them into the temple courts, walking and jumping, and praising God.

---

[27]Ibid., 85-86.

It is significant that, as the apostles are empowered by the Spirit to proclaim the saving name of Jesus Christ, they also heal the sick by this holy name. And the process would continue. According to Morton Kelsey, the healing ministry was a vital part of the early church's life for many centuries, Many church fathers of that time period comment that healing people in the name of Jesus was a normal function of the church.[28] It was not until the age of St. Augustine (ca. A.D. 400) when attitudes about sickness and God's intentions in healing began to change.

In passing we need to confront a theological aberration that has afflicted the Christian church in times past, namely, the thesis of *dispensationalism*. This is a theological belief that all history can be demarked into specific "eras," all of which illustrate the activity of God in different ways. Thus, the era of Christ's ministry, replete with healing miracles and signs of the kingdom of God, is considered to be different than the ages of history that were to follow. Dispensationalism holds that we ought not expect God to present His power today as He did in the first century. This extreme theological position, held by Calvin and others, simply does not accord with the record of the New Testament nor is it even hinted at in the Scriptures. It mistakes God's intervention in the world with cultural change and overlooks what the New Testament clearly teaches: the healing ministry of Jesus is carried on by the Holy Spirit in many different cultural contexts.

All of the apostles appear to be active in healing the diseased as the young church grew in numbers and strength (Acts 5:12). None was more active than Peter whose reputation as a healer was widespread (Acts 5:15-16):

> As a result, people brought the sick into the streets and laid them on beds and mats so that at least Peter's shadow might fall on some of them as he passed by, Crowds gathered also from the towns around Jerusalem,

---

[28]Morton Kelsey, *Healing and Christianity* (New York: Harper & Row, 1973). Chapters 7 and 8 include a thorough review of the healing ministry in the age of the church fathers.

bringing their sick and those tormented by evil spirits, and all of them were healed.[29]

Also engaged in healing were believers who were not apostles, most notably the deacons, Stephen and Philip, who were empowered by the Spirit to heal in Christ's name (Acts 6:8; 8:6). To demonstrate even further involvement by the church, a prayer composed by the early Christian community, known as the *Believer's Prayer,* requests God's blessing upon the healing ministry (Acts 4:29,30):

> Now, Lord . . . stretch out your hand to heal and perform miraculous signs and wonders through the name of your holy servant Jesus.

The apostle Paul is active in healing as well, such as when he healed the cripple at Lystra (Acts 14:8-12). On this occasion when he cried out to the man, "Get to your feet and stand up!" and the cripple jumped up and began to walk, the people thought Paul and Barnabas to be gods and called them Zeus and Hermes. On the island of Malta, after his shipwreck, the apostle laid hands on the father of Publius and healed him of dysentery (Acts 28:8). It was also at that time that Paul astounded the crowd by shrugging off the bite of a poisonous viper (Acts 28:3-6).

Paul certainly had no doubt that the healing of the sick was the work of the Holy Spirit whose presence brought grace and power as the Gospel was proclaimed. Paul wrote to the Galatians: "Does God give you His spirit and work *miracles* among you because you observe the law, or because you believe what you heard" (Galatians 3:5)? It is noteworthy that both Peter and Paul were involved in raising persons from the dead, Peter raising Dorcas of Joppa (Acts 9:36-41) and Paul raising Eutychus who fell from a third-story window while listening to Paul preach (Acts 20:8-12).

In time the healing ministry of the Apostolic Church was to become a more ordered process. We need not conclude that less spiritual power was present in the church but rather that a different expression of this power had evolved. Paul speaks of "gifts of healing"

---

[29]Anthropologists refer to the activity of either touching or entering the shadow of a "holy man" as *baraka*. This tradition has a long history in both the Middle East and in India

as a function within the Body of Christ, the Church (I Cor. 12:9). Likewise, a structured healing ministry emerges in which elders of the church are instructed to pray for the sick and to anoint them with oil (James 5:14-16). We will return to these themes again in chapter seven when we discuss the church and its healing ministry.

It is now necessary to step back and reflect upon the meaning of health as this term has been defined biblically. How do we make use of these accounts in a relevant manner to the practice of medicine and the pursuit of health in our modern day? It is to this subject that we now turn.

Chapter Four

The Biblical Model of Health

It is a fair question to ask: "Suppose God had no design for restoring human health and well-being?" What medical prospects would we have to look forward to on the planet Earth?

From a human point of view, it would certainly be a bleak picture. The efforts of medical science notwithstanding, disease is still rampant in our world and does not appear to be diminishing in the slightest. New strains of viruses continue to appear and are virulent in their effects on human populations. The HIV and E-Bola viruses, which have come out of Africa, may only be the precursors for even more lethal viruses to come. In addition, diseases caused by stress seem to be on the rise even as the rate of mental illness has been increasing in Western societies. Pulitzer Prize-winning author René Dubos adds this sober reminder for those who think that we will establish a "medical utopia" on the planet Earth:

> The concept of perfect and positive health is a utopian creation of the human mind. It cannot become a reality because man will never be so perfectly adapted to his environment that his life will not involve struggles, failures, sufferings. . . . The hope that disease can be completely eradicated becomes a dangerous mirage only when its unattainable character is forgotten.[1]

Fortunately, God has not left us to our own devices in matters of health and healing. He does have a plan concerning health that provides a viable hope for humankind in our present time and a *certain* hope in the world to come. We need to hear this biblical assurance.

The biblical model of health is essentially the *restoration of order* of God's created world. With the coming of the kingdom of God, Jesus Christ began the process of restoration which will continue inexorably

---

[1]René Dubos, *Man Adapting* (New Haven: Yale University Press, 1965), 346.

until the Day of Resurrection. At that time the process of *shalom* will be made complete and God will usher in the fullness of the Kingdom.

In this interim period, however, the God of Healing provides us with many resources of healing to combat the powers of disorder that, although defeated, continue to battle against us.[2] We need to take comfort in the fact that medical systems have improved over time. Our knowledge of the processes of healing has advanced exponentially over the past 50 years. We know a lot more about the patterns of disease, illness, and sickness than we did previously. Medical research in pathology, epidemiology, and mental health continues to mount as more and more studies in medicine, psychology, and human behavior are conducted.

Nevertheless, all of these advances in medicine and therapy are but parts of the grand design of which the biblical model of health is our goal.

The purpose of this chapter will be to set down a philosophy of health that is timeless because it accords with the purposes of God for the human race. It is important to understand God's design by which He will renew His creation to the healthy order He originally intended. As a result, we will be equipped with confidence to deal with disease, illness, and sickness because God in Christ has made all things new in our lives.

The Lord Is the Healer

The foundation of the biblical model of health is that the Lord is the Healer of all humankind. This was the proclamation of the God of Israel who said, *"I am the LORD who heals you"* (Exodus 15:26). Later this proclamation was incarnated in the healing ministry of Jesus Christ who showed mastery over every form of disease.

As the biblical witness makes clear, only the Lord has the authority to cure people of their diseases. No "pretenders" can challenge God's power. No medical system, not even medical science, can ever say that it has harnessed the processes of healing and now holds power over disease. At the most, medical systems can only borrow what God has

---

[2]Martin Scharlemann, *Healing and Redemption* (St. Louis: Concordia, 1965), 87-88. Scharlemann compares the mission of Jesus Christ to D-Day in World War II, which spelled the end of the Nazi tyranny even though the mopping-up operation was to take several more months before the final victory on V-Day.

providentially allowed them to discover and use. Behind all cures stands the Lord who is the Healer![3]

Because He has created the processes by which healing occurs, God is *not* bound to forms. He can heal in any manner He so desires. God dispenses healing through medicine, surgery, and medications which are common means of therapy used by doctors and health practitioners. His healing power can also be transmitted through rituals of healing, through suggestion, through faith, through prayer, through modalities of touch, music, and words, and even through the means of grace.

There is no venue that God cannot use in His love and wisdom to bring healing to the sick in any culture or society. Even those societies that are ostensibly pagan can participate in the healing processes that ultimately come from God and God alone. Healing is no more the private property of Christians than are the sun and the rain. "He causes His sun to rise on the evil and the good and sends rain on the righteous and the unrighteous" (Matt. 5:45). Seward Hiltner expresses it this way:

> The Bible supports whatever leads to a healing direction. Function restored is God's will. God is for, with, and in all healing processes, at any level whatsoever. He is equally present in the surgeon's tools, the psychiatrist's conversations, the internist's nutritional prescriptions, and the pastor's prayer. God is for healing in the sense that restoration of function, with necessary supporting structures, is always desirable.[4]

The Immune System

The basic foundation of healing has already been set in place in the human body, namely, the *immune system*. Those who do research in the area of the white blood cells express amazement at the precision of this

---

[3]The biblical narratives make clear the fact that only God has authority to heal. Those who argue that Satan can also heal because of such passages as Matt. 24:24— "For false Christs and false prophets will appear and perform great signs and miracles to deceive even the elect . . . "—are not convincing in their argument that these signs and wonders actually refer to healing. They rather refer to phenomena other than healing, because healing restores the very order that Satan has distorted. Satan is a destroyer, not a healer. Jesus said to the Pharisees when they accused Him of using Satan's power to heal: "If Satan drives out Satan, he is divided against himself. How then can his kingdom stand?" (Matt. 12:26)

[4]Seward Hiltner, "The Bible Speaks to the Health of Man," in *Dialogue in Medicine and Theology*, ed. Dale White (Nashville: Abingdon Press, 1968), 51-68.

system in which phagocytes monitor the body to detect and de-stroy alien germs. In addition, B and T lymphocytes learn to recognize new pathogens, memorize them, and then create antibodies to attack these germs in the future. This system is beautifully coordinated in that chemical messages are constantly being sent to assess the status of the body's health. It is noteworthy that all medical systems make use of the immune system to restore health by the use of a large variety of medications and therapies.

Perhaps even more crucial than the pharmacopoeia of medical systems is the hope and confidence that these systems generate within the patient's mind and spirit so that the immune system is given optimum support to bring healing.[5] Medical research has demonstrated that the immune system is sensitive to other *stimuli* which include antibiotics, moods, feelings, faith, feedback mechanisms, thoughts, and beliefs. The sensitivity of the immune system to the mental and emotional makeup of the individual makes the "healing process" an extremely complex system to understand. However, this much we know. When we deal with the emotional and spiritual pains of the sufferer, we are at the same time dealing with the maladies of the body. We cannot really separate the disease a person has from the illness that the person feels and the sickness experienced in the social system. The processes of healing run wide and deep.

There is much we still do not understand about healing. Perhaps we will never know all of the intricacies of the "spirit-body" that the God of creation has given to each of us. Added to this is the genetic uniqueness of each single human being that adds complexity of another sort. But none of this should add or detract from the elementary fact that God the Healer provides the processes of healing for our benefit or that He can bring healing in any manner He so desires.

Understanding the immune system helps correct our bias that physical healing is the primary concern of health and healing. The fact that the health of the psyche and spirit are synthesized with the health of the body enlarges our perceptions about health. It is ironic that many traditional medical systems instinctively recognize this truth in that

---

[5]The normal white blood count of an adult is about 7,500 mm. This count fluctuates hourly and is sensitive to emotional moods and stress events. A severe drop in the white blood count signals vulnerability to disease. On the other hand, an attitude of hope and confidence can raise the white blood count, a signal of health because of a strong immune response.

they reach out to all of the needs of the patient instead of only the palpable needs of the body.

As we now take a careful look at the biblical view of health, we will see how this truth is demonstrated in a very persuasive manner.

The Biblical View of Health

What does it mean to be healthy from the viewpoint of Scripture? As we have already referenced in our study of the Old and New Testaments, health is related to the word *shalom* which is best translated as "peace" or "wholeness." *Shalom* refers to the unity of all things under the rule of God. When the ancient Hebrews thought of *shalom*, they thought of the whole warp and woof of their life, their relationships with their neighbor, their dealings with Yahweh God, and even the blessings of Yahweh on their olive trees. *Shalom* meant much more than physical well-being. It also meant personal, social, and cosmic well-being.

Among the Hebrews, to be a "healthy person" meant that one's life relationships were centered in the peace and wholeness of God himself. According to William Watty:

> Health was not considered something physical, but total. In the 23rd Psalm, Yahweh restores my *nephesh*, which means not only spiritual refreshment, but also physical recovery and social rehabilitation. The word for health in Hebrew is *shalom* and the word is the same for "peace," "welfare," "well-being," and "harmony." Health is total. It is personal well-being. It is social harmony and justice. It is walking humbly with God.[6]

Health, then, is more than our physical and mental well-being. Health is the *wholeness* of God's creative love at work in our lives. It is the expression of what God has created us to be—functionally, mentally, emotionally, socially, and spiritually.

To use an example from nature, the lily thrusts toward flowering as an example of its species. Like a budding flower, which is the expression of what a lily is supposed to be—and which is much more than the leaves and roots that sustain it—so wholeness is the expression

---

[6]William Watty, "Man and Healing: A Biblical and Theological View," *Contact.* (Christian Medical Commission, WCC) vol. 54 (December 1979): 5.

of our identity and potential as persons moved by the love of God. It is not how we feel that makes us healthy, but *what we are* as persons.

We can speak of two levels of health in the biblical perspective of wholeness. The first applies to our physical and mental well-being, our ability to function in human society. A term to describe this level is *wellness*. The second level, however, refers to the creative expression by which our personhood interacts with the environment and with others in social relationships. This level can be referred to as *wholeness*, for it is the "flowering" of our spiritual and psychical potential. It is the revelation of "who we are" as persons because we have been touched by the peace of God.

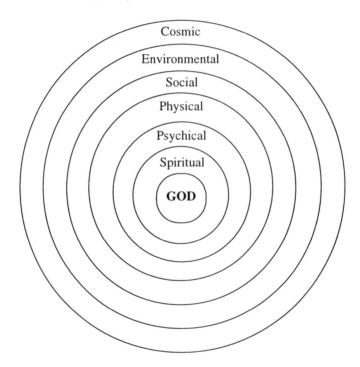

The Biblical Model of Health

The Biblical Model of Health

Look, for example, at the crippled man who was healed by Peter and John at the temple gate in Jerusalem. After his healing in the name of Jesus, we are told that "he jumped to his feet and began to walk" (Acts 3:8). This illustrates that his ability to function was restored. In this respect, we speak of "wellness." But observe what happens as the man walks into the temple: "Then he went with them into the temple courts, *walking and jumping, and praising God.*" Here we discern health as "wholeness" because the man expresses passionately, in the community of believers, that his life has been touched by the peace of Christ. In short, his life has been restored to order.

This concept of health is difficult for people of the Western world to comprehend. We tend to separate the health of the body from the health of spiritual and human relationships. Because we make physical health such a dominant factor, we frequently misinterpret the healing ministry of Jesus Christ. We concentrate on the diseases He healed rather than on the health and wholeness of the people at whom His ministry was aimed.

Biblical health, in contrast, is cosmic because it brings order to the *totality* of our personhood. It also brings order to the community of which we are members.

We see this truth illustrated splendidly in a woman Jesus healed who had been victimized by constant hemorrhaging (Luke 8:43-48). When this woman through faith touched the robe of Jesus in the midst of a crowd, His power rushed out and cured her medical condition. But notice the words that Jesus speaks to this woman: "Daughter, your faith has healed you; go *in peace.*" It is interesting that the Greek phrase reads *eis eirene* which means "into peace." Perhaps a better translation would be: "Go into a *state of peace or wholeness.*" What Jesus was saying to this woman, who was cured physically, was that she was made whole in her personhood. Her life was back in order because God's rule was at the center of her being. To say it another way, Jesus healed her as a total person.

That is the peace or wholeness that is the charter of our Christian faith. I think *wholeness* is a beautiful word. It describes the new reign of God in human hearts through the means of God's forgiveness in Christ. All is now well between God and humankind. In addition, all is now potentially well between every human being on the planet because Christ has broken down the barriers of separation. As one author put it, the wholeness that Christ gives is the confidence that we can be alive for God.

Certainly Jesus healed a lot of people who bore dreaded diseases in their bodies. After all, His mission was to deliver people from their bondage. *Let us not de-emphasize this biblical fact of physical curability* as we speak of wholeness. But at the same time, let us not forget the larger picture of "health" He addressed. Christ came to give us the kingdom of God with all the blessings of *shalom*: "I have come that they might have life, and have it to the full" (John 10:10).

The Meaning of Biblical Health

One of the problems of describing health as "wholeness" is that it seems to include *all* of life in its definition of health. In one sense of the word, that is true because God's order of peace extends to every facet of our existence. But it is possible to explain biblical health in a more concrete fashion. There are at least four ways in which the biblical perspective of health makes an impact on our lives and the world in which we live.

Health in the Physical Environment

In the order of creation God intended our relationship with the *physical environment* to be a healthy one. We recall that the human being was created from the "dust of the earth" so that there is a continuity between humankind and all of nature. Because the whole creation is so interwoven in terms of ecological relationships, it suggests that our daily existence as humans was meant to be in wholesome surroundings. It is significant that God told Adam to work within the Garden and to take care of it (Gen. 2:15). Thus, our concern for environmental health has strong biblical roots because the health of the environment is closely related to our own health and well-being.

One of the tragedies of human history has been a despoiling of the environment with the resultant chaos of allowing disease to run rampant. Water and air pollution have presented major medical problems in much of the world, so much so that people with respiratory disorders are warned not to go outside on certain days of the week. The loss of rain forests and estuaries have created an ecological imbalance that may haunt civilized life in the centuries to follow. Acid rain and toxic wastes, as well, bring a type of pollution that can be lethal to human life. Medical anthropologists also speak of the "diseases of development," which refer to the erection of dams, man-made lakes, irrigation agriculture, and urbanization. Inevitably we discover that such diseases as schistosomiasis, ochhoncerciasis (river blindness), filariasis, and tuberculosis follow in the wake of these cultural interventions. It can be argued that "civilization must move forward," but we must ask the question: "At what price to the health of humans is the success of human progress?"

We cannot continue to treat our environment with impunity because it will exact a fearful consequence on our own health. Now, more than ever, we need to understand the delicate balance of ecological relationships, of which human beings are a part, if we are to live in an harmonious relationship with the environment. The health of nature is directly correlated with the health of humankind.

Health in Social Relationships

What is true in our physical environment is also true in our *social environment*. No person lives in isolation from others but rather in a relationship with fellow human beings. What makes "illness" such a dominant factor in human life is because our relationships with others have become fractured and unhealthy. We may feel a sense of guilt or anger at another person and find ourselves unable to cope with the loss of the relationship. Some persons, in fact, are pushed over the edge and retreat into the world of mental illness. The tragedy of broken relationships makes us vulnerable to disease, whether these losses be divorce, friendship, or bereavement at the death of a loved one.

John Sanford tells the story of a young man who experienced a typical functional disorder due to problems in his social relationships.[7] He was suffering from a pain in his shoulder that gave him no relief. He went from doctor to doctor to find the cause of his pain, but no doctor was able to diagnose any physiological disorder. Finally, one doctor said to him, "Those muscles you say are so painful are the very ones you would use if you were to *hit a person in the jaw*." The young man thought of the hostilities he felt toward certain people, those that he wanted to strike out against. When he was able to release his anger and develop a forgiving attitude toward his protagonists, the pains in his shoulder suddenly disappeared.

God made us to live with others and biblical health implies healthy relationships with those who are members of our family, kin group, and our circle of friends. Medical research has extensively documented the relation between having a support group and well-being. Women who

---

[7]John Sanford, *Healing and Wholeness* (New York: Paulist Press, 1977), 31.

have extensive social contacts live an average of 2.8 years longer than women who do not; the comparable figure for men is 2.3 years longer.[8] One study of men who were heavy smokers revealed that *single* men died of lung cancer at a rate five times that of married men. Other studies demonstrate that people with high levels of social support have fewer complications during pregnancy and childbirth, less susceptibility to herpes attacks, lower rates of myocardial infarction, and lower rates of psychological distress.[9] It should be obvious that health is a wholesome relationship of caring and affection between persons in society.

The Health of the Self

Thirdly, biblical health reflects a *unity of our personhood*, which refers to an integration between the inner and outer lives of the Self. God has made us as persons whose bodies, minds, and spirits thrive when they are in a state of harmony and coordination. Self-worth and self-esteem are related to our personal sense of identity and the acceptance of ourselves as individuals created in the "image of God." But note the chaos that follows when the Self is divided, when we are not honest with ourselves because we are fearful of confronting our failures and inner conflicts. It is hardly surprising that problems of personal identity have accelerated the use of drugs, illicit sex, and alcohol in an attempt to find inner peace. Yet each of these "alternative solutions" leads only to a greater division of the Self and deeper despair. Watty's commentary is appropriate:

> Breakdowns occur in modern society at an unprecedented rate because people's lives are uncoordinated. We wear too many faces. We act too many parts. We allow the several roles which we perform to determine who we are. The result is an inner disintegration, a loss of centre, and a loss of identity. We do not know who we are. We do not know how to use leisure. We fear solitude and self-examination.[10]

The health of the Self is essential if we are to function in a healthy manner. Psychological therapy can be very helpful, especially for those

---

[8]Shelley E. Taylor, *Health Psychology* (New York: McGraw-Hill, 1995), 278.

[9]Ibid., 278.

[10]Watty, op. cit., 7.

who have been victimized by others, such as by rape, sexual abuse, or betrayal. But ultimately the health of the Self is dependent upon the health of the spirit, because the Self finds its true meaning when the Spirit of God is at home in the person. St. Augustine once said: "Thou madest us for Thyself and our heart is restless, until it reposes in Thee."

The Health of the Spirit

Biblical health at its core means a *right relationship with God*. The consummate truth about our humanity is that we are frail and finite creatures, vulnerable to the boundaries of our human mortality. Disease and illness are constant reminders that our own hold on life is slender. We are secure only when a power greater than ourselves holds us in our being. For this reason the biblical proclamation touches humans at the point of their deepest need: "We implore you on Christ's behalf: *be reconciled to God!*" (2 Cor. 5:20)

We pause to remember that Jesus was correcting the distortion of our human nature in His ministry of healing and redemption. His aim was to deliver people from the bondage of evil and to restore wholeness and reconciliation to the broken lives of humankind. Paul said of the redemptive ministry of Jesus (Eph. 2:14-18):

> For He Himself is our *peace*, who has made the two one and has destroyed the barrier, the dividing wall of hostility. . . . His purpose was to create in Himself one new man out of the two, thus making *peace*, and in this one body to reconcile both of them to God through the cross, by which He put to death their hostility. He came and preached *peace* to you who were far away and *peace* to those who were near. For through Him we both have access to the Father by one Spirit.

Biblical health means that the "peace of Christ" resides within us and finds expression in our personality. This peace provides our lives with a center as well as a future. To be spiritually healthy signifies that our whole transient existence is empowered by the presence of God's Spirit. How we relate to the Holy Spirit on whom we daily depend is also a question of health. A life devoted to worship, prayer, and loving service, as we live out our vocations, is a healthy life and one that continues to grow creatively.

Those Who Bring Healing from God

Many different professions and many different types of persons are used by God to bring healing to people. The biblical model of health encourages "medical pluralism" for this basic reason. No single medical system can possibly offer all the resources to combat the ills that oppress our common humanity. The expertise of many different disciplines is required to achieve mastery over disease and illness, a fact that will become obvious in the following survey.

From the perspective of *disease* itself, it is obvious that medical science is essential in order to master the pathogens and functional disorders that attack human bodies. Doctors, nurses, and other medical personnel have been aptly described as the "hands" of God to promote healing and well-being. But medical researchers and technicians are also crucial contributors in God's design in the study of disease and in the development of medications. In a similar context we need to affirm those in the field of public health who provide clean water, dispose of wastes, and destroy disease-bearing organisms and vectors.

It certainly follows that the same applies to those who treat the *diseases of the mind and the emotions*, namely, psychologists, psychiatrists, and therapists whose treatments are meant to overcome the "impotence of the Self" we sometimes experience. We often forget that the disorder of disease enters through the portal of the mind rather than only through the biochemical processes of the body. Schizophrenia, bi-polar disorders, and depression are just as real as cancer and pneumonia and can at times be more painful. It certainly is not a denial of faith in God to consult those mental health professionals whose sole purpose is to assist us in becoming more functional. Elizabeth Skoglund reminds us of this fact:

> Certain Christians actually view psychological counseling as something which should be totally spiritual; they seem to ignore the psychological dimension altogether. Some go so far as to denigrate all counselors. There are two problems here: the inability to see emotional problems apart from spiritual problems, and the mistaken idea that all Christian therapists promote spirituality in their patients and that all non-Christian therapists attempt to destroy their patients' Christianity.[11]

---

[11]Elizabeth Skoglund, *The Whole Christian* (New York: Harper and Row, 1976), 7.

What has been said about psychological disorders pertains also to the illnesses that attack the *human spirit*. These spiritual setbacks not only ravage our fellowship with God; they also erode the meaningfulness of life. If wholeness is to be achieved, the healing of the spirit is essential. In His own ministry, Jesus especially addressed the care of the spirit. As we follow His example, we must address the same in our age. For this reason pastors and other church workers play crucial roles in ministering to people in whom the fruits of spiritual disorder are conspicuously evident.

Perhaps it sounds strange to place pastors at the same level as doctors in terms of health care, but from the perspective of the biblical model of health this is a truism we need to acknowledge. Martin Luther once spoke of the pastor as a *seelsorger*—a carer of souls—a title that, once acknowledged, would do much to advance the art of healing in the Christian church.[12] As Luther understood this term (*seelsorge*), one of the duties of the pastor was to visit the sick in order to give consolation from God's Word as well as to pray and give thanks. It is important to remember that dealing with the "illness" a person suffers, and the sickness that is social, is often as crucial as treating the disease. Because pastors are on the firing line most days of the week dealing with the "illnesses" of their parishioners, they do provide health care in the very process of "caring for the souls" of their flock.

The Purpose of Health

The biblical model of health offers us a clear and unambiguous understanding of the *purpose* of health. We noted it previously when we examined the narrative of the healing of the crippled man by Peter and John. After he had been healed, Luke reports that the man "went with them into the temple courts, walking and jumping, and praising God" (Acts 3:8). In this passage we discern what the functional use of wellness must ultimately lead to: a life that is lived to the praise and honor of God.

Martin Luther phrased the purpose of health in a similar fashion and with theological clarity. According to Luther there was no better way to express the reason for which we strive to be healthy than to seek to *serve God and our neighbor*:

---

[12]Werner Elert, *The Structure of Lutheranism* (St. Louis: Concordia, 1962), 363.

> The Christian should be guided by this one thing alone that he may serve and benefit others in all that he does, considering nothing except the need and the advantage of his neighbor. . . . This is what makes caring for the body a Christian work, that through its health and comfort we may be able to work, to acquire and lay by funds with which to aid those who are in need, that in this way the strong member may serve the weaker. . . . This is a truly Christian life. Here faith is active in love.[13]

Luther's comments demonstrate clearly how our health is to be used in this world: to assist the neighbor who is *in need*—which is everyone! Many examples could be given of persons who characterize this outpouring of Christlike love for the neighbor. Jesus Himself related the Parable of the Good Samaritan as a supreme example of a person who, by binding the wounds of his own social enemy, illustrated the entire purpose of health. In our own generation, no one has exhibited more love for the neighbor than Mother Teresa of Calcutta, India, whose death the entire world mourned. Mother Teresa was for many the epitome of what a healthy life was created to do. To reach out, as she did, to the "poorest of the poor" with the love of Christ constitutes the essence of service to the neighbor. There is hardly a more healthy way to live our lives.

The purpose of health therefore gives an added stimulus to the care of our own physical and mental health. As Luther said: *"This is what makes caring for the body a Christian work."* From Luther's point of view, those who are physically and emotionally hardy have been gifted by God to assist those who have been beset with weakness.

An entire theology of self-care can be established on this biblical concept, which was so well worded by St. Paul: "Do you not know that your body is a temple of the Holy Spirit, who is in you, whom you have received from God?" (1 Cor. 6:19) Rather than abusing the body, which in itself is a creation of God, and which has been redeemed by Christ, Christians have all the more reason to practice the stewardship of self-care. According to James Van Buskirk:

> Religion must not be an excuse for neglect or violation of the laws of hygiene and sanitation; we have no right to expect the Lord to give us good health if we disobey the laws he has ordained. . . . There is no saintliness in failing to take proper care of our bodies. True religion ought to give us a keener conscience to follow the rules of health, the laws of

---

[13]Martin Luther, *The Freedom of the Christian Man.*

God for our good. It is our religious duty to be as healthy as we can, for these bodies of ours are to be "temples."[14]

Health Is More than Wellness

Luther's remarks about the purpose of health also imply a warning that should be mentioned at this time. The pursuit of health must never become an end in itself. If an individual has made health the supreme goal of his life, the "*summum bonum*" of human existence, then health has become an idol of his own making.

Incidentally, this presents a major problem to those health faddists who never get around to asking the question why they spend so much time and energy in health-producing activities. It appears that wellness has become for them the ultimate reason for their existence. In much of America today, the wellness movement has captured more than the minds of people; it has also captivated their hearts. At times we are almost overwhelmed by a panacea of wellness which is symbolized by superbly conditioned individuals who embody tight skin over their cheek bones with gleaming eyes and taut abdominals. But what is the meaning of it all? What is the point of wellness if it has no God-ordained purpose?

This is why a distinction must be made between *wellness*, which means the ability to function, and *wholeness*, which means to live for a purpose. From the Christian perspective, wellness is a desired gift of God, but only in the context of the larger blessing of wholeness in which our lives have been touched by God's grace for a higher calling.

It is instructive to recall that prior to World War II, the youth of Nazi Germany were considered to be the healthiest specimens in Europe. Their tanned bodies and sturdy constitutions, honed by rigorous discipline and competitive sports, characterized them as the zenith of wellness. Those who served in the British army, in contrast, were described as being in relatively poor condition with pallid complexions and bad teeth. But in retrospect, after this bitterly fought war, it was apparent that "health" was personalized by the British who fought for freedom against the Nazi tyranny. The tragedy of Nazi Germany demonstrates so lucidly how the gift of wellness, as used by the forces of evil, can actually become a profound "sickness."

---

[14]James Van Buskirk, *Religion, Healing & Health* (New York: Macmillan Co., 1952), 121.

Wellness, to be sure, is an important aspect of health. Let us never underestimate the benefits of being able to enjoy life as God creatively intended. The human being was created to function, to ambulate, to use his limbs and mental abilities to adapt to the demands of life. It is in the interest of wellness that the United States Department of Health and Human Services makes strategies that affect the well-being of all Americans. Recently this department adopted as one of their three major goals to be accomplished by the year A.D. 2000 *the increase of the span of healthy life for Americans.*[15]

However laudatory these efforts in promoting wellness may be, there is a purpose to health that transcends function. This purpose is a life of wholeness that has been scripted for each of us by God Himself. As Scharlemann makes clear:

> From a biblical point of view, physical well-being is not an end in itself. . . . Any interest in the question of healing must be guided by this fundamental awareness that man is whole to the degree that he is able to command his powers to serve God's intention of having men minister to the needs of others.[16]

The Expression of Wholeness as Health

Perhaps the most useful way to describe the biblical understanding of health is to portray it as a *cause* for which one lives. When Christ healed the sick of His age, He linked them to a cause greater than themselves. He invited them into the kingdom of God, which immediately provided the supplicant with a personal identity, with a destiny to live out their lives, and with a community of faith.

It is within the Kingdom that we live out the stories of our lives. The process of growing, of striving for the cause, is our "story." But

---

[15]*Healthy People 2000: National Health Promotion and Disease Prevention Objectives.* U.S. Department of Health and Human Services, Public Health Services (Boston: Jones and Bartlett, 1992), 45. This goal encompasses the essential elements of health promotion and disease prevention, namely, the prevention of premature death, disability, and disease, and enhancement of the quality of life. Additional or related initiatives can be seen in Robert Amler and H. Bruce Dull, *Closing the Gap: The Burden of Unnecessary Illness* (New York: Oxford University Press, 1987), and *Healthy Communities 2000: Model Standards*, American Public Health Association, 1991.

[16]Scharlemann, op. cit., 76.

this is the very phenomenon that makes life exciting and health-producing. Wholeness means to be vitally involved with the purposes of the Kingdom. It is this vitality that expresses the "health" of our personhood. People who are whole in Christ exhibit the positive hope that Christ, by means of His death and resurrection, achieved for us all.

To illustrate, a woman can live out her life's "story" as a mother of two children and her career as a teacher by healthily devoting her energies to her home and her vocation. But the motivation that compels this woman is the love of Christ who has brought wholeness to her life. She lives not for herself but for the *health* of those whom her life touches.

According to Sanford, what is most significant about becoming whole is the capacity for personal growth, a process by which we discover life's deepest meanings:

> It is impossible to summarize the way a person becomes whole. It is, for one thing, an individual matter, differing with each person. But it can be said that to become whole we must be involved with life. . . . Our life must have a story to it if we are to become whole, and this means we must come up against something; otherwise a story can't take place. . . . If we stand on the sidelines of life, wholeness cannot emerge.[17]

Health as wholeness can be noticed in people as they express themselves. Their personalities show energy and vitality as if touched by a higher purpose. Their intellects demonstrate the capacity to seek out and apply useful knowledge for the benefit of others. Their characters reveal that a Greater One rules within: "Your attitude should be the same as that of Christ Jesus" (Phil. 2:5). It was Chesterton who once said of those who live for a cause: "That which compels man is the beat of the drums." Surely, those who live in the kingdom of God hear the drumbeat of the One who gives humankind wholeness.

Living for a cause is not easy because it involves some risks. Life within the kingdom of God means obedience of faith to Christ's Word which, as a consequence, will bring conflict in its wake. Inevitably, there will be some pain and suffering along the way. Believers in Christ must do battle with evil. Paradoxically, being "healthy" in the biblical perspective may add suffering to our lives. John Sanford adds this important observation:

---

[17]Sanford, op. cit., 19.

Becoming whole does not mean being perfect, but being completed. It does not necessarily mean happiness, but growth. It is often painful, but, fortunately, it is never boring. It is not getting out of life what we think we want, but it is the development and purification of the soul.[18]

But let us lay down an important caveat about wholeness at this point. Wholeness is a term that is also enjoying wide currency in the secular world. It has almost become faddish to talk about the wholeness that is health. We need to be aware that others use this term but shape it to serve their own intentions. For example, some of the psychological literature on wholeness seems to focus unduly on the individual's self-interest only. Thus, wholeness for some seems to have come to mean a kind of psychological "peace," a state of feeling good about oneself, an escape from the struggles of life. For others it carries the New Age meaning of personal identity—"I must become aware of my higher self." Perhaps the most popular use is by those in the wellness movement who describe wholeness as "radiant health," an advanced state of wellness that has spiritual leanings toward Gnosticism.

Interpretations such as these reckon the answer of life to reside *within the individual alone*, not in the Holy Other who stands apart from His creation. None of these should be confused with the biblical perspective of health in which our wholeness is centered in the Christ who came to "proclaim freedom for the prisoners and recovery of sight for the blind, to release the oppressed and to proclaim the year of the Lord's favor" (Luke 4:18-19).

Health Is a Process

Health is a process just as disease, illness, and sickness are processes. People are never totally ill nor are they totally healthy.[19] Every person is somewhere on the continuum between diseased and healthy because life is never static. Change is inevitable and this affects our struggle as we grow toward wholeness.

For example, a person can appear to have achieved a high level of wellness. Her spiritual life may also seem to be mature and deeply fulfilling. Suddenly, an event occurs (a death in the family) that

---

[18]Ibid., 20.

[19]Nancy Tubesing, *Philosophic Assumptions* (Hinsdale, IL: Wholistic Health Centers, 1977), 18.

provokes an extreme amount of stress so that the person becomes "ill." How she resolves this stress will determine whether she moves forward toward health or backward toward sickness.

Health has much to do with the perception of the person who is ill. Health is a process of adapting to the changes of life whether these are crises caused by stress or the onset of disease. In a real sense, health is closely related to our personal coping behavior.

In his book *Anatomy of an Illness*, Norman Cousins writes how he fought back from a crippling collagen disease, *ankylosing spondylitis*, through sheer willpower and by using massive amounts of Vitamin C and laughter.[20] Working in close harmony with his doctor, he decided he needed to take active charge of his own ill-health. Basically what Cousins did was to experiment with the thesis that if negative thoughts create an environment for disease, then, conversely, positive thoughts can create an environment for health. The success of Cousins's experiment has been widely reported in the press and medical community; it has helped change the perceptions of many about the nature of sickness and health.

We are discovering that if patients are encouraged to adopt a positive attitude toward their disease, they will recover much more quickly. In other words, there is a *healthy way to live a disease!* Spiritual and psychological resources can be used to integrate the person toward health. For this reason, some in the field of medicine are suggesting a new model of health, a model which focuses on the health of a person rather than on the disease.

We are discovering that if patients are encouraged to adopt a positive attitude toward their disease, they will recover much more quickly. In other words, there is a *healthy way to live a disease!* Spiritual and psychological resources can be used to integrate the person toward health. For this reason, some in the field of medicine are suggesting a new model of health, a model which focuses on the health of a person rather than on the disease.

Another important truth that has ensued from this change of perception is the fact that a person can still be "whole" despite suffering a physical limitation. In a word, people who are sick are also healthy in other aspects of their being. For example, a man who suffers from hypertension or a woman confined to a wheelchair can still be

---

[20]Norman Cousins, *Anatomy of an Illness as Perceived by the Patient* (New York: W. W. Norton, 1979).

very healthy from the perspective of their spiritual lives. Many handicapped people today demonstrate the wholeness of health in precisely this manner. Regardless of their medical condition, they are a joy to be around; their "aliveness" toward life is contagious. One of the most radiant men I have ever heard speak was the survivor of a colostomy operation. Few individuals could express the joy of being alive and living life as a mountaintop experience as did this man.

There is a reason why wholeness can characterize a person with physical limitations and why such people deserve to be described as healthy. The reason is simply that their "illness" has been healed even though their disease may remain. For such people the pain of the psyche and spirit has been overcome by the greater power of Christ the Healer. When a person lives in the confidence of the Spirit, even though they suffer a loss of function, this is wholeness.

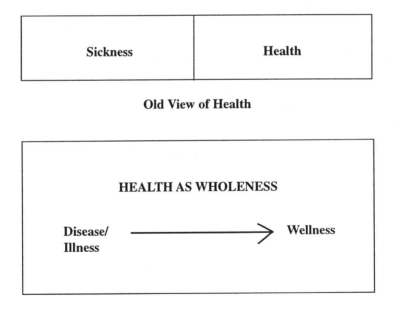

Old View of Health

New View of Health

The Challenge of Biblical Health

The biblical model of health is a challenge to our society today. It enlarges our perceptions of health beyond the narrow confines of the physical and the mental. The biblical perspective encourages us to take a more cosmic point of view. When the spiritual becomes the focus in our understanding of health, we begin to comprehend how the processes of healing stem from and lead back to the One who is the Healer.

The biblical model of health challenges our perceptions of who is really "sick" and who is "healthy." Millions of people believe that health is nothing more than a functioning mind in a functioning body. Such people see no contradiction in the poisonous attitudes and deep-felt resentments they harbor toward others and even toward themselves. They live out of kilter with the healthy design for life God has created. By what stretch of the imagination can we call such people "whole"? By the same token, how can we refer to those people as "sick" who carry on courageously with a limiting handicap but who exhibit a lively interest in life and a deep faith in Christ? We need to carry this "larger" picture of health with us in our journey through life.

The biblical model of health challenges us to ponder the purpose of striving for health and well-being. How healthy are our lives in terms of assisting those who live in pain and who suffer the tragedy of loss? To what degree do we use our own health to help bring restoration to the disorders of humankind? As we move ever closer toward wholeness, we find that our perceptions begin to change.

Chapter Five

The Healing of Persons

The goal of biblical healing is the healing of *persons*. It is not simply the curing of a disease that looms as all-important. Neither is it the mastery of an emotional problem nor the resolution of a psychological crisis. Biblical healing aims at restoring order within the person by healing the whole person. Nothing is more crucial to this goal than the healing of the spirit by which a person is reconciled to God in Jesus Christ.

We often lose sight of this focus in our approach to healing. Because of our cultural training, we tend to become overly concerned about the needs of the body or even about our mental health. While these are major concerns in the healing of the person, they become incomplete unless the spirit is also healed by God's divine power. Jesus once said, *"The eye is the lamp of the body. If your eyes are good, your whole body will be full of light"* (Matt. 6:22). Here is wholistic healing at its ultimate.

It would do us well to observe more closely the manner in which Jesus healed. Jesus never wanted to be known as a "miracle worker." He backed away from the sensational and the quick fix to life's problems. Jesus focused his attention on the whole person and the whole set of relationships that make up life, none more important than the person's relationship to God. What concerned Jesus was the person's health, not the immediate disease or problem that happened to be on the scene at the time.

The purpose of this chapter will be to explore a holistic perspective that focuses our attention on *the person who has the problem*. We need to understand how the Bible defines our personhood, a perspective that is becoming more accepted in our day and age because of the popularity of the wholistic health movement. As we move closer to the concept of the "whole person," we will begin to appreciate how all the needs of a person are integrated in the life of the spirit which only God can make whole.

The Biblical Perspective of the Whole Person

Any discussion of healing the person leads us to the topic of how the Scriptures describe the human being. What does it mean to be human? Are all of us compartmentalized creatures made up of component parts, each component designed to operate on its own? Or are we unitary beings, created by God with different systems but with all of them working together in concert and harmony?

From a biblical point of view, the evidence is clear. We are one, whole and undivided, even as God is one, whole and undivided. There is no hint in the Scripture that we are various parts glued together. Each of us is a totality. I do not have a body. I *am* a body. I do not have a mind. I *am* a mind. I do not have a spirit. I *am* a spirit. We are multidimensional creatures who express ourselves in a unity of being. Such is the biblical view of the person.

There are several anthropological terms in Scripture that refer to the various dimensions of the human being. In the Hebrew language *basar* refers to the body or bodily functions. *Nephesh* has many meanings including the life force or soul. *Ruach* refers to the spiritual dimension but can include the emotions. In the Greek language the complementary terms are *soma*, which refers to the body, *psyché*, which can include the mind and emotions, and *pneuma*, the term that refers to the spirit.

While it is important that each of these terms may signify an activity of the person, each may also refer to the *entire person*. Quite often, the biblical writers will use any one of these terms to refer to the "whole person." For example, the term *basar* can signify the body as well as the whole person (Isa. 58:7). Similarly, the term *nephesh* may refer to the "soul" or to the whole person in his bodily existence (Num. 35:11; Matt. 6:25; Acts 3:23). When Paul said: "May your whole spirit, soul, and body be kept blameless at the coming of our Lord Jesus Christ" (1 Thess. 5:23), he was referring to the whole person. William Watty describes the biblical view of the person:

> One of the basic concepts of man we have in the Bible is one of totality. Man is a psychosomatic being through and through, with all that this entails. In the story of creation we read that God formed man out of the dust of the ground and breathed into his nostrils the breath (*ruah*) of life and man became a living *nephesh*, which may be translated as "soul." The *nephesh* is not something apart from the body, it is the totality of man, a living soul. It is not that the body has a soul; man is a

living soul and it is better to think of him as an animated body, rather than an incarnated soul.[1]

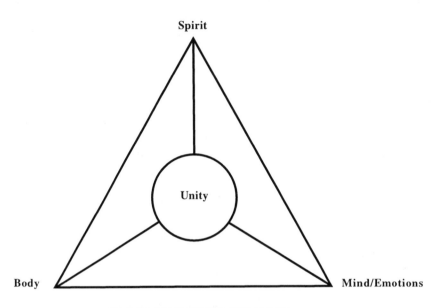

MODEL OF THE WHOLE PERSON

Our own observation from human experience teaches us to think of ourselves as whole persons, not as creatures divided into categories of body, mind, and spirit. On those occasions when something makes us extremely happy, our whole being experiences this happiness, not just one part of us. Trying to find links between body, mind, and spirit may be a fruitless search because there never was a fragmentation to begin with. In actuality, body, mind, and spirit are theoretical constructs just like the terms "ego" or "superego." Our inadequate language to

---

[1] William Watty, "Man and Healing: A Biblical and Theological View," in *Contact*, Christian Medical Commission, World Council of Churches, Geneva, Switzerland (December 1979): 5.

describe human life gives us no reason to break people into parts and act as if one part exists without the others.

We note that many Scriptural statements describe the health of a person in terms of the unity of the various dimensions working in harmony together. Proverbs 17:22 says that "A cheerful heart is good medicine," an observation that has been documented by medical science through much psychosomatic research. Conversely, Proverbs 13:12 says, "Hope deferred makes the heart sick." In Proverbs 15:30 we read: "Pleasant sights and good reports give happiness and health," a statement that would make no sense unless the human being was a "whole person."

When we speak about healing the whole person, we are not denying that any one of our systems may be hurting more than the others. In fact, it is necessary in health care to focus on a problem that may occur in one particular system. For example, a pathogen that attacks the cells of the body must be dealt with by physicians at the level of a person's biochemistry. There are times when an individual may be beset with anxiety and will need the particular skills of a therapist. Nevertheless, the interdependence of these systems is so closely interlinked that it is impossible ever to separate their functions. Elizabeth Skoglund, a Christian therapist, states the point well:

> Convenient as it may be to compartmentalize a human being and say: "This problem is all spiritual or all psychological or all physical," such an attitude is simplistic and can increase a person's difficulties. While people are made up of all these components, each interrelates with the other until they often become blurred and indistinguishable one from the other.[2]

The Spiritual Dimension

As we examine the biblical view of the whole person, it is necessary to understand the function of the spiritual dimension. An anthropological term that is of greatest importance to describe the human being is the biblical word *heart* (Hebrew, *lev*; Greek, *kardia*).[3] It appears over one thousand times and is much more common than the term "soul." The "heart" is presented in the Scriptures as being the indispensable center of human life. Feelings, desires, and emotions are

---

[2]Elizabeth Skoglund, *The Whole Christian* (New York: Harper & Row, 1976), 3.

[3]Ian Hammer, "Pastor, the Gene Made Me Do It!" in *Concordia Journal*, 23, no. 1, (January 1997).

connected with the heart (Ps. 21:2; John 16:6, 22). The conscience bears witness to the law written on the heart (Rom. 2:15).

According to Ian Hamer, the heart is the *religious center* which integrates the entirety of a person's life. It is in the heart in which God deals with every individual as a person. It is in the heart where a person encounters God, either to rebel in hate (Psalm 14:1) or to embrace with grateful love (Luke 2:51).

> The heart, in this Scriptural sense, is not to be pictured as one part or one element in man. The heart *is* the person, and the many functions and activities by which we come to know a person are expressions of the heart. Other expressions of the person are: man is a social being, biological being, neurological, political, economic, and so on. But these are just aspects of his person, expressions of the fact that man is fundamentally a *religious, God-related being* (italics added).[4]

As we approach the topic of healing the person, we do well to note the crucial importance of the spiritual life. *Spirituality* is not simply one of many dimensions that defines our humanity. The life of the spirit is the foundationstone of our human identity and integrates all other aspects of our personhood in the purposiveness of living. If the spirit is alienated from God, this is bound to have consequences in a person's character as well as in a person's health. Jesus confirmed the truth of this process when He said, *"If then the light within you is darkness, how great is that darkness"* (Matt. 6:23).

The healing of the spirit becomes a significant strategy in any approach to the healing of the whole person. Traditional cultures have always understood the significance of this truth because of their acknowledgment that the human being is essentially a religious person. It is encouraging to note how many in medical science are beginning to affirm this belief whereas the practice of wholistic medicine has made it one of the pillars of their philosophy. While we may take issue with how some define *spirituality*, nevertheless, we need to applaud this trend toward treating the whole person. It is only when we behold the person as a total unity that we can truly speak of healing the person.

---

[4]Ibid.

How We Lost the Concept of the Whole Person

The early Christian church pursued a ministry to the whole person and, because of this emphasis on wholeness, the healing ministry of Jesus thrived. We can document quite substantially that the ministry of Christian healing was an effective outreach of the church for at least 300 years. During the Patristic Age, several of the church fathers mention healings done in the name of Jesus. However, by the fourth century A.D., the healing ministry began to fade. About the time of St. Augustine, a platonic or Gnostic view of the person began to dominate the mind of the church, the consequence of which phased the healing ministry of the church into oblivion. This was an era in which it became fashionable to divide the body from the soul. The "soul" was believed to contain the spark of the divine whereas the body was perceived as being a prison. Gnosticism has always sought to release the "real person" from the chains of materiality. With such a divided view of the person, it was only a matter of time before the church's sole concern was simply the care of the soul apart from the body.

During the Middle Ages, little attention was paid to healing people. The church's posture on sickness changed from a focus on healing people to a glorification of sickness as a discipline from the hand of God. The biblical perspective of the person had gone through a radical change. The papacy even forbade the study of anatomy to its priests because it was believed that a concern for the human body distracted from the primacy of the soul. Certainly some attention was paid to the sick during the Middle Ages. The Knights Templars and the Knights Hospitalers were healing orders and cared for the suffering. Convents and monasteries were places of refuge for the ill, but healing was of a secondary activity. The primary concern was to deal with the *suffering* of the individual. All during the Middle Ages, the healing arts, as a means by which God would deliver people from being the hostage of disorder, were all but forgotten. How ironic that the pioneering work of Hippocrates was lost to Europe in these years of darkness while the Arab world had rediscovered him.

At the time of the Renaissance, science could be held in check no longer and broke loose from the church to study the human body. By the seventeenth century, Renee Descartes came to the conclusion that only matter could be empirically studied, the mind and the spirit being ephemeral to the interest of scientific research. Thus developed a philosophy known as *Cartesian dualism*, a perspective in which matter and mind were divided into two distinct entities. It should not surprise us that medical science followed the lead of Descartes and developed its own mechanical model of healing the body. While medical science focused its energies on the needs of the body, the church's primary concern remained the salvation of the "soul."

It is no wonder that, until recently, we have lived with this unworkable division of labor in matters of health and healing. Doctors and other medical personnel were considered to be specialists in healing. At the same time, hospitals acted as the temples in which the science of healing was practiced. Pastors were encouraged to enter, but only to comfort, never to heal. As far as a ministry of healing was concerned, this was a relic of the long-distanced past, known only in the memory of the early church. The only healing activity the modern church engaged in was on the margins of its boundaries, much of which went beyond the pale of orthodoxy and in many instances became cultic.

But then a transformation occurred in medical science which was to change attitudes toward sickness and health in a substantial manner. Two major discoveries tilted the research of medical science away from Cartesian dualism and toward a view of the whole person. The first was the emergence of *psychosomatic research*, an understanding that the mind was an instrumental factor in the causation of disease. The second was the study of *stress* in which new research made clear that human coping behavior was a major reason why the diseases that were crippling and killing people in the Western world were stress related In addition, a third area of research, psychoneuroimmunology which focuses on the relationship between the emotional and spiritual life of the person and the immune system of the body, will also be briefly addressed. It is to these subjects that we now turn.

Modern Medical Research and the Whole Person

Much of the current medical literature emphasizes the study of the intricate system of relationships that make up our personhood. As research into the disease process continues at deeper levels, it is becoming apparent that the *emotional* and *spiritual* dimensions of the person are more involved than previously imagined.

Psychosomatic Research

No one brought this truth more forcibly to the attention of the medical community than Dr. Flanders Dunbar who, as early as 1935, laid the basis for psychosomatic medicine.[5] Dr. Dunbar's extensive research in the interrelationships of body and mind destroyed the concept of a closed mechanical model of the person and pushed medical science to consider the important area of emotions in the process of both disease and healing. Others pursued Dr. Dunbar's lead in researching the effect of emotional states on the individual's health, none more than Dr. Jerome Frank of Johns Hopkins University. Dr. Frank observed the crucial role of emotions in explaining why soldiers in World War II either healed quickly from their wounds or lingered in convalescence. He extended his research to consider the powerful impact of religious healing ceremonials among traditional tribal people, ceremonials in which an emotional catharsis is dominant. According to Dr. Frank, religious healing

> emphasizes the profound influence of emotions on health and suggests that anxiety and despair can be lethal, confidence and hope, life-giving. The modern assumptive world of Western society, which includes mind-body dualism, has had difficulty incorporating this obvious fact and has therefore decided to underemphasize it.[6]

The influence of emotions on health has become the basis of some major research on coronary heart disease. Drs. Meyer Friedman and Ray Rosenman pioneered a 10-year research project involving thousands of test cases.[7] One of their conclusions is that cardiovascular disease is more likely to occur in a person who is a Type A personality—a behavioral and emotional style marked by an unceasing struggle to achieve more and more in less time. Type A behavior is characterized by three components: (1) an easily aroused hostility, (2) a

---

[5]Dr. Dunbar's book, *Emotions and Bodily Changes* (New York: Columbia University Press, 1954), revealed the depth of psychosomatic interrelationships in the person in an exhaustive survey of research. The influence of her work helped establish the journal *Psychosomatic Medicine*. Along this line, see also Roy R. Grinker, *Psychosomatic Concepts* (New York: Jason Aronson, 1973). But, of course, thinking has come a long way since these beginnings.

[6]Jerome Frank, *Persuasion and Healing* (New York: Schocken Books, 1963), 61.

[7]Shelley E. Taylor, *Health Psychology* (New York: McGraw-Hill, 1995), 497-98.

sense of time urgency, (3) competitive achievement strivings. Type B behavior, by comparison, is characterized as more phlegmatic and easy-going. The results of this research demonstrated a correlation between the free-floating anger and frustration of Type A behavior people and the onset of heart disease.[8] Therefore, far from being an organic disorder triggered by pathogens, coronary heart disease appears to be a stress-related disease and illustrates the close correspondence of mind, body, and spirit.

Cancer, as well, is associated with the inability to express emotions in a healthy manner. Dr. Lawrence LeShan, an experimental psychologist, has conducted a lot of research on the psychology of cancer victims. He finds four components in the life histories of those prone to cancer: (1) the patient's youth was marked with feelings of isolation and despair; (2) in adulthood, the patient was able to establish a strong, meaningful relationship with a person; (3) this relationship was then removed with the result being despair, and the pain of childhood returned; and (4) the despair was bottled up, the patient being unable to express how he felt.[9] Some refer to the cancer-prone personality as Type C behavior, which is characterized as responding to stress with depression and hopelessness and the muting of negative emotions.[10] We need to be cautious in promoting a stereotype of the "cancer-prone personality" in that there is current debate over how significant some of these personality factors are in the onset of cancer. However, the data associating poor emotional coping skills and the *course* of the disease in cancer patients is quite substantial. Malignancies may develop more rapidly in individuals who feel helpless, hopeless, depressed, or out of control.[11]

What has been said about cancer and coronary heart disease can also be applied to diseases such as asthma, migraine headaches, arthritis, and other such chronic diseases. For example, it has been

---

[8]We need to remember that correlational studies in scientific research refer to factors that are "significantly" related to the onset of certain diseases and do not necessarily imply a direct cause-and-effect relationship.

[9]Carl Simonton, Stephanie Simonton, and James Creighton, *Getting Well Again* (New York: Bantam Books, 1978), 63.

[10]Taylor, op. cit., 566.

[11]Ibid., 569.

suggested that arthritis may be correlated with repressed anger.[12] Correlation, of course, does not mean that repressed anger causes arthritis; the organic conditions necessary for arthritis must first be present. Repressed anger is rather what is called, in medicine, a "precipitating factor," the trigger that stimulates the disease process.

Research on Stress

Studies in the effect of *stress* on the physiology of the human body have likewise moved medical science closer to an appreciation of the whole person. Dr. Hans Selye, the world's authority on the study of stress, says that stress is the wear and tear of everyday life. He states that many common diseases are largely due to errors in our adaptive response to stress, rather than to direct damage by germs or other external agents. He refers to such diseases as high blood pressure, gastric and duodenal ulcers, and certain types of rheumatic, allergic, cardiovascular, and renal diseases as essentially *diseases of adaptation*.[13]

According to Dr. Selye's extensive research, stress is a physiological response to the events of life. Every stress reaction, whether it is good stress (eustress) or bad stress (distress), triggers biochemical changes in the body by activating the autonomic nervous and endocrine systems. Essentially what the stress response is designed to do is to prepare the person to meet the stressful situation; afterwards, the function of the body returns to a steady state.

However, poor coping skills or sustained exposure to a specific stressor allow stress to have a deleterious effect on the body. It is at such times that we become vulnerable to disease. Elizabeth Skoglund describes some of the biochemical changes that occur in typical distressful situations:

> Most of us have experienced the destructive effects of the mind upon the body: the tight muscles and dry mouth right before a public appearance or an examination; the fast heartbeat and accelerated muscular

---

[12]Personal conversation with Dr. Ken Bakken in 1981, when he was a member of the medical faculty of Johns Hopkins Medical School.

[13]Dr. Hans Selye, *The Stress of Life* (New York: McGraw-Hill, 1956), viii. Additional resources beyond the work of Dr. Selye of recent vintage include the excellent text by George S. Everly, Jr., *A Clinical Guide to the Treatment of the Human Stress Response* (Northvale, NJ: Jason Aronson, 1986).

movements right before an automobile accident; and the numb feeling of shock that occurs after the pronouncement of a tragic message such as the death of a loved one or a bad medical prognosis. Like it or not, our bodies are constantly affected by our minds for both good and bad.[14]

Skoglund goes on to say that it is imperative to emphasize the *reality* of physical disorders which arise from stress. Many people illogically think that if stressful emotions cause a physical problem, the pain can be turned off with an act of will much as one turns off a light with the flip of a switch. In actuality this lack of understanding of psychosomatic problems only adds to a person's stress and compounds the physical ailment. Our major need is to learn how to cope with the stress before it translates itself into a physical disorder.

Living in a society in which competition and achievement are prized cultural goals has undoubtedly added to the number of stressors that daily affect us. We ought not to be surprised that heart disease, cancer, and stroke—all stress-related diseases—are the three major killers of Americans and have ranked in that manner for a number of years.[15] Nevertheless, experts in stress have suggested that succumbing to the medical problems of stress is not an inevitable process. Relaxation techniques to help effectively cope with the stressors of life has become the subject of stress workshops all over the American continent. None has become more popular than Dr. Herbert Benson's *The Relaxation Response*, in which the author's research suggests that certain techniques can counteract the harmful effects and uncomfortable feelings of stress.[16]

Dr. Hans Selye has even suggested a philosophy of life that he feels best deals with the effects of stress, namely, the feeling of *gratitude*. He argues that gratitude, more than any other emotion, possesses characteristics that are aimed at human survival and which are designed to protect the person from stressful situations:

---

[14]Elizabeth Skoglund, *The Whole Christian* (Harper & Row: New York, 1976), 54.

[15]U.S. Department of Health.

[16]Herbert Benson, *The Relaxation Response* (New York: William Morrow, 1975). According to Dr. Benson, the relaxation response refers to the inborn capacity of the body to enter a special state characterized by lowered heart rate, decreased rate of breathing, lowered blood pressure, slower brain waves, and overall reduction in the speed of metabolism.

> Gratitude is the awakening in another person of the wish that I should prosper, because of what I have done for him. It is perhaps the most characteristically human way of assuring security. It takes away the motive for a clash between selfish and selfless tendencies, because, by inspiring the feeling of gratitude, I have induced another person to share with me my natural wish for my own well-being.[17]

It is significant that a medical scientist of international renown is led to a *philosophic-religious* conclusion about how to effectively deal with the disease process. Selye comes close to a biblical perspective of the whole person and, on the basis of scientific research regarding gratitude, seems to echo the wisdom of the Preacher of Ecclesiastes: "If your enemy is hungry, give him food to eat; if he is thirsty, give him water to drink. In doing this you heap burning coals on his head, and the LORD will reward you" (Prov. 25:21-22).

The Study of Psychoneuroimmunology

One of the most exciting new fields of study in medicine focuses on the relationship between the emotional and spiritual life and the immune system of the body. This new field of study is called *psychoneuroimmunology* (PNI), and has been defined as the manner in which the mind and nervous system interact with and affect the immune system.[18] More specifically, it is the way in which our beliefs, expectations, and personality patterns affect the natural killer cells which survey the body for pathogenic germs.

Many consider these revelations as a major breakthrough in understanding the unitary composition of our personhood. It means nothing less than that nerve centers and chemicals in our bodies respond to our fears, to the things we imagine, and to the full range of our beliefs and emotions. Said another way, it means that our religious faith is somehow connected with the cells of our body and the state of our physical well-being.

For many years now, medical professionals have been giving serious credence to a new theory of cancer known as the "surveillance

---

[17]Selye, op. cit., 285.

[18]Judith Green and Robert Shellenberger, *The Dynamics of Health and Wellness: A Biopsychological Approach* (Fort Worth, TX: Holt, Rinehart and Winston, 1991), 8.

theory." According to this theory, cancer cells develop daily in our bodies, but are also disposed of daily by our bodies. As long as the immune system is alert and healthy, white killer blood cells attack and destroy these colonies of cancer cells. Why, then, does the immunological system break down in some people and not in others? The evidence points to emotional stressors as well as negative beliefs which weaken the immune system. The result is that the disease pathogens gain an upper hand and begin the process of growth.

Some of the pioneering work in psychoneuroimmunology was done by Robert Ader, who discovered that T lymphocytes in rats could be conditioned the same way that Pavlov's dogs were conditioned to salivate at the sound of a bell.[19] Ader concluded that if key actors of the immune system could be so conditioned to aversive stimuli, then it must follow that mental and emotional states can have a powerful effect on immunity.

The field of psychoneuroimmunology is a young field and extremely complex because of the relationship between the psyché, nervous system, and immune system. Nevertheless, some of the recent studies have helped us understand how people who are "ill" are more at risk in developing disease. Natural killer cells are more active in individuals with positive personality traits than those with negative traits. We are not surprised to learn that women who were recently bereaved had lower killer cell activity than women of a control group of the same age.[20] The same was true for women who were recently divorced and for students who were taking final exams.

The more we learn about the complex interrelationships at work in the whole person, the more we can appreciate the strategic role of religion and the process of health. There are some health practitioners who say that *all* disease, at its base, is related to the spiritual and emotional attitudes of the person. Dr. Arthur Kleinman, of Harvard University, on the basis of placebo research, said that we are being led to a new understanding of the human being. How does the body know the difference between "hope" and "despair" except that, as Kleinman

---

[19]Ibid., 121.
[20]Ibid., 124.

says, all human events are mental, physical, and spiritual at the same time?[21]

Medical research in the field of mind/body relationships is having far-reaching implications for practitioners of the healing professions. No longer can we assume that the body is the sole territory of medical doctors, nor the mind the sole province of psychotherapists, nor the spirit the singular category of pastors and priests. The stressors that attack us do not remain in the neat little compartments that we may assign them. We have been holistically created even as the process of healing is holistic at its core.

The Wholistic Model Of Health

It has been referred to as a "revolution" by some whereas others speak of it as simply a shift of focus. Wholistic (or holistic) health care is an approach to health and healing that respects and treats all of the dimensions that make up the human person—the spiritual, the social, the emotional, as well as the physical. Perhaps the most characteristic feature of the wholistic model is that it seeks to heal the whole person by concentrating on the *unity* and the total personhood of the individual.

The wholistic model of health is actually a *philosophy* about health rather than a specific procedure. Many wholistic doctors use drugs and surgery in their practices, but they differ in that they use other alternatives and techniques as well. According to Dr. James Gordon, wholistic medicine does not seek to supplant allopathic or modern medicine but attempts rather to expand its vision:

> This model is a corrective to the excesses of biomedicine, a supplement to its deficiencies, and an affirmation of its deepest and most enduring strengths. It sets our contemporary concern with the cure of diseases in the larger framework of health care, enlarges and enriches the roles of both health care providers and patients, and provides a framework

---

[21]Robert Hahn and Arthur Kleinman, M.D., "Belief as Pathogen, belief as Medicine: 'Voodoo Death' and the 'Placebo Phenomenon' in Anthropological Perspective," *Medical Anthropology Quarterly* 14, no. 4 (August 1983): 18.

in which many techniques—old and new, Western and non-Western—may be used.[22]

Because it emphasizes the unity of the person, the wholistic model has brought about a change in the manner in which patients are treated. It focuses on *health* rather than disease. Most wholistic practitioners stress the need to turn the patient's attention from the disease to the positive goal of wholeness. "Don't focus on the pain" is the credo. Focus instead on health, on life, on growing to a higher dimension of well-being.

Changing the focus from disease to health does not mean that we sweep away the severity of a person's medical problems. But it moves beyond the immediate physical problem to the spiritual, integrative needs of the person, namely, the individual's relationships with other people and with the cosmos. This perspective helps patients to understand that health is much more than the absence of disease. Health becomes more a process of centering oneself on the purposiveness of life. Dr. Paul Tournier, a Christian physician who affirms the wholistic principle, writes about "positive health" and says that it is expressed as a "quality of life, a physical, psychical and spiritual unfolding, an exaltation of personal dynamism."[23]

Because it places the emphasis on health, the wholistic model states that sickness itself can be a learning experience for the person. By means of the illness experience, a person is able to sort out what is truly important in life. Thus, each of us can learn new directions by which to focus our energy and recover our potential as persons who have been created by God.

A major emphasis of the wholistic model is that the capacity for healing resides within every person, namely, the immune system which is sensitive to signals from the mind and spirit. It therefore follows that every person is responsible for his or her own health, at least to some degree within the confines of human frailty and ambiguity. Doctors and other medical personnel are "enablers" rather than authority figures whose prescriptions must be followed without thinking.

---

[22]James S. Gordon, M.D., "The Paradigm of Holistic Medicine," in *Health for the Whole Person: The Complete Guide to Holistic Medicine*, eds. Arthur Hastings, James Fadiman, and James Gordon (Boulder, CO: Westview Press, 1981), 15.

[23]Paul Tournier, *The Healing of Persons* (Harper & Row: New York. 1965), 185.

Kathleen Deierlein interviewed several persons who went to wholistic practitioners and asked them why they selected wholistic healing. Among the many responses she received, the feeling of self-responsibility was frequently mentioned:

> [With this healer and therapy] the person helps you but you have a lot to do for yourself. It's not like "you heal me." You have to take responsibility for yourself and help heal yourself. American people go to the doctor, they say "heal me, but I'm not going to do anything for me. You take the responsibility for making me better, but I won't. . . . It's your job."[24]

The wholistic model is not a new model. Almost all of the early approaches to healing were concerned about the unity of the person, and the same is true among all traditional peoples of the world. According to Norman Cousins, even Hippocrates was a wholistic practitioner because "he insisted that it was natural for the human body to heal itself."[25] However, through the passage of years and a multitude of scientific research, this model has become expanded to include some new features which have appealed to the general public.

James Gordon has listed at least 17 characteristics that are included in the modern "paradigm of holistic medicine." We have taken the liberty to select nine of the most important principles from this list in order to explicate its philosophy more clearly:[26]

> *(1) Holistic medicine addresses itself to the physical, mental, and spiritual aspects of those who come for care.*
> *(2) Holistic medicine emphasizes each patient's genetic, biological, and psychosocial uniqueness as well as the importance of tailoring treatment to meet each individual's needs.*

---

[24]Kathleen Deierlein, 'Ideology and Holistic Alternatives," in *The Healing Experience: Readings on the Social Context of Health Care*, eds. William Kornblum and Carolyn Smith (Englewood Cliffs, NJ: Prentice-Hall, 1994), 180.

[25]Norman Cousins, *Anatomy of an Illness* (New York: Bantam Books, 1981), 111.

[26]See the discussion by James S. Gordon, M.D., "The Paradigm of Holistic Medicine," in *Health for the Whole Person: The Complete Guide to Holistic Medicine*, eds. Arthur Hastings, James Fadiman, and James Gordon (Boulder, CO: Westview Press, 1981), 3-27.

(3) A holistic approach to medicine and health care includes understanding and treating people in the context of their culture, their family, and their community.

(4) Holistic medicine views health as a positive state, not as the absence of disease.

(5) Holistic medicine emphasizes the promotion of health and the prevention of disease.

(6) Holistic medicine emphasizes the responsibility of each individual for his or her health.

(7) Holistic medicine uses therapeutic approaches that mobilize the individual's innate capacity for self-healing.

(8) Physical contact between practitioner and patient is an important element of holistic medicine.

(9) Holistic medicine views illness as an opportunity for discovery as well as a misfortune.

Many Christians have affirmed the wholistic model because of its close parallels with the biblical perspective of the person and the biblical model of health. Because it is a philosophy rather than specific procedure, it is possible to be in agreement with some of the principles without necessarily endorsing them all. Edgar Jackson, who has written extensively in the field of religion and health, believes that the healing ministry of Jesus is an affirmation of the holistic approach:

> There is nothing incompatible between the healing power of Jesus and the knowledge that can be gained through science or the larger perspective that can develop from a holistic perspective on human nature. In fact, it may be that the climate is right at this time to bring together what may have seemed to be conflicting forces to a new synthesis that can best serve the interest of a healing ministry.[27]

Nevertheless, from the viewpoint of confessional theology, we need to exercise caution about the concept of "spirituality" as this term is used in wholistic medicine. We are not in agreement with how some holistic practitioners use the term "spiritual"; at times it appears as if this term includes anything from Native American spiritualism to

---

[27]Edgar Jackson, *Your Health and You: How Awareness, Attitudes, and Faith Contribute to a Healthy Life* (Minneapolis: Augsburg, 1986), 100.

Eastern mysticism.[28] This is discomforting to those who want to be faithful to the Scriptures, but who, at the same time, espouse the wholistic model. For confessional Christians there can be no compromise with biblical revelation: reconciliation to God can only be accomplished through the atoning work of Jesus Christ. But the fact that various avant-garde healing approaches, for example, New Age, claim to be wholistic does not in itself invalidate the wholistic model any more than atheistic doctors, who believe only in materialism, invalidate the biomedical model.

Throughout this book I have been using the term "wholistic" (or "holistic") in a manner that corresponds to the biblical model of health and healing. The scriptural narratives are rich in their description of whole person health care for an obvious reason. They provide the essential ingredients for the restoration of health and wholeness which includes fellowship with God through Jesus Christ.

Alternative or Complementary Medicine

One of the major premises of the wholistic model is the use of therapeutic techniques which may differ from the traditional Western medical approach of drugs and surgery. These modalities, believed to be effective on the body's innate capacity for healing, are commonly referred to as *alternative medicine.*

Some of these healing techniques are quite old and are imports from other cultural traditions such as China and India: they include acupuncture, massage, fasting, herbal remedies, and the like. Other alternative techniques are relatively new and focus on psychotherapy, hypnosis, nutrition, vitamins, biofeedback, and relaxation therapies such as bioenergetics and meditation. Wholistic practitioners have also been experimenting with the use of music and sound in health as well as the impact of color and therapeutic touch on the healing process. Because of its unique approach in healing the sick, "faith healing" also qualifies as a modality of alternative medicine.

---

[28]Paul C. Reisser. M.D., "Alternative Medicine," in *Christian Research Journal* (Sept.-Oct. 1997): 31-37. Reisser takes wholistic healing to task because of those practitioners whose approach to spirituality sometimes includes monism and other Eastern mystical approaches that are hostile to the teachings of the Old and New Testaments. It is significant that Reisser does not take biomedicine to task for its philosophy of materialism, which has no room for spirituality.

It needs to be made very clear that "alternative medicine" does not eschew the use of drugs and surgery in the treatment of the sick. On the contrary, medical practitioners who make use of alternative medicine only do so if traditional methods are not effective or if they sense that there is a better alternative than intrusive medicine.[29] Some doctors and health practitioners prefer the term *complementary medicine* to alternative medicine because of the fact that the former term seems to indicate clearly that alternative techniques should be used only as a complement to traditional procedures.

Many doctors are beginning to selectively use some of these alternative modalities in their own practice. For example, one Los Angeles doctor, an associate professor of neurology and internal medicine at the University of Southern California School of Medicine, treats sufferers of chronic headaches with a multiple modality approach.[30] He may prescribe aromatherapy, physical therapy for head and neck, biofeedback training, hypnotherapy, psychotherapy, or acupuncture as well as tranquilizers or muscle relaxers. At a cancer workshop I attended, I heard one practitioner advise the use of meditation, biofeedback, and color *in addition to* the standard techniques of chemotherapy and surgery.

On the other hand, there are some in the field of medicine who believe that alternative medicine is fraught with problems and regard the success of this new approach to healing as dangerous to medical practice.[31] One of these concerns is that cures are being promoted, such as healing through subatomic energy fields, which may not have been subjected to controlled scientific research. Such concerns are valid because many health claims are being made which need to be looked at with close scrutiny. The American public is quick to jump on so-called "miracle cures," a typical American cultural pattern which seems to seek quick solutions to the problems of life. The federal government is understandably very picky when it comes to making a link between any product or treatment modality and the treatment and prevention of disease. For this reason, the U.S. Food and Drug Administration undertakes a thorough examination of all new products before giving

---

[29]Drugs and surgery may have undesirable side effects. One of the problems of some drugs is that they may be addictive or else they may cripple the patient from taking an active role in their own healing.

[30]Barbara Thomas, "Health," *Los Angeles Times,* September 22, 1997.

[31]Reisser, op. cit., 35-37.

approval for public use. The usual procedure is a randomized, controlled intervention trial in which a group of subjects receives the nutrient whereas a similar group receives a placebo. The two groups are then followed for a length of time and are compared.

Notwithstanding this caution about the use of alternative medicine, there can also be a danger in closing one's mind to what can potentially be a host of valid healing techniques. The Quakers had a proverb which is applicable to this discussion of experimenting with a new approach: *It is better to light a candle than to curse the darkness.* The truth of the matter is that we are only now beginning to understand the complexity of the healing process. The God of healing cannot be contained in a narrow, mechanical model which refuses to consider that there may be knowledge of healing that human minds have yet to ponder. It is helpful to remember that Jenner was once mocked for his smallpox vaccination as was Simmelweiss for his urging doctors to wash their hands before delivering a baby. Alternative medicine may open some doors to the future that will come to bless our approach to healing because it dares to enlarge our vision of restoration from disease.

A Strategy for Whole Person Health Care

When an individual is sick, several things are happening at once. The person is struggling with a disease while at the same time trying to deal with the pain of being ill. The person is likewise enduring the rigors of the sick role. Most frequently, this means being treated by concerned physicians and nurses. Perhaps surgery or other therapy is involved; medications are certainly a part of this regimen. There may also be support in the form of pastoral visits or visitations from friends and family.

What is essential in this whole procedure is that the *sick person* is not "lost" in the treatment process. The danger exists that all of the patient's needs will be attended to except the most critical ones. As we referenced in chapter 1, perhaps the most crucial factor in any person's experience with ill-health is *illness*. How the person is dealing with the meaning of the pain and suffering is really at the heart of illness. Those of us who have spent hours by the sickbeds of suffering people know well the depth of the fears and anxieties that such persons feel. They feel lonely, alienated, and fearful about their future. They miss their families. Their self-esteem has suffered a colossal jolt. It should be obvious that any strategy for treating the sick must deal with the whole person, not simply the disease. Said simply, the ill person needs compassion, understanding, and encouragement.

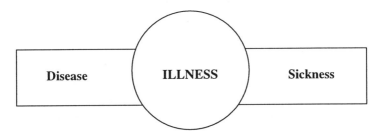

According to Dr. Arthur Kleinman, medical practice earlier in this century exhibited this personal touch. "Western physicians were interested in treating both disease *and* illness—the way the patient perceives and experiences his disorder, in the context of family and society."[32] However, as their ability to control disease began to increase, physicians began to limit their care to the cure of disease.

One of the problems that has contributed to this division of labor has been the extraordinary "success" of medical technology. The American public continues to marvel at the scientific mastery of the processes of biochemical and physiological healing. The precision by which laser technology can remove a gall bladder in the morning and return the patient to his home in the afternoon astounds us. We stand in awe at the speed by which Cat-scans see anomalies in our bodies or the efficiency by which antibiotics break a raging fever. But what Cat-scans and X-rays do not reveal are the toxins and spiritual maladies that lie deep within the person. Here reside the anguish of pain and the sinister face of sin. These are the other faces of disease. These are marks of our human distortion as well.

A modern doctor recently pointed out the problem of treating only the disease and overlooking the deeper-seated needs of the person:

> In general, modern medicine takes disease to be an anatomico-pathologic fact. We tend to see illness as an objective entity that is located somewhere anatomically or that perturbs a defined physiologic process. . . . Clearly much has been gained by this approach. It is our heritage and must not be frivolously denied. *But has not something been lost?* Having

---

[32]Arthur Kleinman, M.D., "The Failure of Western Medicine," *Human Nature* (November/December, 1978): 63.

worked so hard to objectify illness, do we not have trouble confronting the fullness of the human context in which illness occurs. Have we not, in some consequential way, made disease our focus instead of sick people? (emphasis added)[33]

Despite the problems of the past, we can only be encouraged that whole person health care has begun to capture the imagination of many who are members of the medical profession. Christian doctors and nurses, because they are committed to the healing of the spirit, can especially relate to the words of Henri Nouwen who believes that *hospitality* is a key Christian virtue in dealing with the sick:

> Hospitality is the virtue that allows us to break through the narrowness of our own fears and to open our houses to the stranger, with the intuition that salvation comes to us in the form of a tired traveler. . . . Hospitality is the ability to pay attention to the guest.[34]

Nouwen's metaphor is appropriate in restoring a human touch to the technological mastery that pervades the medical market-place today. To care for the sick as "guests within our house" creates a symbol of Christian health care that sets apart Christian doctors and nurses as different from the norm. It is to walk in the tradition of the Healer Himself.

Health care, however, involves more than the ministry of doctors, nurses, and other medical workers. Pastors play a crucial role in the healing process and deserve the appellation of "healer" far more than most men of the cloth dare imagine. A skill that many pastors have in abundance is the capability of helping the sufferer work through his *illness*. I refer especially to those occasions when a person finds it difficult to cope, when discouragement sets in, or when an individual is struggling with the prospect of death. This is an area of pastoral care in which the minister can share the suffering of the patient and apply the healing resources of the Gospel of Jesus Christ.

---

[33]Richard Baron, M.D., "I Can't Hear You While I'm Listening," in *The Healing Experience: Readings on the Social Context of Health Care*, eds. William Kornblum and Carolyn D. Smith (Englewood Cliffs, NJ: Prentice Hall, 1994), 24-25.

[34]Henri Nouwen, *The Wounded Healer* (Garden City, NY: Image Books, 1979), 89.

On some occasions, pastors will hear confession of sins in the sickroom and will proclaim the absolution of Christ's forgiveness. Luther referred to such private confession as the "consolation of the brethren." At such a time, when the ill person seeks to make restitution for his spiritual waywardness, the forgiveness of Christ is a true healing experience. As the pastor enables the person to achieve this experience, he characterizes himself as a "carer of souls."[35]

But pastors can make a difference in matters of health that touch upon the body as well. Granger Westberg, founder of wholistic health centers in church settings, believes that pastors can minister to the sick in ways that transcend the capability of doctors:

> Before, when I was teaching seminary students clinical pastoral care in a hospital setting, I found that they were so in awe of physicians that they depreciated their own value and expressed the wish that they could be doctors. . . . Now, in the Wholistic Health Center setting, they had quite the opposite point of view. They observed how often the care which a doctor gives sick people is only temporary, symptomatic treatment which really doesn't get to the heart of the problem. They now experienced themselves as ministers dealing with more basic problems and assisting people to rethink ways of living that could bring about health to the body.[36]

If problems have existed in modern medicine in treating the whole person, similar problems have plagued the church. Perhaps the primary offense that pastors have been unwittingly guilty of in the care of the sick is their own fear of illness and disease. Seeking to avoid the painful reality that stares him in the face, the fearful pastor resorts to a breezy, conversational style that attempts to assure the sufferer that "everything will be all right," even though the patient knows better. Or else the pastor masks himself with a "professional mannerism," whose obvious intention is to build a chasm between the minister and the patient. In either case the pastor has failed to be a healer because he has forsaken the model of the Healing Christ—he has failed to identify with the pain of the sufferer.

---

[35]Werner Elert, *The Structure of Lutheranism* (St. Louis: Concordia, 1962), 365. The phrase "consolation of the brethren" is found in Smalcald Articles III, 4.

[36]Granger E. Westberg, "From Hospital Chaplaincy to Wholistic Health Center," in *Health and Healing: Ministry of the Church,*ed. Henry Letterman (Chicago: Wheat Ridge Foundation, 1980), 112.

Henri Nouwen gets to the heart of this problem and, by contrast, informs us what it means to minister as a wounded healer:

> If there is any posture that disturbs a suffering man or woman, it is aloofness. The tragedy of Christian ministry is that many who are in great need, many who seek an attentive ear, a word of support, a forgiving embrace, a firm hand, a tender smile, or even a stuttering confession of inability to do more, often find their ministers distant men who do not want to burn their fingers. They are unable or unwilling to express their feelings of affection, anger, hostility or sympathy.[37]

Whole person health care is not an easy task as those who daily participate in the "front-line trenches" know all too well. Caring for the *person* who is sick demands a premium of our patience and compassion, and the willingness to suffer. It challenges each of us, whether doctor, nurse, or pastor, to "bind up our own wounds" in anticipation of the time when we will be called to bind up the wounds of others.[38]

John Sutherland Bonnell relates a story about a young physician from his congregation who was convalescing in a hospital after a serious operation.[39] Although he had already acquired a large practice as a young man, he had never shown any marked interest in the church. For 20 minutes Dr. Bonnell conversed with the physician but had offered him no spiritual help. As he was about to leave, he became conscience-stricken. How could he introduce to a doctor the subject of faith in a manner that was not artificial or formal, yet would touch the doctor's needs? An inspiration suddenly came to him. He would give the doctor a "prescription."

"When you make a professional visit to the sick, you generally leave a prescription, don't you?" asked Pastor Bonnell. "Quite often," replied the physician. "Well, I am going to give you a prescription now," responded the minister. On a piece of paper he wrote the words, "The Lord is thy keeper . . . He that keepeth thee will not slumber. He that keepeth Israel shall neither slumber nor sleep." Underneath the text, Rev. Bonnell wrote: "To be taken at bedtime." When he was about to leave, the physician gripped his hand and said earnestly, "Thanks for

---

[37]Nouwen, op. cit., 71.

[38]Ibid., 82.

[39]John Sutherland Bonnell, *Psychology for Pastor and People* (New York: Harper & Brothers, 1948), 148-49.

what you have done for me. I shall take the prescription exactly as you have advised."

Dr. Bonnell concludes the story by saying that he saw the physician's eyes filled with tears as he left the room. This hospital visit marked a turning point in the spiritual life of the young physician.

No greater task faces our world today than the healing of persons. As we shall discover when we discuss the ministry of healing in chapter 8, this also is a task of the Christian congregation. For this ministry we need a clear understanding of the relationship of faith and healing, the subject of the next chapter.

Chapter Six

Faith and Healing

Let us begin by saying that *faith* is a good word. We ought not be fearful of a word with such strong biblical roots, a word that illustrates the intimate relationship between a person and God. Neither is it possible to do justice to the biblical approach to healing if we do not clearly comprehend the nature of faith.

Jesus affirmed the faith in those whom He healed. In His encounters with the sick and diseased, He consistently mentions this word "faith." In healing episode after episode, Jesus took pains to underscore the importance of faith in the healing process. One particular narrative from the Gospel of Matthew makes this point clear (9:27-30):

> As Jesus went on from there, two blind men followed Him, calling out, "Have mercy on us, Son of David." When He had gone indoors, the blind men came to Him, and He asked them, "Do you believe that I am able to do this?" "Yes, Lord," they replied. Then He touched their eyes and said, "*According to your faith* will it be done to you," and their sight was restored.

In this passage, the subject of "faith healing" is introduced to the reader. The two blind men were healed *according to their faith.* They confessed their belief that Jesus was able to heal them. Then, after He touched their eyes with His hands, they were able to see.

It is ironic that the subject of faith healing has become troublesome in modern times. No doubt many abuses and excesses have occurred in the name of Christian faith healing. Some of these practices have become so outlandish and fraudulent that sensitive people can only wince at these calumnies. For this reason, in the minds of many, the term "faith healing" reeks of magic and superstition. It conjures up visions of tent services at which people throw away crutches and back braces. For others there is a sense of discomfort that traditional healing methods, such as physicians and medications, have been disdained.

Because of the confusion that modern faith healers have brought to this topic, we will have occasion to discuss these distortions later in the chapter.

But, as always, hasty judgments can be unwise. Rather than turning a deaf ear to the subject of healing and faith, we ought to seek an understanding of biblical faith and how it is applied. Then we will be better able to separate the wheat from the chaff.

A major objective of this chapter will be to explain the concept of faith as it pertains to the Gospel accounts of healing. But as we do so, it will also be necessary to explore the notion of the "faith factor" as this term has been applied in modern medical therapy.[1] Much of the current medical literature discusses the effect of human suggestibility and expectancy on physical health. The use of the placebo is well known in the practice of medical research. As a result, the word "faith" has become a popular term among writers, journalists, doctors, and others who extol its use in the practice of medicine.

This raises important questions for an understanding of biblical faith. In what ways is biblical faith essentially different from medical faith or the "faith factor"? On the other hand, are there some similarities between biblical faith and the "faith factor" that help us better understand the process of healing?

It will be our task to sort out the many different interpretations that have accrued to this word "faith" in order to set forth a clear exposition of faith and healing in its biblical context.

---

[1] See the discussion of the "faith factor" in Edgar N. Jackson, *The Role of Faith in the Process of Healing* (Minneapolis: Winston Press, 1981), 22-31. For a compendium of research articles discussing "faith," see Dale Matthews, David Larson, and Constance Barry, *The Faith Factor: An Annotated Bibliography of Clinical Research on Spiritual Subjects* (Rockville, MD: National Institute for Health Care Research, 1993); David Larson, *The Faith Factor: An Annotated Bibliography of Systematic Reviews and Clinical Research on Spiritual Subjects* (Rockville, MD: National Institute for Health Care Research, 1993); and Dale Matthews and David Larson, *The Faith Factor: An Annotated Bibliography of Clinical Research on Spiritual Subjects* (Rockville, MD: National Institute for Health Care Research, 1995). See also the classic, Carroll A. Wise, *Religion in Illness and Health* (New York: Harper and Brothers, 1942).

Faith and the "Faith Factor"

Perhaps it is well to begin by discussing "faith" as a general term and then to describe how this term is used by the medical community. This will provide the contrastive background to later examine biblical faith.

Faith can be said to have three basic elements, namely, (1) the cognitive, 2) the emotional, and (3) the volitional. The first of these, the *cognitive*, refers to the intellectual assent of a belief. For example, a person may believe that Vitamin C is necessary for good health. Much of human life is sustained by beliefs such as these, beliefs we hold to be true and abiding. Another way to describe the cognitive domain of faith is to refer to it as the *content* of faith.

The second element of faith is the *emotional* or psychological domain. In this domain, a person commits himself to the belief emotionally. An attitudinal response takes place in which the individual feels strongly about the belief. Here the terms "suggestibility" and "expectancy" come into focus. The suggestion is firmly rooted in the person's mind that Vitamin C is good for human health. In addition, the person literally expects this to occur in respect to his own health.

In the third domain of faith, our attention is turned to the element of *volition* which refers to the human will. The importance of the will is demonstrated by the fact that, if faith is to be operative, a person must "want" this belief to take place. Thus, a person so strongly desires the therapeutic results of Vitamin C that he will make the necessary effort to obtain it for himself. We note a behavioral movement on the part of the person toward the object of his faith.

Any discussion of "faith" needs to involve all three of these elements, each of which is a necessary part of the equation. It is significant that biblical faith maximizes these three elements and it does so in a manner that distinguishes it from the "faith factor" or medical faith. As we will discuss later in this chapter, biblical faith emphasizes the content of faith because of its insistence that the object of faith is Jesus Christ. At the heart of biblical faith is the relationship between God and the person, a relationship so dominated by the activity of God that it can be described as a theocentric relationship.[2] To be sure, biblical faith contains both the psychological and volitional

---

[2]Gustav Aulen, *The Faith of the Christian Church*, 20.

elements of faith, but these are acted upon only after the revelation of God has become dominant in the human heart.

By contrast, medical faith seems to emphasize mainly the psychological elements of faith, especially the factors of suggestibility and expectancy. In much of the medical literature about faith and healing, little if any emphasis is given to the content of faith and in some respects, the object of a person's faith is so belittled that literally anything—a doctor, a friend, a family member, the medication—can effectually act as the object. Of paramount importance for advocates of the "faith factor" are the psychological processes by which the patient believes he can become well.

As early as 1901 when Dr. William Osler wrote the basic textbook for medical science, *The Principles and Practices of Medicine,* he also wrote an article for the *New York Sun* called "The Faith That Heals." Dr. Osler stated that only three or four drugs were really useful in medicine and he urged a return to psychical matters of healing. His use of the word "faith" was anything that was suggestive to the patient, be it God, liver pills, or the doctor. In a sense, Dr. Osler set the tone for a generalized use of the word "faith" in the medical community.

Since that time many well-known doctors have attempted to study the effect of the "faith factor" in the healing process. As can be expected, the emphasis has been on the psychological domain of faith. No less an authority than Dr. Jerome Frank of Johns Hopkins University Medical School has stated what many in medicine hold to be the crucial element of "faith," namely, the expectancy generated by the mind:

> The apparent success of healing methods based upon all sorts of ideologies and methods compels the conclusion that the healing power of faith is in the patient's mind, *not in the validity of the object* (emphasis added).[3]

A similar message has been promoted by Dr. Bernie Siegel, who has written many popular books on the healing effect of the patient's frame of mind. Dr. Siegel emphasizes especially the healing power of hope and love and cites numerous examples of patients who were cured

---

[3]Jerome Frank, *Persuasion and Healing* (New York: Schocken Books, 1961), 60.

where medicine and surgery failed.[4] A careful analysis of Siegel's books reveals that these mechanisms of healing, which on the surface seem to be spiritual, are actually generated psychologically by the person himself.[5]

What is beguiling about these descriptions of "medical faith" is not that they are false or that they do not work. On the contrary, they do *work* and they are, in and of themselves, valid methods of healing. The troublesome fact is that these psychological approaches to healing are perceived by some to be "faith healing" when, in fact, they are not. They are actually a work of the human ego.

According to Dr. Norman Shealy, the use of the mind in healing is not faith healing but rather *work healing*.[6] What we refer to as the power of positive thinking in vernacular speech is in reality the work of the ego. That healing occurs through psychosomatic mechanisms such as positive thinking is well known. Simply wishing to get better can stimulate the healing processes of the body so that the person does improve medically. The mind can make a person well. Experiments in biofeedback have demonstrated that human suggestion is a powerful stimulus in the biochemical processes of the body. In cancer research, mentally "imaging" that the cancer has been overcome by the white blood cells has proven to be therapeutic for the patient.[7] So are other wholistic practices such as biogenics, a form of mental meditation in which the mind sends healing messages to all parts of the body.

But none of this is "faith healing" as we refer to this term. In reality these psychological methods are a form of mental gymnastics that

---

[4]See his discussion in Bernie Siegel, *Peace, Love, and Healing* (New York: Harper & Row, 1990), as well as *Love, Medicine, and Healing* (New York: Harper & Row, 1986).

[5]It is important to question the source of "spiritual" power that is discussed by medical authors. Is spiritual power a gift that is received from without, that is, from God? Or is it a power that is released from within? Edgar Jackson in his book *The Role of Faith in the Process of Healing* seems to speak for many in the field of medicine when he says: "The power of true release is from within. It may be approached by psychological drives and easy formulas of repetition, but they are always the symptoms of the real power that is waiting to be released when the full meaning of life is realized" (146).

[6]Personal conversation. Holistic Health Conference, Seven Springs, PA, November 1989.

[7]Carl Simonton, Stephanie Simonton, and James Creighton, *Getting Well Again* (New York: Bantam, 1980). See especially 151-74.

appear to be closely related to the healing process. It is a cause for elation that we now possess a better understanding of how psychological processes can affect the healing of the body. Biblical healing, however, constitutes a different essence and its consequences go much deeper.

A Further Look at the "Faith Factor" in Medical Healing

It will be helpful to further explore the subject of the "faith factor" in medical healing for the purpose of learning how many in the field of medicine explain the function of faith. According to Dr. Jerome Frank, three major components of the "faith factor" are suggestion, expectancy, and personality structure.[8]

Suggestion and Faith

The first of these, *suggestion,* needs little introduction. We all have experienced the pleasant results of the suggestive power of language. For example, a chance remark by a friend regarding our physical appearance can sometimes have important bearing about how we feel about ourselves. This, in itself, can be health-producing. The effectiveness of suggestion depends partly on the person offering the suggestion. The fame or prestige of the suggester are important factors. For this reason we may be more receptive to suggestions from the doctor because of the prestige of the medical profession. In certain cases, disease can be treated by suggestion therapy alone.

Emile Coué (1857-1926) popularized the use of suggestion for treating illness with his belief that if an idea was repeated many times to an individual, the suggestion would sink into the subconscious mind. Coué's advice to his patients was to have them say every morning and every evening, *"Every day in every way I am getting better and better."*[9] According to Coué, the power of the imagination produced by the suggestion would control the subconscious mind with beneficial consequences for the body. He also felt that a suggestion made as an

---

[8]Edgar N. Jackson, *The Role of Faith in the Process of Healing* (Minneapolis: Winston Press, 1981), 25. There is a fourth component, namely, *status*, which refers to the power of the group to condition a person to respond to the suggestion of healing.

[9]Leslie Weatherhead, *Psychology, Religion, and Healing* (New York: Abingdon-Cokesbury Press, 1951), 128.

aside, "Of course, you're going to get better," rather than made in an authoritative manner, was more likely to get past the critical defense mechanisms of the mind. Coué's approach became quite popular in Europe with thousands of advocates who were convinced that his method worked. Over the years it has continued to generate affirmative response because it demonstrates how suggestion sheds some light on psychosomatic healing.

Can suggestibility be considered an aspect of biblical healing? Undoubtedly, it is connected in some manner with the healings reported in the New Testament. Many of the people who clamored to touch Him were responding to the suggestion that Jesus had power to heal. But all people are suggestible to some degree; it is part of our human condition. For this reason, suggestion may play some role in the psychological domain of faith, but it is certainly not a key factor in understanding biblical faith.

Expectancy or the "Placebo Effect" and Faith

Expectancy has long been associated with the healing process and it is sometimes referred to as the "placebo effect." A positive expectation that something beneficial will happen can have a powerful effect on the physiology of the body, so much so that it has become standard procedure in medical research to test the efficacy of new drugs.

An illustration of the power of expectancy can be demonstrated in the following example. Research was conducted on two groups of patients with bleeding ulcers.[10] One group was informed by a doctor that they would receive a new drug that would, with certainty, produce relief. The second group was informed that they were receiving an experimental drug about which little was known of its therapeutic effects. In actuality, the *same drug* was given to both groups. What were the results? The first group showed 70% significant improvement in their ulcers whereas the second group showed only a 25% significant improvement. The only real difference was the *positive expectancy* of the first group.

Most placebos used in medical research are inert "sugar pills" that have no therapeutic effects; in such a manner, researchers can determine the power of the placebo in comparing it with a pharmacol-

---

[10]Simonton, Simonton, and Creighton, op. cit., 24.

ogically active drug. According to one study, placebo therapies have an average significant effectiveness of 35.2%.[11] Almost anything can act as a placebo including bleeding the patient, touching the patient, expecting the medication to be effective, or the expectancy of the doctor that the medication will produce results. It is probably true that no medical therapy is undertaken without the placebo effect being involved in the process.

Dr. Jerome Frank, who has achieved prominence in writing about the effect of the placebo, is convinced that it is the power of expectancy that explains "faith healing" and the so-called miracles that are attributed to faith. As the following quote will illustrate, he gives scant attention to the spiritual content of a belief:

> There is a good possibility that the emotional state of trust or faith in itself can sometimes rapidly produce far-reaching and permanent changes in attitude and bodily states, though the occurrence of these phenomena cannot be predicted or controlled. The major evidence for this lies in the realm of religious conversions and so-called miracle cures. . . . Since it is the state of hope, belief, or faith which produces the beneficial effects rather than its object, one would expect to find the same phenomenons in a non-religious framework, and this is in fact the case.[12]

This emphasis on expectancy to explain how "faith healing" occurs is crucial in our discussion of faith and healing. I personally raised my doubts about this explanation with Dr. Frank at a medical conference in New York City several years ago. Were we to follow his thesis to a logical conclusion, we would have to conclude that Jesus healed people for the simple reason that they "expected" or "hoped" to be healed.

Much more light has been shed on the subject of the placebo by Dr. Arthur Kleinman of Harvard University who takes a wholistic perspective about the phenomena of hope and expectancy and its effect on physiological functions.[13] Kleinman believes that we are "wired" to react to the events of life both physiologically and psychologically. In brief, we cannot separate the mind from the body. *The mind is embodied, the body mindful.* If Kleinman is correct, then expectancy or

---

[11]Robert Hahn and Arthur Kleinman, "Belief as Pathogen, Belief as Medicine: 'Voodoo Death' and the 'Placebo Phenomenon,'" *Medical Anthropology Quarterly* 14, no. 4 (August 1983): 17.

[12]Quoted in Jackson, op., cit., 24.

[13]Hahn and Kleinman, op. cit., 18.

its opposite, despair, are simply emotional states by which humans respond to the exigencies of life. Something else must be at work to stimulate the whole person in the direction of hope, something no less than the belief itself! Kleinman's thesis brings us closer to the content of faith.

Just as with the factor of suggestion, expectancy can be considered to play some role in biblical healing. Many of those healed by Jesus can be described as highly expectant such as the woman with the issue of blood who said to herself: "If I only touch His cloak, I will be healed" (Matt. 9:21). But expectancy can hardly be operative without a substantial belief that validates and releases the power of a positive expectation. Psychological explanations for healing can enlighten the topic of healing, but they do not explain.

Personality Structure and Faith

One of the factors that has emerged as an important variable in the "faith factor" is the type of *personality structure* a person has. Thus, some people seem to have a greater ability "to accept suggestion than others and to respond to the kind of stimuli that the use of a placebo involves."[14]

There is no doubt that there is some truth in the assertion that personality types and the capacity to be healed are correlated. People who are rigid and inflexible by process of upbringing and cultural experiences tend to be more suspicious of good things happening to them. They are less accepting and responsive to external stimuli because they are withdrawn within themselves. Such personality types erect defense mechanisms to protect themselves from the pain of failure and, as a result, they pattern themselves to expect the worst.

Taken at face value, it would seem to suggest that rigid personality types are at a disadvantage as compared to optimistic personality types. According to studies of the "faith factor," the former have much less capability for "faith" and "hope" than do the latter. But is this really true? Cannot faith bloom even in those who seem to have a closed mind toward life?

Take a look at the case of the father who brought his demoniac son to Jesus (Mark 9:14-29). Perhaps it was the father's rigid, pessimistic personality that explains his statement to Jesus: "*If* You can do

---

[14]Jackson, op. cit., 29.

anything, take pity on us and help us." The phrasing of the father's plea for help was hedged with a doubt that Jesus could heal his son. No wonder Jesus responded to this doubting and closed-minded posture with the challenge, "*If you can?* Why, everything is possible for him who believes."

As this example demonstrates, rigid personality types can yield to the power of Christ's healing. Jesus not only reminded the father that He had the authority to heal, but He also challenged the father to *want* to believe. In other words, the power of Jesus' authority activated the volitional domain of faith, so important in biblical healing. When the father said to Jesus, "Lord, I do believe, help me overcome my un-belief!" his defense mechanisms gave way to the flowering of faith.

There is much more at work in biblical healing than the "faith factor" is willing to admit. Because those who espouse the "faith factor" lean so heavily on psychological explanations, they overlook or minimize the "content" of faith as well as the "volition" of faith. The result is that Jesus the Healer becomes little more than a talented therapist who can make people hopeful and expectant.

Obviously, the New Testament narratives present a completely different picture.

Beliefs and the "Faith Factor"

A new approach to the "faith factor" has been gaining much popularity in the medical field, namely, the work of Dr. Herbert Benson, head of Harvard's Mind/Body Institute. Benson, who has been actively engaged in research on the relationship of meditation and healing, believes that human beings are "wired for God." Unlike many others in the field, he is persuaded that "personal" beliefs are a crucial part of a person's health and well-being.

According to Benson, "What I am saying is not that faith heals, but that belief heals, and the belief may or may not be religious."[15] Without a doubt, Benson is moving much closer to the cognitive domain of faith because he focuses on the substantive power of the belief itself to heal. He takes seriously the fact that people's religious beliefs are "real" for them and are not simply fluff.

---

[15]Beth Baker. "The Mind-Body Connection: Putting the 'Faith Factor' to Work," *AARP Bulletin* 38, no. 7 (July/August 1997): 20.

But lest we become too enthused about this shift in emphasis, we need to realize that Benson's approach to spirituality is so vague that any religious or personal belief will work. In his approach, "God" is simply a force that a person can identify with, a feeling that some sort of presence or power or energy exists. This spiritual force might even be a doctor or a meaningful relationship; however, since most people in America are religious, this belief will most likely take the form of a spiritual power.

Benson, who has worked with the Dalai Lama of Tibet, claims that beliefs combined with relaxation, pack a medical wallop and can stimulate healing. "I am not saying that God exists or not—I don't know. But what I am saying, from a medical point of view, we're in a win-win situation when people are believers of some sort."[16] Typically, Benson will have a Christian patient meditate on the statement, "Christ, have mercy on me," or, if a Muslim, "Allah is good," or again, if Jewish, "The Lord, our God, is one." He refers to this combination of beliefs and relaxation as the "faith factor" in medicine and cites considerable medical research in his favor.

Benson is plowing new ground with his focus on beliefs, but there is little evidence that his approach is anything more than the "power of positive thinking" in a new dress. It seems essentially to be a mentalistic form of healing, a psychosomatic procedure that can produce medical results, but which falls considerably short of the biblical model of faith; that is, it is not wholistic in our understanding of things.

Biblical Faith and Healing

As we turn our attention to biblical faith, we need to recall that Jesus affirmed the faith of the sick people whom he healed. Some of Jesus' most dramatic healings were accomplished in the context of great faith—for example, the daughter of the Canaanite woman (Matt. 15:21-28) and the servant of the Roman centurion (Matt. 8:5-13). Frequently Jesus would commend the person's faith as He did to the Samaritan leper who returned to give Him thanks: "Rise and go; your *faith* has made you well" (Luke 17:11-17).

Jesus not only affirmed the faith of the sick who reached out to Him, but on some occasions He would coax and cajole these sufferers

[16]Ibid., 17.

until their faith burst forth in a lively confession. The examples of the Canaanite woman and the father of the demoniac son come to mind.

It should not surprise us that Jesus expected faith from those who sought His healing power. As we have already referenced in chapter 3, Jesus' healings were signs that the kingdom of God had come to the world of humankind. The purpose of His healing ministry was to restore the broken to a spiritual relationship with the Father in the kingdom of God. For this reason, *faith* was the means by which people would enter into the Kingdom and receive the gifts of healing and wholeness.

Biblical faith, more than anything else, refers to a *relationship* between God and the person. According to Luther, it is impossible to talk about faith unless it is first understood that God Himself has entered into a fellowship with the believer. Luther's famous words from the Large Catechism—"These two, God and faith, belong together and must be conjoined"—imply that biblical faith is much more than a psychological or a sociological phenomenon but rather a theological phenomenon.[17] In short, it means that God and the believer are in a relationship with each other as 1 John 1:3 reminds us: "And our fellowship is with the Father and with his Son, Jesus Christ." Wherever this relationship ceases to exist, faith has also ceased to exist.

From the viewpoint of biblical faith, God is immediately present and active in the life of the believer. In the realm of faith God is the ruler and His will is supreme. Faith means to be subdued and dominated by God. Faith is not some sort of anthropocentric approach which makes the human central and God the obedient servant of human needs and self-esteem.[18] Faith is entirely a work of God and exists only because of God's activity.

Because God and faith belong together, it is important to understand that faith has its basis in God's *revelation*. The God who subdues us also reveals Himself to us. It is through this revelation of Scripture that He reveals His heart and His will by which we can know Him and the mystery of His love. But this revelation of God must be perceived by *the eye of faith alone*.[19] In other words, it is faith that

---

[17]Gustav Aulén, *The Faith of the Christian Church*, 20. For a fuller exposition of biblical faith and healing" see R. K. Harrison, "Healing, Health," in *The Interpreter's Dictionary of the Bible*, vol. 2 (Nashville: Abingdon Press, 1962), 541-48.

[18]Ibid., 20.

[19]Ibid., 24.

opens our eyes to discover the living God and His acts of grace. By virtue of our own human reason, we could never fathom nor apprehend the mysteries that God reveals to us. Luther once remarked about this process: "The Word, of course, I take hold of with the intellect, but agreement with that Word is the work of the Holy Spirit, not of reason, which always seeks its own righteousness."[20]

Faith is therefore saying "yes" to the God who has overwhelmed us with His grace. From this God we can no longer flee. Perhaps the most profound aspect of faith is to discover that our "seeking" after God is nothing more than that the Father is "drawing us" to Himself (John 6:44).

With this background, we are now able to look at biblical faith from the viewpoint of its three elements, namely, the cognitive, the emotional, and the volitional.

The Cognitive Basis of Biblical Faith

When we consider the cognitive element of faith, we focus on the object of our faith, the One in whom we believe. Biblical faith is firm and certain of its object, namely, the God who revealed Himself in Jesus Christ.

It is significant in so many of the healing episodes that the supplicant addresses Jesus as the One in whom their faith is rooted. For example, blind Bartimaeus cried out to the Healer, "Jesus, Son of David, have mercy on me" (Mark 10:46). Even the demoniac in the synagogue acknowledges the authority of Jesus: "What do You want with us, Jesus of Nazareth? . . . I know who You are—the Holy One of God" (Mark 1:24). The content of faith is in reality nothing else than the God who has revealed Himself.

Luther spoke of faith as assenting to the truth of God's revelation, saying a "yes" to God and to His work and promise. For this reason, a characteristic of biblical faith is its *certainty,* the confidence that God is true and can always be depended upon. As Luther points out, "This is the reason why our theology is certain: because it snatches us away from ourselves and places us outside of ourselves lest we rest upon human strength, conscience, feelings, character, our own works."[21]

---

[20]Werner Elert, *The Structure of Lutheranism* (St. Louis: Concordia, 1962), 84.

[21] Aulén, op. cit., 94.

Because faith is faith in divine revelation, not in personal experiences, the certainty of faith does not come and go. As a result, faith can persist even in the midst of tribulation and distress. Because faith is not a faith of experiences, but altogether a faith in God alone, it can live under those circumstances when God seems remote and can carry us on to new experiences.

For some of us, the most insightful story of healing in the Gospels is the very human story of the woman with an issue of blood (Matt. 9:20-22; Luke 8:43-48). This woman had endured a lot of distress. But so certain was this woman of the authority of Jesus that she held one thought in her mind: "If I only touch His cloak, I will be healed." Her certainty literally pushed her through a crowd of people to touch the hem of Jesus' robe. Nor did she run away when Jesus demanded that the person who touched Him come forward. Trembling at the feet of Jesus, this woman confessed in front of the crowd why she had touched Him and how she had been healed. For this bold action of faith, Jesus commended her and said: "Daughter. Your faith has healed you. Go in peace."

The Emotional Basis of Biblical Faith

While faith is an assent to the God who has revealed Himself to us, it must be more than a bare intellectual assent of the mind. It must also be an emotional attitude of the heart.

Sometimes the psychological conception of biblical faith is referred to as *"fiducia cordis,"* the *confidence of the heart*. Faith in Christ becomes truly faith when the believer can say with confidence—faith is the certainty that this applies to "me."[22] In other words, the Christian is certain that Christ is for him or her in the midst of all the billions of people who live on the same planet.

A psychological understanding of faith is understood as having certain feelings and attitudes that flow from the fact that a person is in the fellowship of God. Among these are the attitudes of trust and confidence in God's promises as well as a vibrant hope and expectancy in the goodness of God. The believer not only knows the promises of God, but there is in his heart an emotional response to these promises. They affect him, he wants them, he lays hold on them, and applies them to his personal need.

---

[22]Elert, op. cit., 68.

Of all the people that Jesus healed, none seems to have demonstrated greater confidence in the authority of Jesus than the Roman centurion whose servant lay ill of a serious fever and was close to death (Luke 7:2-10). So confident was this man in Jesus' authority to heal his servant that he even sent friends to Jesus with the message: "Lord, don't trouble Yourself, for I do not deserve to have You come under my roof. . . . But say the word and my servant will be healed. For I myself am a man under authority."

The centurion went on to explain how he had the authority to tell soldiers and servants to do whatever he bade them to do. By simply making the command, the deed was done. It was a metaphor of his own confidence that Jesus had the authority to banish the power of sickness by simply making the command. So amazed was Jesus at the magnitude of the centurion's faith that He responded: "I tell you, I have not found such great faith even in Israel."

We gain something of understanding the confidence of faith when looking at its opposite which is *fear*. On more than one occasion, Jesus scolded His disciples for their attitude of fear in the face of distress: "You of little faith, why are you so afraid?" (Matt. 8:26). Fear immobilizes faith because it destroys the confidence of the person in God's ability to overcome the threat of disaster. The amount of faith a person possesses is not the crucial factor in biblical healing. A mustard seed, Jesus said, is the measure of a faith required to move mountains (Matt. 17:20). What is important is the "movement of faith" toward its true object, the confidence of the heart that never wavers nor rebels despite the situation.

The Volitional Basis of Faith

When we say that a person *wants* the good things that God has promised to all believers, we are referring to the volitional element of faith. Many of the promises that Jesus made were conditional according to the desire of the person to receive them: "Ask and it will be given to you; seek and you will find; knock and the door will be opened to you" (Matt. 7:7).

Faith is certainly not characterized by a passive or tenuous attitude. Attitudes of resignation and fatalism are *not* faith but are rather adversaries of faith. The popular aphorism "whatever will be, will be" is nothing more than an admission that God's power is limited and finite. Faith, by its very nature, is active and seeks a change from the situation which now exists to a situation which should exist.

In times of sickness, it is only natural for a person to supplicate the God of grace to be *released* of disease and suffering and to be made whole. Here we see faith as asking, pleading, beseeching, begging, and appealing to God for mercy. This is a common usage of faith and one that occupies many of the narratives of the Old and New Testaments.

The volitional element of faith is illustrated by *tenacity*, an attitude that refuses to give up despite the barriers that one faces. Perhaps the most illuminating example of this truth in the Gospels is the Canaanite woman whose daughter was possessed with a demon (Matt. 15:21-28). When Jesus refused to speak with her, she pestered the disciples to heal her daughter. Undaunted by their refusal to assist her, she again approached Jesus and pleaded for help. His challenging remarks to her would have discouraged a lesser person but not this woman. She persisted in her request, stating that "even the dogs eat the crumbs that fall from their master's table." When Jesus saw the full flowering of faith in that utter act of dependence, He said to this woman, "Woman, you have great faith! Your request is granted."

We also recall that beautiful parable Jesus told of the persistent widow who kept beating on the judge's door asking for justice (Luke 18:1-8). Once again we are given an example of a woman who didn't give up when first denied. She stayed with her request until she was vindicated. In this parable Jesus teaches us that our prayer life should exhibit this same tenacious characteristic. We should never give up if our request is in accord with the will of God and is for a just cause. We are encouraged to pray that God's goodness and wholeness will be revealed in our lives. Praying is an act of faith. As Jesus makes clear at the conclusion of the parable, "And will not God bring about justice for His chosen ones, who cry out to Him day and night?"

Faith is characterized by boldness that sets it apart as distinct from the ordinary. Persons of faith possess a tenacity that does not give up the struggle and are firm in their resolve that God will vindicate their requests in a timely manner.

God Solicits Our Faith in Him

Biblical faith is our lifeline to God. We are never so far from God that we cannot approach Him in faith when we are in any trouble.

Indeed, God desires that we come into His presence with our needs, no matter how insignificant that may appear to be.

Throughout the Old and New Testaments, we learn that the heart of God is open to the troubles of His people. God is genuinely moved by our suffering and sets in motion a plan to restore us from the forces of disorder. To Moses God said: "I have indeed seen the misery of My people in Egypt. I have heard them crying out . . . and I am concerned about their suffering" (Exodus 3:7).

In His own ministry, Jesus urged people to come to God with their troubles. He tells us that we should be persistent in asking what we want from God, never faltering or doubtful, because the Father desires to give us those good things we need to sustain ourselves. According to Jesus, even human fathers do not deceive their children but give them what they need: "If you, then, though you are evil, know how to give good gifts to your children, *how much more will your Father in heaven give good gifts to those who ask Him!*" (Matt. 7:11).

This truth is important because it teaches us that the Father desires to give us those things that are *good* for us. I find it significant that when He healed the man with the withered hand, Jesus replied to His audience: "Which is lawful on the Sabbath: *to do good* or to do evil, *to save life* or to kill" (Mark 3:4). Healing is a good gift, according to Jesus, for it restores the person to a life of wholeness.

But Jesus does expect the needy person to *ask* for these good gifts. It is obvious that God knows our needs, better than we do ourselves. However, in the mind of God, the process of asking for help is, in itself, an act of faith! It is an act of faith because it shows dependency on the mercy and goodness of God who alone can supply us with what we truly need.

The careful reader will note that Jesus commended the recipients' faith because they dared to ask Him for healing despite the barriers they may have faced. It was not easy for the two blind men to make their requests to Jesus (Matt. 9:27-31). Jesus didn't stop when they first cried out to Him; He kept walking. Sightless, they struggled after Him into a house where they repeated their requests. Faith is also an act of courage.

In times of sickness, or even when we are somewhat ill, God invites to pray for our healing. It matters not whether our sickness is in some way deserved or whether its origin is unknown. It matters not whether we are praying for our own need or for the need of a loved one. God will hear and respond positively to our need in some manner. For He is moved by our repentance and by the cry of our faith.

Healing and the Prayer of Faith

How do believers in this present age demonstrate their faith in the healing power of Christ? There is only one way to pray for healing and that is to pray the prayer of faith. According to the apostle James, the prayer of faith is a major activity of the Christian congregation: *"Is any one of you sick? He should call the elders of the church to pray over him. . . . And the prayer offered in faith will make the sick person well; the Lord will raise him up"* (James 5:14-15).

The prayer of faith is the supplication of the church for the ill person in its midst. As God's servants, we pray that the Healer will share His goodness and mercy with the sufferer. We pray that God will release the sick person from the oppression of the disease and will grant healing to the totality of his personhood. We especially make a plea to God to grant the sick person the gift of wholeness and to fill the heart with peace.

This means that we will pray aggressively, confidently, and tenaciously.[23] Because we live in a spiritual relationship with God, our Father, we have every right to approach Him with the things that trouble us in body, mind, and spirit. Biblical faith takes God at His word: "Call upon Me in the day of trouble; I will deliver you and you will honor Me" (Psalm 50:15).

Not everyone may agree with all the sentiments of the following statement, but we cannot disagree with the writer's plea that prayer for healing means to be honest and forthright:

> Prayer is a great resource at times of illness. We are invited to take our trouble to God. We are to be honest and open, complaining and direct, persistent to the point of being obnoxious. We are to ask for what we want and not be willing to settle for second-best. If we want health, we should ask for it. If we want full recovery, we should not hedge our bets by asking only for "the serenity to accept whatever comes," or suggesting

---

[23]There is no biblical mandate that healing prayers need to be prefaced with the phrase "if it be Thy will." See Leslie Weatherhead, *Religion, Psychology, and Healing* (Nashville: Abingdon-Cokesbury Press, 1951), 440-41. Weatherhead says that previous to the fifth century A.D. "the conditional 'if it be Thy will'—so common a feature in modern prayers for healing—is altogether absent from these early Christian prayers."

that "nevertheless, your will be done." Most of us have been conditioned to be realistic, laid back, less than optimistic in our prayers. We look around and see what is possible and ask for them instead of what we really want. We expect our prayers not to be answered, and they usually are not.[24]

The prayer of faith is a bold prayer because we dare to take God seriously. It was this thought that James had in mind when He said (1:6-7): "But when he asks, he must believe and not doubt, because he who doubts is like a wave of the sea, blown and tossed by the wind. That man should not think he will receive anything from the Lord."

Christians who pray for healing are also alert to the use of physicians and other medical resources. To walk in faith also means to walk in wisdom! For it may be through the ministry of a caring doctor or the application of an antibiotic that God chooses to exercise His healing power. It is an encouraging sign that some Christian doctors and nurses are beginning to pray with their patients. Healing prayer, of course, includes more than the physical malady. The prayer of faith is aimed at all the needs of the ill person.

What happens when it does not appear that an affirmative answer will attend our prayers for healing? This topic will be discussed at length in chapter 7. Nevertheless, the posture of the Christian is always the posture of faith! No matter what the situation or exigency of life, faith in Christ is not frustrated because it leans on the certainty of God's loving presence. There is no other way that God would have us live (2 Cor. 5:7). Yes, even in our darkest hour—when we walk through the valley of the shadow of death—we walk by faith!

The Problem of "Faith Healers"

A discussion of faith and healing cannot help but bring to mind those who are known popularly as "faith healers." Perhaps nothing has impeded a salutary Christian ministry of healing more than those whose methods and claims of healing seem to be at odds with the biblical interpretation of healing.

---

[24]Daniel Simundson, "Health and Healing in the Bible," in *Word & World: Theology for Christian Ministry* 11, no. 4 (Fall, 1982): 336. See also L. K. Graham, "Healing," and P. W. Pruyser, "Health and Illness," in *Dictionary of Pastoral Care and Counseling* (Nashville: Abingdon Press, 1990), 497-505.

Who are these "faith healers" who appeal to many in the marketplace of healing today? Most are men and women who occupy the fringe areas of orthodox Christianity, operating as independent healers rather than representing a denomination. Their theological positions may vary to some degree, but all of them seem to possess interactive skills by which they successfully work their audiences. They attract large crowds not only by virtue of their charismatic personalities, but also because they bear the nostrum of healing, a desired priority in American culture.

Most faith healers appear to share several basic assumptions about faith and healing. The first of these is that an individual will be *physically* healed from disease if he or she has sufficient faith in Jesus Christ. This assumption is based on a belief that God wants all people to be healed and will always reward true faith by healing diseases. Such healers make scant mention of the healing of the spirit nor of the healing of the whole person. In a manner that is typical of a theology of glory, the emphasis is the healing of the body.

A second assumption is that healing must occur in the same miraculous fashion as in the ministry of Jesus Himself, that is, by spontaneous remission. For this reason, their healing services are usually highlighted with melodramatic and histrionic effects, each of them staged to produce an aura of expectancy and hope. The audience itself is encouraged to participate in the healer's intention that the crowd be of "one mind and one will" so that suggestion will be maximized.

Finally, there is the assumption that failure to be physically healed is because of lack of faith in God or disobedience to His Word. Behind this assumption is the belief that faith is a human activity that can be increased by human effort. Encouragement is given at these services to "believe!" and to "claim the healing!" If no healing has occurred, the onus is placed squarely on the sufferer—"If you had enough faith, you would be healed."

No doubt there have been some people who have been physically healed through the ministry of the so-called faith healers. We will have occasion to discuss how such healings might be achieved. On the other hand, there have been scores of failures which have caused Wade Boggs to make this observation:

> It is probable that this spiritual and mental tragedy overshadows the physical, for no disappointment can equal the disappointment in the

promises of God. It is a very serious thing to raise the hopes of multitudes of sick people with assurances that God will always reward true faith by healing diseases, and then to lead the great majority of these people through disillusionment to despair.

Furthermore, if it cannot be demonstrated that God has promised to heal all the sick, then to try to arouse people's faith in a promise God never made would be a wicked and tragic thing.[25]

Boggs is among those who have been highly critical of the operation of faith healers as have other theologians, such as Theodore Graebner. It will be helpful for the reader to survey these criticisms because, to a large extent, they explain why a deep suspicion about spiritual healing still lingers in the minds of pastors and laypersons today.

Boggs attacks the theology of faith healers because of their assertion that the healing power of God must occur in the same "supernatural" and miraculous manner employed by Jesus.[26] He objects to such terms as "natural" and "supernatural" because the healers imply that the healing power of God is at work in the latter—in the form of dramatic miracles—but not in the former, in which God heals through doctors and medicines.[27] In this criticism, Boggs is certainly on target and his objections are valid. Whether God heals spontaneously or by means of medications and therapy, the healing is from His hand and should be honored.

Nevertheless, Boggs shows his own theological bias in his belief that faith healing has no place in the modern Christian church. Like many who follow in the footsteps of Calvin, Boggs is essentially a dispensationalist who believes that the healing ministry of Jesus was for the purpose of establishing His church. Since the miraculous cures of Jesus accomplished this goal, believers in Christ no longer have a need for this type of divine intervention. Boggs is of the opinion that the manner in which God heals today is through the profession and technology of modern medical science.

Theodore Graebner opposes faith healers on quite different grounds and cites many reasons why they should be avoided by Christian

---

[25]Wade Boggs, *Faith Healing and the Christian Faith* (Richmond, VA: John Knox Press, 1956), 30.

[26]Ibid. See his discussion of the claims of faith healers in chapters 1 and 2.

[27]Ibid., 182.

believers.[28] First, the healers parade miracles and wonder-working before the public in a dramatic manner, an activity typical of the "enthusiasts" whom Luther scorned as manipulators of the Holy Spirit. Although Luther himself was involved in the healing of the dying Melanchthon, he was ordinarily contemptuous of signs and wonders and relied instead on prayer for the sick.[29] Graebner argues that although the healers promote miraculous healing, they are not consistent with the Scriptures. Consistency demands a continuation of other healing gifts such as casting out devils, taking up serpents, and raising the dead, activities that healers are ordinarily not engaged in.

Another objection that Graebner makes is that faith was not always present when Christ healed the sick. Some of those whom Christ healed did not demonstrate faith, for example, the man born blind who did not know who Jesus was at the times of the healing (John 9:35-38) or the man with the withered arm (Matt. 12:9-13). Graebner wonders why faith healers exhort people to have faith if God is not limited in His power by the attitudes of people.

Further, Graebner is persuaded that faith healing is not always the best means by which God produces spiritual fruit in believers. Although he admits that God hears our prayers and can intervene through divine healing, he argues that suffering is the medium by which God's triumphs are more perfectly performed. In this regard, Graebner takes a position more in keeping with the medieval and pietistic traditions that have emphasized God's activity in suffering rather than in healing. Accordingly, Graebner argues: "God in His infinite wisdom and love sees that we need to be made perfect by the things which we suffer, and that He will not lift the cross, no, not while life lasts, when He knows that only so may we be kept in the faith and prepared for the unending joys of heaven."[30]

---

[28]Theodore Graebner, *Faith-Cure: The Practice Sometimes Miscalled "Divine Healing"* (St. Louis: Holy Cross Press, 1921).

[29]Ibid. It can be argued that Luther evolved in his attitude toward healing. The early Luther appears to be convinced that God did not heal in the same manner as He did at the time of Christ. However, the later Luther spoke approvingly of laying on hands with prayer for the healing of the sick. An example of Luther's suggestion for a congregational approach to healing appears in chapter 8.

[30]Ibid. Graebner's emphasis on the benefits of suffering is typical of the church, which has long given up on the ministry of healing. The entire issue of suffering and faith will be dealt with in chapter 7.

Both Boggs and Graebner have merits in their criticisms of faith healers, but their arguments are defensive and illustrative of their own attitudes about healing. One wonders why they have failed to mention a major biblical problem of the healers, namely, the emphasis on physical healing rather than the healing of the whole person. To focus on physical healing, as the healers do, is to minimize the healing power of the forgiveness of sins, certainly the divine means by which God brings wholeness to broken people. This is a major shortcoming of the faith healers and indicates their distortion of the Scriptural teaching about healing.

Again, the healers can be criticized for their distortion of the nature of faith: faith is a gift of God, not a human activity. It is distressing that the healers do not mention faith as a relationship with the God of grace nor the joy of living in His kingdom. What is so often lost in their healing services is this comforting message of God's grace, the truth that God loves us despite our sicknesses and that His grace has secured for us the gift of eternal life.

A major problem of the healers is their emphasis on a theology of glory rather than the theology of the cross. Where is the "wounded healer" among the faith healers? Where is the identification with the pain and suffering of the sick, the willingness to sacrifice one's own well-being on their behalf? The emphasis of the healers on the dramatic and miraculous can have the effect of presenting a false Christ to the world, a Christ who knows only triumph but never the shame of the cross.

Finally, we can raise the argument that the Christian healing ministry is really the ministry of the congregation and not a spectacle to be showcased to the world. While it is true that Jesus and His disciples preached the kingdom of God on the streets, the later writings of the New Testament make it clear that gifts of healing were activities of the Holy Spirit in local congregations. In this respect, the healing ministry is part and parcel of the total ministry of the church, not a unique ministry to itself.

An important question to be raised at this time concerns the successes of the faith healers. How can we explain the fact that healings do occur at the hands of the healers? Graebner holds to the opinion that these so-called faith cures are actually mentalistic healings in which people are healed through the power of suggestion:

With the joining of soul and body in such an intimate and perfect union, we have a safe starting place for the discussion of mental healing. We know the agency of these interactions is the nervous system, especially the sympathetic nerves which operate and control the organic activities of the body. Aside from all suggestion from without, the mind, working unconsciously through the nervous system, possesses curative power. The divine healers depend on this curative power of the mind in many cases.[31]

Graebner is convinced that the entire operation of faith healers is nothing but a naturalistic and psychological process in which the power of suggestion produces hope and confidence in being healed. The manner by which the healers succeed is a procedure that every physician knows about and uses in his practice. To call such healings "miracles" he terms preposterous and arrogant. "You have seen how they are worked. . . . When did Jesus and when did Paul conduct a three-hour service in order to work up his hearers to a stage of excitement? The healers cannot accomplish a thing without these psychological preparations. I believe that religion has nothing whatever to do with their cures."[32]

An interesting research study on individuals who attended Pentecostal healing services reveals that "faith healing" may be a psychological buffer that helps people deal with the harsh realities of their sickness.[33] According to Mansell Pattison and his associates who worked with Pentecostal responses to the MMPI, those members who had been "healed" were relying heavily on the psychological defense mechanism of denial. Because they believed that they were putting their full faith in God, they acted as if they had experienced a healing *regardless* of the presence or absence of physical symptoms afterwards. As Pattison says, "Hence, it is not surprising that a zealous religious service could prime individuals to accept a group's own interpretation of how they *should* be feeling and how they should perceive their physical state."[34]

---

[31]Ibid.

[32]Ibid.

[33]Marc Galanter, *Cults: Faith Healing and Coercion* (New York: Oxford University Press, 1989).

[34]Ibid., 4

Pattison and his colleagues therefore concluded that the primary function of faith healing was not necessarily to heal sickness, but to reinforce the group's religious perspective and thereby provide sick people with a means of avoiding harsh realities.

Sometimes the gifts of God can be distorted from their divine intention and, instead of bringing a blessing, they cause confusion. I believe this to be the case with so-called faith healers whose ministries have done little to advance the cause of Christian healing. To a large extent, they have created barriers for a biblical understanding of faith and its role in the healing process. But perhaps the lesson we have learned from the faith healers is that people will look elsewhere for answers to disease and illness if orthodox churches are not attentive to those needs.

It is for this reason that I believe that the church needs to recover the legacy of its healing ministry. In chapter 8, "The Ministry of Healing," it will be my purpose to demonstrate how the church can again become attentive to matters of health and healing. As we present some biblical guidelines for a congregational healing ministry, surely this can be a symbol that the restoration of order is occurring in our own day.

Chapter Seven

Sickness and Suffering

Not everyone is physically healed of their sickness. Some remain chronically ill for the balance of their lives. Others may improve for awhile, but then their condition worsens and they die. It is appropriate that we focus on this topic of suffering in the aftermath of our discussion on faith and healing. A polyannish optimism about health, which seeks avoidance of all pain, certainly does not describe the reality taught by Scripture nor the experience of human life.

In Greek mythology there is the story of Chiron's wound. Chiron was a centaur who was wounded by one of Hercules' poisoned arrows. Unfortunately, the wound proved incurable and relief could only come through death. But Chiron was not allowed to die. He was made to bear his wound until finally he was allowed to enter the underworld. Since that time the "Chironian wound" is known as the wound that will not heal.[1]

Despite the advances of medical science, many people are not cured, no matter how sophisticated the technology or heroic the efforts of medical professionals. Many more pray for a healing of their malady but experience no deliverance. Current statistics of the American populace reveal that 9% of our nation suffers a chronic disorder, either a physical handicap or a mental or physical impairment that compromises their capacity to function normally.[2] As we ponder the

---

[1]John Sanford, *Healing and Wholeness* (New York: The Paulist Press, 1977), 33.

[2]*Healthy People 2000: National Health Promotion and Disease Prevention Objectives*. U.S. Department of Health and Human Services, Public Health Services (Boston: Jones and Bartlett, 1992), 73. About 33 million people have functional limitations that interfere with their daily activities, and more than 9 million have limitations that prevent them from working, attending school, or maintaining a household. The underlying impairments most often responsible for these conditions are arthritis, heart disease, back conditions (including spinal curvature), lower extremity impairments, sand intervertebral disk disorders. For those under age 18 the most frequent causes of activity limitation are asthma, mental retardation, mental illness, and hearing and speech impairments.

plight of chronic sufferers, we find ourselves coming face to face with one of the universals of human life.

A major objective of this chapter will be to examine the theme of suffering from a biblical perspective, especially as it relates to sickness. I believe that there is ample evidence in the Scripture to demonstrate that the Healer does bring healing to those whose lives are chronically impaired. The healing Christ is *not* silent! God's power can come in other ways than physical healing.

The Problem of Pain

Here is the problem before us. We have read the stories of healing in the Bible. We have heard God's invitation to come to Him for help and healing. We have prayed the prayer of faith and have dared to expect divine intervention. In addition, many other people are praying for us. Yet the healing does not come. Our disease, our illness, and our sickness persist.

As we ponder our situation, doubts begin to creep into our mind. We wonder if God truly cares. The pain remains and there seems to be no answer from the One who so compassionately healed others. We may feel like the psalmist who cried: "How long, O LORD? Will You forget me forever? How long will You hide Your face from me? (Psalm 13:1)

At times like these, some of us may become disillusioned about the efficacy of prayer. We have come with great expectations, believing the promises, and the answer seems to be "no." What then are we to do? Should we abandon our prayers? Should we give up all hope that God is concerned about our sickness? Should we become critical of "faith healing," which seems to promise too much? Obviously not.

The biblical approach to chronic disease and suffering is a very positive and faith-oriented approach. It is one of the profoundest truths in all of Scripture because it is centered in the grace and mercy of God.

But before we examine the biblical approach, it is necessary to look at a popular approach to suffering that provides a completely different answer, the answer of *fatalism*. There are those who take the point of view that God wants them to be sick or else they would not be suffering as they do. We need to carefully scrutinize this unbiblical attitude and the false comfort it gives.

Is Sickness the Will of God?

It is time to do battle with that old conundrum that keeps popping up whenever we talk about faith and sickness—*is it God's will that we be sick?*

I remember the time when an elder of my church was ready to undergo surgery for stomach cancer. As I sat by his bedside the night before his operation, I said to him, "Ron, let's pray for your healing." He turned to me and responded, "But what if this is the will of God?" I could only look at him in amazement and think to myself, "Ron, if it's the will of God that you have cancer, then why are you getting an operation? Why are you having one of the best oncologists in Pittsburgh operating on you if God wants you to be sick? That makes no sense. It's schizophrenic!"

I am convinced that there is no greater obstacle to the healing power of God than the misplaced attitude that God *wants* a person to be sick. Such a fatalistic attitude is a far cry from the biblical faith Jesus once described: "If you have as small as a mustard seed . . . nothing will be impossible for you" (Matt. 17:20). Such an attitude is not even remotely close to voluntarily accepting a cross and bearing it to God's glory. To believe that God *wants* us to be sick is an attitude of resignation, a pessimistic fatalism that one's lot in life is to be sick if sickness occurs for whatever reason.

Is it not significant that not once does the idea of God willing our sicknesses appear in the record of the Gospels? To which sufferer does Jesus even suggest that it would be better for that person to remain sick than to be healed? On the contrary, Jesus considered healing to be a "work of God" and looked with compassion upon those who came to be delivered of their diseases. On that occasion when the leper cried out to the Healer, "If You are *willing*, You can make me clean." Jesus reached out and touched the man. "*I am willing,*" He said. "Be clean" (Mark 1:40-41).

Much of this problem of fatalism about sickness we can trace to early medieval times when the church suddenly changed its perception of the person. Gnosticism split the soul from the body with the corollary belief that the soul was the spark of life whereas the body counted for little. With this emphasis on the spirituality of the soul apart from the body, it was but a small step to phase out what once was a vibrant ministry of healing. Interest in matters of health began to wane and was replaced with a new focus upon the glory of suffering.

As the body suffered, the soul was believed to prosper. Soon the attitude developed that sickness was actually a good experience because it was a palpable sign that God was chastening the believer. Far removed from the hostility Jesus felt toward disease, medieval piety rather believed that the sicker a person was, the more God loved him. With God now the "heavy" in matters of sickness, the belief that sickness was the will of God eventually became dominant in the church and has been with us to this day. Modern books of prayer continue to contain prayers that God "disciplines" us through sickness.[3]

Years ago I received a phone call from the Abbess of a Cistercian Abbey in Tucson, Arizona, one of the strictest orders of the Roman Catholic Church. In her request for me to speak to the nuns of the Abbey about Christian healing, she specifically asked me to "bring them out of the Middle Ages." I presented a series of talks to these Cistercian nuns on "the Christian ministry of health and healing" and witnessed an amazing transformation. Many of these nuns had believed that their illness was a sign of God's chastening discipline. In point of fact, their practice was to stay cloistered in their cells, nourishing the illnesses they were certain God wanted them to have. When challenged by the truth that Christ brought the blessing of healing and wholeness with the kingdom of God, their minds began to change. One old nun said to me after the final seminar, "I wish I had known this 25 years ago."

Now, none of this discussion denies the fact that God can produce spiritual growth *by means of* disease and handicaps. There is much truth in the fact that life's infirmities can become a medium to achieve exceptional accomplishments. We are well aware of the "success stories" of those who, like Helen Keller, overcame tremendous handicaps to secure wholeness. There is even truth in the axiom that, had these adversities not come, their towering achievements probably would not have occurred.

---

[3]Leslie Weatherhead, *Religion, Psychology, and Healing* (Nashville: Abingdon-Cokesbury Press, 1951), 440-41. "The idea of divine chastisement is not found in any of the liturgies and prayers for healing before the fifth century. . . . The Christians of the first centuries had a clearer conception of the power of the healing Christ than has ever been manifested by the church of later ages, and perhaps a deeper sense of the responsibility owed by the body of Christian believers to their brethren in sickness. The sick were not, in their eyes, victims of divine chastisement, but victims of a 'disorder' which follows the violation of God's will. . . . It is not surprising, therefore, that the conditional "if it be Thy will"—so common a feature in modern prayers for healing—is altogether absent from these early Christian prayers."

But we need to avoid the conclusion that there is something "good" in disease and misfortune that has produced these monumental victories. The argument that God wants us to be sick in order for us to prosper is not a fair argument. It subtly makes us believe that the power for good is in the disease rather than in the God who works through it. When Joseph was sold into captivity by his own kin, he overcame his handicap and rose to become second only to Pharaoh in Egypt. Later he said to his brothers: "You intended to harm me, but God intended it for good to accomplish what is now being done" (Gen. 50:20). The obvious lesson here is *not* that suffering is good but that *God is good.*

Why glorify the power of disease and the distortion it brings to our human nature? It is far more reasonable that we fix our attention on the Healer who produces order out of disorder and who can transpose divine triumphs out of the nefarious power of evil.

I believe that the answer to the riddle of suffering is to discern what God truly wants in respect to our personhood and what He will allow to achieve that purpose. Certainly it is true that God wants *wholeness* for each of us because wholeness is the blessing of the kingdom of God. It is also true that He can and does bring wholeness by permitting us to endure what may appear to be tragic and disturbing at the time. In brief, God the Healer can bring health to our lives "in spite of" the malady we struggle with. All of this demonstrates that the power of God's grace and the strength of His love are greater than the power of disease. As the apostle himself proclaimed: "And we know that in all things God works for the *good* of those who love Him, who have been called according to His purpose" (Rom. 8:28).

Paul and His "Thorn in the Flesh"

The apostle Paul's experience with his "thorn in the flesh" provides us with a good example how God works his gift of grace through a human handicap (2 Corinthians 12:7-10). The affliction Paul suffered must have bothered him considerably because his prayers about this problem were persistent. Paul prayed three times for this dreaded handicap, which some think to be a disease of the eyes, to be taken away.[4] Perhaps Paul even argued with God, as some do in their prayer

---

[4]Some scholars believe that Paul suffered from malaria whereas others conjecture that he had a vision problem, perhaps hinted at in Gal. 6:11, "See what large letters I use as I write to you with my own hand."

life, that he could accomplish much more in the work of the kingdom if this affliction were to be removed.

Sometimes it is easy to forget that Paul was an amazingly successful apostle. Not only was he an effective preacher, but he had spiritual experiences reserved only for a few such as himself—"(he) was caught up to paradise. He heard inexpressible things, things that man is not permitted to tell" (12:4). Paul had even been healed of blindness at the time of his conversion and had healed others in the name of Jesus. He knew personally the power of God in its dramatic expressions.

Yet God's answer to Paul's prayers was simply, "My grace is sufficient for you, for *My power is made perfect in weakness*" (12:9). The apostle was now to experience God's power through the medium of his own physical weakness. As Paul struggled with his handicap, he learned a lot about himself and his spiritual life. He was obliged to come to terms with his own conceit and pride, which is a painful process in itself. He found himself forced to depend upon only one thing—the power of God's love and grace.

Paul does not say that his "thorn in the flesh" came from God. On the contrary, he says that it was "a messenger of Satan to torment me" (12:7). What Paul relates to us so vividly in this experience is that, no matter how much Satan seeks to separate us from God, God can use the same experience to draw us even closer.

There are times when all of us are forced to feel the reality of pain and learn that there is only one thing that our lives must depend upon— the *grace* of God. When those situations of life come, and they will, when the suffering will not cease despite our many supplications to God, what then? The answer of faith in circumstances such as these is to *accept* the suffering and learn from it. Paul Tournier's words are appropriate here:

> So the Christian answer to suffering is acceptance. Through accep-
> tance, suffering bears spiritual fruit—and even psychical and physical
> fruit as well. Resignation is passive. Acceptance is active. Resignation
> abandons the struggle against suffering. Acceptance strives without back-
> sliding, but also without rebellion. There is no greater testimony to the
> power of Christ than that which shines from the bed of a sick person who
> miraculously accepts suffering. There is no attitude more impossible for

man—without the miraculous intervention of Christ—than the acceptance of suffering.[5]

God can work through our sicknesses to develop within us a profound, Christlike maturity. This is a graceful acceptance of sickness and turns our attention from the suffering to a healthy, purposive attitude. It allows for the presence and involvement of God in the outcome of the sickness. Even if healing (from a specific bodily function) does not come, this is not a sign of God's absence. On the contrary, God works even in our misfortunes, our limitations, our weakness. As God said to Paul, "My grace is sufficient for you for My power is made perfect in weakness" (2 Cor. 12:9).

In those cases of chronic suffering, such as Tournier describes, *faith is not frustrated*, because God can accomplish spiritual triumphs in such situations. It is hardly necessary to point out that this is evidence of a deep spiritual healing. The shaping of a Christlike life through the anvil of pain and suffering is an argument for the power of God who overcomes the power of disease with His grace. The psalmist says confidently, "My flesh and my heart may fail, but God is the strength of my heart and my portion forever" (Ps. 73:26).

What is vital for the chronic sufferer is to keep the conversation open with God. God gives us permission to say what we want to say, that we are disappointed, that we feel His absence, and that we feel alone. But in this process we find ourselves drawn closer to God and a need for His gift of grace.[6]

No matter what we say about it, suffering is not easy to bear. The Christian depends on God's grace in any situation, and embraces each new day with the confidence that the Lord will provide the strength and courage to persevere. Paul's statement to the Philippians is a statement of faith: "I know what it is to be in need, and I know what it is to have plenty. I have learned the secret of being content in any and every situation. . . . I can do everything through Him who gives me the strength" (Phil. 4:12-13).

God's ability to work good out of evil is a truth in which Christians ought to rejoice. To make that statement is not to soften the hostility we bear toward disease. It is rather to acknowledge the

---

[5]Paul Tournier, *The Healing of Persons* (New York: Harper & Row, 1965), 143.

[6]Daniel Simundsen, "Health and Healing in the Bible," *Word and World: Theology for Christian Ministry* 2, no. 4 (Fall 1982): 336.

strength of God's love in any situation. Leslie Weatherhead adds a provocative comment:

> It is also realized that God can use suffering to his glory and man's blessedness, and that by a right reaction to it, men can become saints. But if suffering were a condition of saintliness, Christ would not have fought it. Indeed, its normal result is rebellion, depression, and despair.
>
> It is not suffering, but *a heroic reaction to it*, that has made sufferers into saints. Suffering is not essential to a right reaction to life and to God. If the person is unimpaired by disease, he can offer himself as a perfect instrument for God's purposes in the world (emphasis added).[7]

These comments about responding to the grace of God in situations of suffering provide a spiritual answer to those who are bearers of the "Chiron wound." But there are larger questions about sickness and suffering that press upon us, and which seek answers as well. For example, can we distinguish between a suffering that seems to have a purpose and one that does not? If so, how do we deal with such suffering?

A Further Look at Sickness and Suffering

A candid survey of the Scriptures makes clear the truth that no one is exempt from suffering. There is no life in which from birth till death one does not endure pain, injustice, injury, and disappointment. Suffering is one of the consequences that derives from living in a universe permeated with brokenness and disorder. Accidents, epidemics, automobile wrecks, airplane crashes, and tornadoes are all illustrations of the fact that we live in a world in which the "ground is cursed" until Christ returns again (Rom. 8:22-23).

But *not all suffering is the same.* There is a kind of suffering that seems meaningless and difficult to bear, especially when borne by a child or when the pain is of such an intensity that death is seen as a better alternative. On the other hand, there is a kind of suffering that Paul says we should rejoice in: ". . . but we also rejoice in our sufferings, because we know that suffering produces perseverance; perseverance, character; and character, hope" (Rom. 5:3-4). It seems as if a distinction should be made between the suffering that is the consequence of living in a broken world and the suffering that is

---

[7]Weatherhead, op. cit., 227.

voluntarily undertaken because of commitment to faith in Christ. Stanley Hauerwas describes this difference:

> It is important that we be able to distinguish between those forms of suffering that derive directly from the way of life occasioned by our faithfulness to the cross and those forms of suffering that do not. The suffering to which Paul refers to in Romans is the suffering that those who followed Jesus were to expect: social ostracism, persecution, unjust jailings, even martyrdom. . . . The suffering that follows living a faithful Christ-life has a different valence than that which does not. At least we can understand what is happening. This kind of suffering takes place within a history that has a *telos*.[8]

The Suffering of Persecution

From the biblical perspective, the suffering of persecution is purposive because the promise of persecution for faithfulness to the cross is made clear in Scripture. Jesus forewarned His disciples that they would suffer many things in His name. "Blessed are you when people insult you, persecute you and say all kinds of evil against you because of Me" (Matt. 5:11).

We do not always appreciate the fact that persecution is often related to the onset of disease and illness. Sitting in a cold, damp Roman dungeon with poor sanitation, a situation many of the apostles and early Christians were forced to endure, provides an environment in which disease flourishes. Paul mentions the deprivations he sustained as Christ's apostle, including floggings, beatings, anxiety, and nutritional stress (see 2 Cor. 11:23-29). It is a marvel that he did not die from the persecution he endured.

There is a *purposiveness* to this kind of suffering that is done for the sake of Christ and for the advancement of the kingdom of God. Those who live in countries that resist the rule of God know full well the physical consequences of proclaiming the Christian Gospel. In modern Western culture persecution is more likely expressed in milder forms, usually a type of persecution more accurately labeled "emotional stress." For example, in America we note the subtle discrimination against those who seek to honor Christ in the workplace or the anger produced when Christian obedience is applied within the

---

[8]Stanley Hauerwas, *Naming the Silences: God, Medicine, and the Problem of Suffering* (Grand Rapids, MI: Eerdmans Publishing, 1990).

home. These can become daily battles for those who carry the Christian cross. What is obvious in these contexts is that emotional distress in the service of Christ can be disease-producing and just as lethal as physical incarceration. Whether the wounds originate in physical conditions or are produced psychosomatically is really a moot point. The reality before us is that sickness has resulted because a person was courageous enough to follow Jesus Christ.

Because of persecution for the sake of the Gospel, this type of suffering is described as a *discipline* in the Scripture. The writer to the Hebrews speaks of believers submitting to the chastening love of God "because the Lord disciplines those He loves, and He punishes everyone He accepts as a son" (12:6). Suffering in this manner has a "*telos*" and, for this reason, it is more easily borne.

However, we need to exercise care in interpreting this important passage from the book of Hebrews. To use this passage to validate the normal experience of disease and sickness, so common in medieval piety, is theologically indefensible. To say to a person suffering from cancer that God is "disciplining" that person is to lay upon the individual a burden that is grievous beyond words. It portrays God as a cruel martinet who delights in our suffering. When the church attempts to "comfort" the sick with such an unbiblical caricature of God, she has completely lost sight of the Healing Christ who touched the sick with loving compassion.

It is obvious from the context that the writer to the Hebrews is speaking to Christians who were *undergoing persecution*, not those who were diseased or in pain from the consequences of everyday life. He encourages them to remain true to Christ despite the severity of their suffering. The words "In your struggle against sin, you have not yet resisted to the point of shedding your blood" (12:4) make the point very clear that their suffering was for the sake of the cross.

Suffering that Seems to Have No Purpose

If suffering persecution for Christ has a purpose, what about suffering that seems to have *no purpose* and that, on the surface, seems to portray God as being unconcerned or far distant from the agony of the sufferer? Sometimes this is referred to as "the Problem of Job." For example, the experience of a small child who is dying of an incurable disease? Hauerwas again says:

Yet for a child to die of a disease seems to serve no purpose. It is a blackness before which we can only stand mute. The cross here is not explicable. . . . It is crucial for us to recognize that, while it is perfectly appropriate for us to discover the suffering we experience in illness to have a telos in our service to one another in faith, it is not appropriate for us to try to force that account on another. If we try to attribute these terrible results to God's secret providence, that cannot help but make God at best a tyrant and at worst a cosmic torturer. What we must finally do in the face of suffering of [such persons] is to show the patience that does not try to discern any "purpose" behind the suffering, but without in any way caring less for them. [9]

There is no greater challenge to the medical caregiver or pastor than to try to bring comfort and healing to a person whose disease seems to have no redemptive purpose or design. What does one say to a young mother with three small children who has just been informed by her doctor that she has inoperable cancer? Or to a young man who, because of an automobile accident in which he was a passenger, is now a paraplegic? The traditional bromides of well-intentioned persons that such a wasting disease is "the will of God" or that "this is for your spiritual good" fall like sparrows to the ground. These high-minded bits of counsel bring no comfort, only despair. They remind us of the "friends" of Job whose advice only tormented this long-suffering man of God.

When there is no purpose to the suffering that is sickness, *it is best not to invent one.* We can only care for these sufferers in their pain even as did Jesus, the Healer. Here we approach the grace of God that typifies the theology of the cross.

It is on occasions such as these when the Christian response must essentially be one of *love* and compassion for the sufferer. Perhaps the most powerful of Jesus' parables, from the perspective of the theology of the cross, is the Parable of the Good Samaritan (Luke 10:30-37). The Samaritan asked no questions nor did he give any advice when he saw the wounded man. But he gave of himself in love for his fallen neighbor and he bound up his wounds.

In this sense the medical profession, including doctors, nurses, and other paramedics, are fellow workers with Christ because they impart the compassion that exemplified the ministry of the Healer. So also are those in allied professions, such as the pastoral ministry and social

---

[9]Ibid.

work, who have devoted their lives to the relief of human suffering. It is significant that on the Day of Judgment, our earthly deeds of visiting the sick and providing food for the hungry will be the criteria by which our faithfulness to Christ will be measured (Matt. 25:34-40).

As Paul Tournier has said, *"To fight against suffering is to be on God's side."*[10] We sometimes become oblivious to the insidious nature of disease and the pain that terminally ill patients bear. In American culture we hide those who suffer pain from public view, partly because we ourselves are so paranoid about pain. But it is a sobering experience to walk through the halls of a hospital ward in which the terminally ill are located and to view this reality with one's own eyes. Or to visit a Third World country where suffering is a daily occurrence and where the sick are on public display. To go through life and to remain impassive to the suffering wrought by the forces of disorder is to be blinded to the healing ministry of Jesus who tenaciously fought the power of evil.

In our own day and age, there is hardly a more cogent example of suffering than those who have suffered the loss of a loved one. *Bereavement*, by any definition, is one of the most profound illnesses that a human can experience. To lose a spouse, a parent, or a child is to suffer in a very painful way—it is as if a limb were cut from your body. The trauma is so great that many never resolve the loss, no matter how long the passage of years.

The bereaved person grieves for the loved one because he or she *loved* that person. It is the nature of love to suffer even as God suffered when He gave His own Son up to the cross. The way to minister to the bereaved is not to avoid the sufferer but to share with him your love. However, be aware of the cost . . . sharing oneself in love can become *painful*. Henri Nouwen adds an important thought: "Compassion is born when we discover in the center of our own existence not only that God is God and man is man, but also that our neighbor is really our fellow man."[11]

"Never tell a bereaved person that the death of their loved one is 'not really so bad.' Because it is. Death is awful, demonic. . . . What I need to hear from you is that you recognize how painful it is. I need to

---

[10]Tournier, op. cit, 142.

[11]Henri Nouwen, *The Wounded Healer* (Garden City, NY: Image Books, 1979), 41.

hear from you that you are with me in my desperation. To comfort me, you have to come close. Come sit with me on my mourning bench."[12]

There Is No Medical Utopia

While all health and healing come from God, no physical healing will ever make us immortal. After we have done everything possible to improve our health, it is healthy to know that we are not at home in this world. We live here only for a time as sojourners and pilgrims. What is healthy is to acknowledge that the time will come when the greatest meaning of life will be to surrender our life to God and to die in peace.

A Christian posture of health is to live confidently and realistically in a world of which Paul said "its present form is passing away" (1 Cor. 7:31). We know that this life is not all that there is. All human beings must die. No one has the promise of perpetual good health in this life. If we are fortunate to live a life that is marked with many years, the aging process soon begins to make its mark and we discover that we lack the vitality of our youth. We too are passing away.

Incidentally, medical science is in agreement with the Scripture that there never will be a medical utopia on the planet earth. René Dubos, Pulitzer Prize winner in health, points out the fallacy of an imagined future in which no disease will exist:

> The hope that disease can be completely eradicated becomes a dangerous mirage only when its unattainable character is forgotten. It can then be compared to a will-o-the-wisp luring its followers into the swamps of unreality. In particular, it encourages the illusion that man can control his responses to stimuli and can make adjustments to new ways of life without having to pay for these adaptive changes.[13]

DuBos argues that such a prospect cannot happen because disease is a part of the human body. Each of us carry within our bodies pathological organisms which constantly interact with our body's immune system. As long as these organisms remain, there will be disease and sickness. Even if we kill off some of the more virulent strains, other strains soon develop in their stead.

---

[12]Quoted in Hauerwas, op. cit., 76.

[13]René Dubos, *Man Adapting* (New Haven: Yale University Press, 1965), 346.

We are discovering this truth especially with the effectiveness of antibiotics. New strains of disease are evolving because the drugs that were so effective against the older strains are now proving ineffective against the newer strains. In addition, new viruses are appearing against which medical science seems to be powerless, for example, the HIV virus that emerged from Central Africa and whose reservoir is the green monkey. The HIV virus, which attacks the most important member of the immune system, the Helper T, was a benign virus until human beings began to invade the ecology in which it lay dormant. Virologists are seriously concerned about the emergence of other lethal viruses as human civilization continues to upset the delicate man-land relationships that obtain on the planet Earth.

Certainly we must continue to wage war on disease and not be deterred by the grim future of the plethora of diseases which refuse to go away. Dubos's comments simply bring us back to reality, a reality that the Scripture affirms most emphatically in its description of the groaning of all creation under the bondage of sin (Romans 8:21-23).

So there must be more than this life if God's promises about healing are to be kept. If God's intention for us is wholeness, *shalom*, we need a life beyond this one in order for that to be accomplished. Indeed, the promise of the resurrection is that a Day of Sabbath Rest is sure to come when Christ will make all things whole. The New Testament points our eyes to an "end time" when all the forces of disorder will be defeated and the order of God's rule will prevail over all things. Paul says (1 Cor. 15:24-26, author's translation):

> Then the end will come. Christ will overcome all Spiritual rulers, authorities, and powers, and will hand over the Kingdom to God the Father. For Christ must rule until God defeats all enemies and puts them under His feet. The last enemy to be defeated will be death.

Faith and Death

In some cases, we may be so bold as to say that death itself is healing. In some situations it may be the only healing possible. For death is the means by which God receives the believer to Himself and prepares that person for the greatest of God's healing miracles, the resurrection from the dead. For this reason, it is possible to say that when a Christian dies in the Lord, such a person experiences a *holy death*. According to the promise of the book of Revelation: "Blessed are the dead who die in the Lord from now on." "Yes," says the Spirit, "they will rest from their labors, for their deeds follow them" (Rev. 14:13).

In actuality all of life is a movement toward death. To deny this reality is to make it difficult to live in the fullness of health throughout the years of our lives. Only those who are unafraid to die are those who are unafraid to live in the confidence of their future in Christ.

But death is approached by Christians even as life is approached, through faith in the Christ who promises us an eternal hope. In ministering to those who are dying, there is no need to be defeatist or fearful. We approach our death in the faith that God will overcome this enemy and grant us a place within His kingdom of glory. Martin Marty's comments are appropriate here:

> The believer dies very much alone *and* the believer dies in company. Luther: "We have all been ordered to die, and no one will be able to die for another. But each one will be obliged to contend against death in his own person." " No Christian should doubt at his end that he is not alone when dying, but that very many eyes are looking at him." These are the eyes of God, Christ, angels, saints, and the congregation.[14]

Why Heal?

It is obvious that some will raise the question, Why seek to heal people if death is our inevitable destiny? This question cuts to the heart of all our inquiries about health and healing. It is a logical question, but it is not a humane question.

Within each of us there is an instinctual need to preserve life at all costs. Why else do we observe such heroic efforts when a neighbor's life is in danger? Why else do we take every measure to preserve the life of a loved one who is dying? Not only those in the field of medicine battle the inevitability of death; each of us is prepared to fight to the end as well. Perhaps the crowning achievement of our humanity is that we see life as our friend and death as an enemy.

Why then do we heal? According to the third and most important principle of the Hippocratic Oath, the doctor is to sustain life in every form. Martin Scharlemann, however, provides an answer that reflects

---

[14]Martin Marty, *Health and Medicine in the Lutheran Tradition* (Philadelphia: Fortress Press, 1982). See also Martin Marty and Kenneth Vaux, editors, *Health/Medicine: An Inquiry into Religion and Medicine* (Philadelphia: Fortress Press, 1982).

the richness of the biblical teaching about health: "[We heal] because life and healing are the very province of God, and men are privileged to share in this power." [15]

Christians are involved in healing because God, who is whole, desires that we be whole. For such a reason Christ, the Healer, came to usher in the kingdom of God. This is why the church has been commissioned to proclaim His kingdom to the world and to share with all people the gift of healing and wholeness.

God's gift of healing also emphasizes our personal stewardship in taking care of our health for as long a time as we have been granted to live on earth. It was the psalmist who said: *"Teach us to number our days and apply our hearts unto wisdom"* (Psalm 90:12, author's translation). This is good theology as well as good science. According to the Scriptures, our days have been numbered in the sense that the forces of disorder will one day bring our lives to an end. Nevertheless, we should strive to live as wisely as we can as long as life has been granted us by God. But the other side of the coin is that, by living wisely and practicing the principles of good health, we can lengthen our days. "Have reverence for the Lord and you will live longer," says Proverbs 10:27, "the wicked die before their time" (author's translation).

In a very incisive account of our human vulnerability to death, Hans Selye says that every member of the human race dies from some disease, but never from *old age*. In his book, *The Stress of Life,* Dr. Selye, who has performed many autopsies, states that he has never yet encountered a person who has died of old age:

> To die of old age would mean that all the organs of the body would be worn out proportionately, merely by having been used too long. This is never the case. We invariably die because one vital part has worn out too early in proportion to the rest of the body. Life, the biologic chain that holds our parts together, is only as strong as its weakest vital link. When this breaks—no matter which vital link it be—our parts can no longer be held together as a single living being. . . There is always one part that wears out first and wrecks that whole human machinery, merely because the other parts cannot function without it.[16]

---

[15]Martin Scharlemann, *Healing and Redemption* (St. Louis: Concordia, 1965), 94.

[16] Hans Selye, *The Stress of Life* (New York: McGraw-Hill Book Co, 1956), 27.

It is Dr. Selye's belief that our bodies are designed to live much longer than they do (perhaps as long as 300 years), but because of the stresses of life, much of which is under our own control, we all die prematurely. Is it not significant that as much as we abhor suicide, many of us may actually be guilty of systematic suicide by the perverse ways we do violence to our bodies? Here is the question each of us must answer—unless someone takes our life from us, who else is doing the damage that brings on death but ourselves?

No less a medical authority than Dr. Elliot Dacher, chief of the Georgetown University Community Health Plan in Reston, Virginia, says that we are going to die the way we have chosen to live. The diseases of our culture—heart diseases, cancer, mental anguish, obesity, high blood pressure—which no drug can cure because they are the diseases of Western civilization, are the result of our own destructive lifestyle.

There are, of course, many extenuating circumstances that enter into this picture of death that have not been mentioned. A three-year-old child who dies of leukemia or a policeman who is shot in the line of duty hardly fit into this model of Christian self-care. Tragedies occur in this world that we have no control over and which are not easily answered. Nevertheless, disease and death serve the purpose of reminding us that the forces of disorder are still viable among us. We do not live in a medical utopia. The Day of Sabbath Rest is yet to come.

But in this interim period we are not without hope. We still live with the power of the Healing Christ. The Christian ministry of healing is a biblical answer to a world that struggles with disease and illness. It is to this subject that we now turn.

Chapter Eight

The Ministry of Healing

Ever since the Fall of humankind, God's design has been to restore the Order. When Jesus initiated the kingdom of God, this restoration of the brokenness of the human race began with dramatic clarity. The New Testament writers noted the marvelous outpourings of healing bestowed as the Healer overcame the powers of evil in His mission of redemption. In a similar fashion, they observed how the distortion of human nature, symbolized by the power of disease, gave way to the healing power of God.

In our current age, the Holy Spirit continues to bring God's rule to human hearts. Surely it is not too fanciful to suggest that similar blessings can be evidenced in the modern church.

In this chapter we want to suggest the manifold ways in which the congregation can function as a healing community. Where else except in the local congregation do we find such abundant resources from God to bring restoration? The Gospel of the Kingdom is "good news" to everyone, but it is especially good news to the ill. We need not wonder why this is so. God brings healing and wholeness through the power of the Gospel to those who are the victims of sin's oppression.

For years members of Christian congregations have heard the Gospel narratives of the Healing Christ and of His compassionate treatment of the sick. But until recently, the church seems to have lacked sufficient motivation and direction to move into the mainstream of the healing enterprise.

All this is now changing. The church is discovering how much it has to say about human health and well-being. Many congregations are conducting workshops and seminars devoted to the topic of healing. It is no longer a stigma to lay on hands while praying for the sick nor even in anointing the sick with oil. Healing services, once the exclusive province of "faith healers," are being established in mainline churches. Indeed, as the church seeks to apply the theology of health to the Christian life, topics such as nutrition, exercise, and meditation have become lively points of discussion in a health-oriented church.

We live in exciting times. As we share the Gospel of the Kingdom, we are at the same time sharing God's gifts of healing with those who are sick and ill.

The Congregation as a Healing Community

It seems simplistic to say it, but it is true. The Christian congregation is a *healing community*. For a person to be whole, he must move out of isolation and live in fellowship with other men and women. In the fellowship of Christ, believers share the Word of God and sacraments with one other. But they also share their faith with each other in a context of healing and wholeness.

St. Paul frequently described the church as a "household" (e.g., Eph. 2:19). By using this term, Paul was describing how Christ's love creates a fellowship of people who are "related" to one another in a fictive manner. The Christian exists not for himself or herself, but as a "brother" or "sister" to others who share this household of faith. In fact, the Christian community can be likened to a "tribe" that we read about in traditional cultures and with all the attendant responsibilities of being a member of the tribe. Paul Tillich says it this way:

> Everyone is potentially a tool of healing for anyone else. The fact that Jesus gave the disciples responsibility for healing and casting out devils does not constitute a special prerogative on the part of the minister. Every Christian received this charge, and each of us should take it seriously in our relation to one another. Everyone should accept his priestly responsibility for everyone else.[1]

A Model of Community Healing

We are taught a powerful lesson about the corporate nature of healing in the curing of the paralytic (Mark 2:1-12). In this episode, Jesus commends the faith of the four people who carried the paralytic

---

[1]Paul Tillich, *Healing: A Spiritual Adventure*, 24. An exposition of the church as a healing community is given in such resources as Karin Granberg, *Healing Community* (Geneva: WCC Publications, 1991), and in an early work of Howard Clinebell, Jr., *Mental Health through Christian Community: The Local Church's Ministry of Growth and Healing* (Nashville, Abingdon Press, 1965).

to Jesus. Because of a large crowd at the entrance of the door, the four friends dug a hole through the roof and lowered the paralytic on his mat into the room. Mark's description stirs our emotions: "When Jesus *saw their faith. . . .*"

It is clear from this account that healing faith can be demonstrated in a corporate manner with dramatic results. The restoration of the paralytic takes place within a *group* situation. According to Scharlemann, this account can serve as a model for the congregation as a community of healing:

> Here the individual is not alone, especially not in his illness. For the very presence of the illness provides the opportunity for corporate service. . . . When men and women offer their services to the sick in their midst, they are presenting their lives to Christ. They enter that wholeness, so to speak, into which they have been drawn by faith. Here is the fellowship of the body of Christ which is the means of loving one another and having all things, including sickness, in common.[2]

Many other accounts are mentioned in the pages of the New Testament about the involvement of the Christian community for the sake of the sick person. In the first few centuries after Christ, the church was intensely involved in a healing ministry. These included intercessory prayers, visitations, and other rituals of healing. In all of these activities, the "communion of saints" was in action, functioning as a community that took seriously the presence of the Healing Christ in their midst.

No passage in the New Testament, outside of the Gospels, states the corporate ministry of healing as clearly as the pericope of James 5:14-16.

> Is any one of you sick? He should call the elders of the church to pray over him and anoint him with oil in the name of the Lord. And the prayer offered in faith will make the sick person well; the Lord will raise him up. If he has sinned, he will be forgiven. Therefore confess your sins to each other and pray for each other so that you may be healed. The prayer of a righteous man is powerful and effective.

---

[2]Martin Scharlemann, *Healing and Redemption* (St. Louis: Concordia, 1965), 100-1.

Many elements of a healing ministry are included here that give directions how to specifically deal with the sick and ill in the congregation. Prayer for the sick is mentioned as well as confession of sin and absolution. We note also the anointing of oil and (by implication) the laying on of hands. All of this is done in the context of faith with the supplementary statement that by means of this procedure the sick person will be healed.

What looms as important in these instructions is that the church is encouraged to become intimately involved in the sickness of its members. James by no means is presenting an ironclad formula for healing the sick. He is certainly not saying, "This is how a healing ministry *must* be done." James rather teaches us how a community of faith can reach out to the God of healing on behalf of the sick. He shares with us an orderly procedure by which the church may be an instrument for restoration to health.

Throughout this chapter, it will be necessary to refer to this passage to some degree because it presents guidelines about how the congregation can minister to the sick. Our discussion will now survey many of the basic fundamentals that are involved in a congregational healing ministry.

Healing through Word and Sacraments

The foundation of the healing ministry is the healing power of the Gospel. God comes to us with the amazing pronouncement that He wants to heal the broken relationship that obtains between us. As a gift of His love and grace in Jesus Christ, He offers us forgiveness of our sins and fellowship in the kingdom of God. Here the process of healing begins. When we are reconciled to God through the power of the Gospel, we begin our walk in the wholeness of Christ.

The *forgiveness of sins* by God is the most potent healing medication known to humankind. When a person is forgiven, the consequences touch not only the life of the spirit but the emotions and physical processes as well. As modern psychology affirms, when we love ourselves, we find it possible to love other people. By means of the forgiveness of Christ, we learn to forgive others; this cures our anger. By the same token, when Christ's forgiveness impacts our inner Self, we learn to forgive ourselves—and this cures our guilt.

The assurance of forgiveness in Christ makes God's love a joyful reality. Our self-worth is restored. The meaning of life is renewed.

Remember what Jesus said when He healed the paralytic, "Son, be of good cheer. Your sins are forgiven" (Matthew 9:2, NKJV). Note the accent of joy that accompanies the proclamation of forgiveness.

The healing power of the Gospel is proclaimed in many venues in the life of the congregation. We look first at the proclamation of the Gospel in Christian worship and in the distribution of the sacraments.

Healing in Christian Worship

The worship service itself is a supreme healing event. A medical doctor once said that more healing occurs in the hour of worship than any other hour of the week. When we consider the healing effect of the Scripture, the sermon, the hymns, and the sacraments—all of which signal that the Risen Christ is in our midst with His offer of *shalom* (peace)—it is difficult to dispute the doctor.

The atmosphere of the worship service is conducive to healing. The symbols of love, hope, and peace permeate the service in a myriad of ways. The architecture of the building and its appointments help focus the mind on the deeper, enduring meanings of life. The people at worship are motivated by means of the service to reach out to each other in a spirit of love.

I personally believe that a well-delivered sermon, presenting Christ as the Redeemer from sin and the Hope of the Ages, is as valid a healing experience as the church can perform. Contrary to public opinion, people do listen to sermons. When they find the comfort and peace of Christ in the spoken word, they encounter healing. Should a member say to the pastor after church, "I really enjoyed the sermon today. It had a special meaning for me . . ."—that person has had a healing experience. We should thank God for it.

Incidentally, it is during the Pentecost half of the church year when many of the Gospel readings contain the stories of the healing miracles. Such stories symbolize how the Christian's life under the Holy Spirit is filled with the regenerative and recreative power of the kingdom of God. When pastors preach on these healing pericopes, they should plan their messages carefully. These are opportunities to address the sicknesses and illnesses of the members in a realistic manner and to speak to them about the Healing Christ and His gifts of healing. As always, the Gospel of God's forgiveness should be at the heart of these sermons. It is well to remember that members face the frailties of life day after day and are encouraged when these topics are addressed from the pulpit.

Music and Worship

A much overlooked aspect of healing transpires in the music of the worship service. There are powerful images of health in the hymns. When the congregation participates in the hymnody of the church, we catch a glimpse of God's *shalom* at work. Nor should we overlook the healing power of musical instruments which, of course, include the human voice. Whether we experience the message of peace through the peal of the organ or a greater awareness of God's love by means of a stirring choir anthem, God is sharing His *shalom* in a special way. It is worth nothing that the psalms were originally meant to be sung to the accompaniment of musical instruments.

Music has long been associated with mental and emotional health. We recall the pleasant results when David played the harp for King Saul, "Then relief would come to Saul; he would feel better, and the evil spirit would leave him" (1 Sam. 16:23). The Greeks also used music in the preparation and performance of their healing rituals. In the Western world, music has played a dominant role in our social institutions. Reference here is made to liturgical music in worship as well as to martial music used to inspire shared emotions in military ventures.

Research in the field of music and health demonstrates a strong correlation between music and the emotional life. According to Helen Bonny, music has the capability of detouring the ego control and directly contacting the emotional center of the brain; by means of this process music can stir up latent conflicts and emotions which may be expressed through the music.[3] Because music reflects so accurately the moods and emotions of people, it is being used increasingly for psychotherapeutic use, especially for relaxation and guided imagery exercises. Music that has a calming and quieting quality apparently helps produce molecules called peptides that relieve pain by acting on

---

[3]Helen Bonny, "Music and Sound in Health," in *Health for the Whole Person*, eds. Arthur Hastings, James Fadiman, James Gordon (eds.), (Boulder, CO: Westview Press, 1981), 278.

specific receptors in the brain.[4] The healing effect of music on the immunological system is also being currently researched.

Congregational worship committees ought to focus more attention on the relationship between music and health. Because the worship life reflects the hope and joy of the Gospel, planning music that embellishes these themes with the appropriate emotional expression can be a far-reaching investment in the health of members.

Healing and Baptism

We might say of Baptism that it is the original healing event that we experience. In Baptism the person experiences a new birth given by the Holy Spirit. This is the beginning of wholeness because, by means of this covenant, the individual is made a member of God's Kingdom of joy.

As the new Christian now walks in the life of the Spirit, this wholeness in Christ develops and grows. In a very real sense, Baptism encourages a sense of health and well-being. The Christian is made mindful of daily repentance as he remembers his Baptism. This prompts the person to confess readily to God those sins which otherwise might be allowed to fester within the heart.

But Baptism also brings blessings to the whole person. Since it is a seal of God's promise of eternal life and the resurrection from the dead, the baptismal covenant has a claim upon the whole person, including the body. It can therefore be suggested that Baptism is a stimulus for Christians to practice the stewardship of health. Luther speaks to this point:

> Since the water and the Word together constitute one Baptism, body and soul shall be saved and live forever: the soul through the Word in which it believes, the body because it is united to the soul and apprehends Baptism in the only way it can. No greater jewel, therefore, can adorn our body and soul than Baptism.[5]

Baptism thus sounds the keynote for Christian healing. It all starts here and it all comes back to this. In the baptismal covenant, believers are yoked to the healing Christ as well as to fellow believers of the

---

[4]Ibid., 278.

[5]Martin Luther, *The Large Catechism.*

Christian community. The life of faith becomes a life of wholeness that each shares with the other.

Healing and the Lord's Supper

Holy Communion is a powerful healing sacrament of the church. Not only do the recipients of this Supper receive assurance that their sins are forgiven, but they are promised life and salvation in the name of Christ. Such promises of God intensify and strengthen the experience of wholeness.

Just as in Baptism, the blessings of the Lord's Supper affect the whole person. We need to focus on the benefits to the body as well as the spiritual life of the person in considering the healing properties of this sacrament. This is not merely a spiritual eating and drinking but the giving of Christ's body and blood to the sick and ill for the strengthening of the whole person to salvation. As Luther puts it in the Large Catechism:

> We must . . . regard this sacrament . . . as a pure, wholesome, soothing medicine which aids and quickens us in both soul and body. For where the soul is healed the body has benefited also.[6]

One way to understand this healing activity of God is that we are compelled to leave all our anxieties and frustrations at the Lord's Table. In this sacrament Christ assures us, by means of His bodily presence, that His gift of peace stands guard over our lives. When the pastor releases us from the Table and says, "Depart in peace," this phrase can also be translated *"Depart in a state of health"* (see Luke 8:48).

Martin Scharlemann emphasizes the power of healing in the horizontal dimension of the Lord's Supper as the people of God share with one another these sacred mysteries.

> It is here that men and women draw close together to each other in corporate action as they express their fellowship with the Head of that community of which they were made a part at Baptism. Those who gather at this table come together to heal each other in body and soul; for where there is love for one another, the sickening power of envy, hatred and

---

[6]Ibid..

malice is broken. In this way the Lord's Supper counteracts neurotic anxiety and its concomitant psychosomatic symptoms. [7]

Perhaps it is necessary to emphasize at this point that the Lord's Supper is becoming to be recognized as a healing experience by those who are active in the healing ministry. Both physical and mental healings are reported as occurring through the salutary use of this sacrament. But why should this surprise us? The more we become aware of the intricate relationships of the spiritual, the mental, and the physical dimensions of our personhood, the more we are able to comprehend the meaning of Christ's words in Matthew 6:22: "If your eyes are sound, your whole body will be full of light." Healing of the spirit can and does affect healing in the body as well.

But the converse is also true. Human pride and hostility toward others can affect a person's bodily health in a negative manner. At Corinth Paul scolded the members of this congregation for their lack of care and concern for the weaker members of the congregation while participating in the Lord's Supper (1 Cor. 11:17-32). Such behavior, he made clear, constituted a contempt for the body of Christ and made them guilty of profaning the Lord's Body. The judgment of God against this sin of pride resulted in the fact that many of the offenders became sickly and others died.

Congregational Prayer for the Sick

Perhaps no ritual of the church has been more applied for the restoration of the sick than congregational prayer. In the pericope of James 5, the apostle suggests that the congregation pray for the suffering person: *"Is any one of you sick? He should call the elders of the church to pray over him. . . . And the prayer offered in faith will make the sick person well; the Lord will raise him up"* (vv. 14-15).

There are two ways that prayers for the sick may be actualized in the congregation. One method is intercessory prayer and the other is to pray with the sick. Let's look at these more closely.

---

[7]Scharlemann, 65-66.

Intercessory Prayer

Intercessory prayer occurs when the congregation prays in public assembly for the sick in their midst. As a common procedure in all congregations, this type of prayer is usually observed at every Sunday worship service. Intercessory prayer is in keeping with St. Paul's admonition to "pray always for God's people" (Ephesians 6:18, author's translation) and is a prioritized responsibility for any Christian community that is alert to the needs of its members. Whether in public intercession or in special prayer groups or even through personal devotions, the priesthood of believers demonstrates that it is a healing fellowship.

A reading of the New Testament reveals that the early church was actively engaged in intercessory prayer for the sick. It is helpful to repeat the prayer we mentioned earlier, the *Believer's Prayer,* which requests God's blessing upon the healing ministry of the congregation:

> Now, Lord . . . stretch out Your hand to heal and perform miraculous signs and wonders through the name of Your holy servant Jesus. (Acts 4:29, 30)

Intercessory prayer, in whatever context it is used, makes mention of the believer's name and implores the God of grace to restore the sick person to health. Such prayers may include the naming of the particular malady that the person is suffering. We need to say clearly that prayers for the sick are not "bothering" God nor are they informing Him of something He already knows. In the Parable of the Persistent Widow (Luke 18:1-8), Jesus instructs His disciples to continually bring their needs to God in order that something may be done about them. In that same parable, Jesus stated that persistent prayer is a demonstration of the *faith* of the Christian community. We pause here to mention that intercessory prayer for the sick is a major healing function of the church.

One of the most effective uses of intercessory prayer I have observed was when a pastor turned to face his seated congregation. He simply began to talk about the members of the congregation who were sick; he also rehearsed the state of their illness. All eyes were glued upon him as he shared the seriousness of their disorder. Then he asked the congregation to kneel, as he himself kneeled before the altar, and began to pray in intercession for those in need.

Praying with the Sick

A second way in which prayers for the sick are expressed in the Christian parish is during a visitation to the sick person's home or at the hospital. This is a powerful use of prayer because the congregation is not only praying *for* the sick person but is also praying *with* the sufferer. Whether this prayer is performed by the pastor, a layperson, or a group of laypersons, the procedure will be much the same.

Usually such a prayer is accompanied by the laying on of hands of which more will be said later. The prayer itself will emphasize the gift of wholeness for the sick person. We dare not dictate to God what He must do in the healing process nor do we "claim the healing" as if this were a magic charm that marshals God's power to our bidding. The prayer for the sick should include this higher purpose of being released from disorder in order to better serve God's intentions in worship, service, and living. What we are praying for is that the full measure of Christ's wholeness may touch the supplicant and equip him or her for holy living.

Healing prayers do not cringe at the sight of an excruciating and disabling disease. We dare not approach the sick with more confidence in the power of the disease to kill than the power of God to heal. We approach the God of grace humbly but with the *confidence* that He can liberate the sufferer from the chains of this disease and from the consequences of its pain. As we pray we remember the promise of Jesus Christ, "I tell you the truth, if you have faith as small as a mustard seed, you can say to this mountain, 'Move from here to there,' and it will move. Nothing will be impossible for you" (Matt. 17:20). It is always a good practice to read some appropriate Scripture before laying on the hands in prayer and personally to encounter the promises of God.

Healing prayers focus especially on the forgiving love of Jesus Christ, whose death and resurrection bring assurance that God's salvation is freely given to the sick person. This was the practice of the psalmist who, after making confession of his sin, prayed that God would have mercy upon him in his suffering (Psalm 41:3-4). In praying for the sick, we pray that God's love and peace may be received by the patient and that his life may be opened to the healing power of God.

Healing prayers are not rushed nor are they compressed within a certain time period. In situations of a grave illness, a considerable amount of time, in fact, several hours, may be spent in concentrated prayer or meditation. Some congregations practice the *prayer vigil* in which members may pray for a seriously ill person for a period of 24 hours without ceasing. At the conclusion, there is a quiet confidence that God will bring healing in the manner He deems to be wisest.

We must realize that there are several factors involved in the healing purposes of God. The disease process frequently must run its course. Sometimes the patient becomes worse before he becomes better. In our approach to the sick, we therefore pray in faith, and we pray fervently, but we leave to God both the time and the method as to how He will touch the healing process and give His wholeness.

Healing in Christian Confession

Yet another channel of healing in the congregation is the confessional, which has been sadly neglected in the modern church to its chagrin. The apostle James, in his instructions to the church, mentions the confession of sins in the context of praying for the sick: *"If he has sinned, he will be forgiven. Therefore confess your sins to each other and pray for each other so that you may be healed"* (5:15-16).

As we have already noted, it was standard procedure in the Old Testament to make confession of sins while pleading to God for deliverance from sickness. Perhaps we need to visit this theme more seriously in our modern day. We cannot assume that every person who becomes sick is a purely innocent victim and has not, in some way, brought about the sickness that now consumes him. It can even be suggested that some individuals, on their sickbeds, would welcome the opportunity to "clean the slate," to make confession of those festering sins that have now come home to roost.

Luther, in the doctrine of the Office of the Keys, gives guidelines for making confession of sins to the pastor:

> Before God we should confess that we are guilty of all sins, even those which are not known to us, as we do in the Lord's Prayer. But in a private confession, before the pastor, we should confess only those sins which trouble us in heart and mind.[8]

---

[8]Martin Luther, *The Small Catechism.*

Note the emphasis on the sins "which trouble us in heart and mind." These are the poisonous toxins of bitterness, resentment, guilt, and anger which need release and cleansing by the healing balm of Christ's forgiveness.

Let's amplify on this theme a bit more. One of the major reasons we have problems with ill health is because we are not willing to confess the unhealthy emotions that block our quest for wholeness. Frequently we are not willing to face up to the fact that we do have problems. Quite frankly, it can be a very painful process to admit to ourselves that we have been harboring unhealthy attitudes. When a person has constructed a grudge against another individual that endures for years and years, and has rationalized a defense of this grudge, there will inevitably be a terrible struggle to let that anger loose and become clean. Confessing a deep-seated sin such as a grudge can be quite painful. How well I remember one man with chronic back pain who prayed daily for healing but with no results; however, he could never bring himself to release the bitter hostility he felt towards members of his family.

For this reason, Jungian psychology contends that the route to wholeness must pass through the crucible of pain. If a person is to be purified of his selfish instincts and achieve wholeness, the only remedy is to make confession. Incidentally, the New Testament gives virtually the same counsel. The way to the cross is through repentance which brings pain to the psyche. But it is only by means of this process that wholeness and healing can occur.

Healing and Absolution

Dr. Paul Tournier, the Swiss physician, has said that it is a waste of time to counsel people who are unwilling to confess their sins. Furthermore, it has been his experience that medical advice has little effect on changing the attitudes and behavior of people. The only way to change people is from within, in the heart, where the spiritual revolution takes place. According to Tournier: "I feel that the deepest meaning of medicine is not in counseling lives but in leading the sick to a personal encounter with Jesus Christ, so that, accepting it, they may discover a new quality of life, discern God's will for them, and receive the supernatural strength they need in order to obey it."[9]

---

[9]Paul Tournier, *The Healing of Persons* (New York: Harper & Row. 1965), 212.

Dr. Tournier demanded of all his patients that they come to terms with the toxic resentments and guilt that dominated their attitudes. He told them that there could be no healing unless they allowed Christ to release them from the slavery that made them ill. What they needed was a new centering, and this centering could only come through the Gospel of Christ's forgiveness and love.

The following is a portion of a letter that Dr. Tournier received from one of his patients, a young woman who, at first, resisted his counsel, but later received a deep spiritual healing when she accepted Christ's gift of wholeness:

> I was nervous and high-strung, going rapidly from a period of enthusiasm to one of depression, always having ups and downs—tiring both to myself and to those I was with, and finding lack of sleep very hard to bear. My digestion was bad; I used to eat too quickly and was easily and often sick. I suffered from skin eruptions. I was a terrible glutton, even though I fought against it . . . I had very little self-control and used to give way to all my feelings . . . anger, enthusiasm, or despair—not without a certain violence, in a way that was painful to the people about me. I began to pray, to obey, and my life began to be centered on Jesus Christ.
>
> There came a day when I realized a new balance had been established in my body—an evenness of temper. . . . My health is my personal testimony. But it has happened all by itself, I might say without my knowing it. This new state of mine depends upon my regular quiet times and my surrender to God. It isn't something acquired once and for all, but it remains and lasts in the measure to which I obey God, confess to Him and am freed from my sins. The health of my body depends upon the health of my soul. [10]

This letter is an example of the gift of wholeness that can be achieved when a person's life is centered on Jesus Christ. It is not our desire to oversimplify the complex matter of achieving a state of health. Processes such as these often take a great deal of time and patience. But consider the therapeutic result. In confessing her need for help and centering her life on Jesus Christ, a balance in her life had been achieved.

---

[10]Ibid., 221-22.

Luther and the Ministry of Healing

Luther in his later years began to emphasize the ministry of healing as an outreach to the members of the parish who were sick. On June 1, 1545, he wrote a letter to Pastor Severin Schulze of a village near Leipzig. A member of Pastor Schulze's congregation was suffering from a severe case of melancholia. Following is the letter of counsel Luther sent:[11]

Pastor Severin Schulze
Venerable Sir and Pastor:
　　The tax collector in Torgau and the councilor in Belgern have written me to ask that I offer some good advice and help for Mr. John Korner afflicted husband. I know of no worldly help to give. If the physicians are at loss to find a remedy, you may be sure that it is not a case of ordinary melancholy. It must rather, be an affliction that comes from the devil, and this must be counteracted by the power of Christ and with the prayer of faith. This is what we do, and that we have been accustomed to do, for a cabinetmaker here was similarly afflicted with madness and we cured him by prayer in Christ's name.
　　Accordingly you should proceed as follows: Go to him with the deacon and two or three good men. Confident that you, as pastor of the place, are clothed with the authority of the ministerial office, lay your hands upon him and say, "Peace be with you, dear brother, from God, our Father and from our Lord Jesus Christ." Thereupon repeat the Creed and the Lord's Prayer over him in a clear voice, and close with these words:
　　"O God, Almighty Father, who has told us through Thy name, He will give it to you: who has commanded and encouraged us to pray in His name, 'Ask and you shall receive,' and who in like manner has said, 'Call upon Me in the day of trouble: I will deliver thee, and thou shalt glorify Me,' we unworthy sinners, relying on these Thy words and commands pray for Thy mercy with such faith as we can muster. Graciously deign to free this man from all evil, and put to nought the work that Satan has done in him, to the honor of Thy name and the strengthening of the faith of believers; through

---

[11]Original text in Latin: W.A. Br. (letters) XI, M/112.

the same Jesus Christ, Thy Son, our Lord, who liveth and reigneth with Thee, world without end, Amen."

Then, when you depart, lay your hands upon the man again and say, "These signs shall follow them that believe; they shall lay hands on the sick and they shall recover." Do three times, once on each of three successive days. Meanwhile let prayers be said from the chancel of the church, publicly until God hears them. Insofar as we are able, we shall at the same time unite our faithful prayers and petitions to the Lord with yours.

Farewell. Other counsel than this I do not have.

I remain, etc.

(Martin Luther)

Luther's remarks offer some helpful guidelines in establishing a healing ministry within the parish. We note that members of the congregation are involved as a therapeutic community under the guidance of the pastor. The Word of God is effectively at the center of the healing therapy. In addition to prayer for the sick, Luther employs the laying on of hands. Although Luther's counsel is rudimentary in its structure, this approach to healing comprises the basic elements of biblical healing.

Rituals of Healing in the Congregation

Until it is brought to their attention, most people do not realize that there are few rituals of healing practiced in the modern church. Yet the early church displayed palpable evidence to the world that it was indeed a healing community. The symbols of *anointing with oil* and the *laying on of hands* have a long history in the Christian tradition and were means by which the early church reached out to the sick. Perhaps it is time to revisit these time-honored symbols of healing. We do not wish to invest in these symbols more than the love and compassion of Christ that they symbolize, nor to construe to them any spiritual powers of their own. Nevertheless, we ought not disavow the fact that, if God chooses to work through them, He most certainly will.

Anthropologists have long noted that rituals of healing play a dominant role in traditional societies. A ritual, by definition, refers to "a patterned, repetitive activity that conveys a meaning." Inherent in all rituals is a power that draws people together into a community and which symbolizes the group's shared values. Indeed, the richness of a culture can be seen in its long-standing rituals, which are brimful with treasured meanings and keepers of its collective consciousness.

Perhaps the greatest value of rituals is their ability to communicate the deepest mysteries of faith. By virtue of the fact that they can include in a simple gesture or in a sensory experience such a wealth of shared meaning, rituals evoke within the person a sense of communicating with the divine. We need only think of the bread and wine in the Lord's Supper to appreciate this truth. Singing the carols at a Christmas Eve service is highly ritualistic and, at the same time, deeply moving for the worshipper. Rituals touch the emotions as few other social phenomena do.

It is an encouraging sign that Americans are beginning to reassess the value of rituals. Facing the losses of life all *alone*—especially the loss of health or the loss of a loved one in death—has caused many to yearn for the sense of community that simpler societies possess. I have heard more than a few Christian ministers express envy of the "bereavement rituals" of the Jewish faith that help their members through a time of grieving. Such rituals perform the function of healing the bereaved and incorporate the suffering person into a supportive group.

It can be argued that we need *more*, not fewer, rituals in our autonomous, fragmented society. Rituals of healing can be a powerful means by which a Christian ministry of healing reaches out to the sick with the love of God and affirms these sufferers in their time of need.

The Laying On of Hands

Laying hands on the sick occurs as a dominant ritual in the New Testament. It takes place so frequently that we are surprised only by its absence.

During His earthly ministry, Jesus almost always laid His hands upon those whom He healed. Frequently He placed His hands directly on the bodily location of the malady, whether the disease was habituated in the eyes, the ears, or the limbs. In His instructions to the disciples before He left their midst, Jesus told them that "they will place their hands on sick people, and they will get well" (Mark 16:18). We note that Paul was healed of his blindness when Ananias laid hands on him (Acts 9:17).

Touch remained important even in the early church. St. Irenaeus (ca. A.D. 150) reported that he and others "still heal the sick by laying hands on them and they are made whole."[12] It has been suggested that this practice ceased only because it was impossible to touch everyone. Thus, the practice of the "outstretched arms" accompanying the benediction at the end of a service became established. The outstretched arms of the pastor symbolize the laying on of hands of the entire group.

Laying hands on a person is a symbol of *compassion*. What mother does not wrap her child in her arms when the child is hurt or ill? To touch a person who is suffering is a sign of concern from fellow believers and from friends. Touching provides a point of contact that breaks through the barrier of loneliness and fear; it is a message of reassurance. In times past, as some have observed, ministry to the sick was characterized by a stiff formality. More recently, however, "touching" the sick person has come into vogue. Thanks especially to the personalized care provided by nurses, we are discovering that touching has powerful consequences in giving patients hope and reassurance.

But touching is more than a symbol. It is also a natural healing gift, and like all natural gifts, the Lord can channel its energy to bring healing. Modern medical research is beginning to exemplify a correlation between laying on of hands and a stimulation of the healing process. Dr. Dolores Kreiger, for example, has demonstrated clinically the therapeutic use of touch by measuring a significant rise in hemoglobin levels in the blood of patients who receive this treatment.[13] In addition, she notes that touch affects brain waves, relieves pain, and produces a generalized relaxation response. After publication of these medical results that derive from simple "human touch," Dr. Kreiger was invited to teach 3,000 doctors, nurses, and therapists how to lay hands lovingly on their patients and thus transmit healing energy from themselves to a sick person.

In the context of the Christian church, the laying on of hands has been used on occasion as a means by which healing prayer can be

---

[12]Irenaeus, *Contra Haeresis* II:32, 4-5. Even the secular psychotherapeutic world increasingly acknowledges the value of rituals, such as that of touch. See, for instance, Evan Imber-Black and Janine Roberts, *Rituals for Our Times: Celebrating, Healing, and Changing Our Lives and Our Relationships* (New York: Harper-Collins, 1992).

[13]Dolores Kreiger, *The Therapeutic Touch* (Englewood Cliffs, NJ: Prentice-Hall, 1979), 16.

focused. Leslie Weatherhead describes how some have used it in England.

> The pastor begins with a silent meditation after giving the person a constructive thought to hold to about the love and good purpose of God to heal. A short simple prayer is then said, asking God to heal. Stand then in front of the person who is kneeling and lay the right hand on the forepart of the head and the left on the back of the head. Then comes the Laying on of Hands and Prayer:
> "Our Lord Jesus Christ who gave authority to His disciples that they should lay hands on the sick that they might recover, have mercy upon you and strengthen you in body, mind, and spirit, and give you faith in His power to heal. And by His authority committed unto me, I lay my hands upon you that you may recover your full health and strength, in the name of the Father, and of the Son and of the Holy Spirit."[14]

A word of caution should to be included here about the use of this method. The laying on of hands is not a magic technique to be used when all else fails. Neither should people see this method as a substitute for medicine and medical care. It is rather a healing ritual by which the Christian community can express its faith in love for the sick person.

Laying hands on the sick can be a symbol of divine love-making contact with the human spirit. In a powerful way it enables the patient to share the faith of fellow Christians. It also helps those who lay on hands to focus on the prayer for healing that accompanies this act.

The Anointing with Oil

Anointing the sick with oil has its roots in the practice of the early church as is evident in the pericope from James 5:14-16. The instructions from James are rather straightforward and seem to be a general congregational procedure in A.D. 48, when this letter apparently was written: "Is any one of you sick? He should call the elders of the church to pray over him and *anoint him with oil in the name of the*

---

[14]Leslie Weatherhead, *Psychology, Religion, and Healing* (New York: Abingdon-Cokesbury Press, 1951), 133. See also W. V. Arnold, "Blessing and Benediction," in *Dictionary of Pastoral Care and Counseling* (Nashville: Abingdon Press, 1990), 100-101.

Lord. And the prayer offered in faith will make the sick person well; the Lord will raise him up."

Oil in Hebrew anthropology was the symbol for life. The Hebrews used it for cooking, for light, for medicinal purposes, and as a symbol of God's blessing. In the passage from Luke 7:46 we learn that when a guest came to the house of another, he was anointed on his head as a symbol that he was *included in the group*. It was a form of blessing to assure the house guest that he was not excluded from the community of people in the house. This appears to be a valid interpretation of the meaning of the anointing with oil. Anointing with oil conveyed to the sick that, as members of the fellowship, they were included in all of the blessings God desired to share with His people. It is important in this context to remember that Jesus instructed His own disciples to anoint with oil in their ministry to the sick (Mark 6:13).

The Tradition of Anointing with Oil

The Eastern Orthodox Church has always used the anointing in their ministry to the ill. After a long hiatus, the Roman Catholic Church has recently restored the anointing of oil to its original meaning in this church as a healing sacrament. For hundreds of years it had been used as a sacrament for the dying, known as the Last Rites or Extreme Unction.

It will be helpful to the reader to survey this subject more comprehensively. The new Roman Rite for Anointing has made two major changes. The first change involves the intent that the ministry of healing is a function of the congregation. The second change emphasizes that the anointing of oil is for the purpose of healing the sick:

> 1) Ideally, anointing is to be a *communal* rite utilizing not only the priest's but also the lay people's prayers for healing;
> 2) Anointing is a rite for *healing* the sick rather than preparing the dying for death. The old Rite stressed the priest's prayer for a happy death and not the lay people's prayer for healing. In the new Rite, the priest returns to the early Christian tradition and invites the lay people to pray with him.[15]

---

[15]Barbara Shlemon, Dennis Linn, & Matthew Linn, *To Heal as Jesus Healed* (South Bend, IN: Ave Maria Press, 1978), 18-19.

According to some Roman Catholic commentators, physical healing was foremost in the minds of the early church fathers when they prayed for the sick and anointed with oil. "All 13 blessings of oil still in existence from that period mention physical healing. The five most ancient blessings for the sick mention only physical healing and do not explicitly refer to spiritual effects."[16]

In the traditional manner of anointing the sick with oil, a prayer was first spoken which involved the Blessing of the Oil. The following prayer of a bishop was recorded by Hippolytus in A.D. 197.[17]

> *Lord God, loving Father, You bring healing to the sick through Your Son Jesus Christ.*
>
> *Hear us as we pray to You in faith and send the Holy Spirit, man's Helper and Friend, upon this oil, which nature has provided to serve the needs of men.*
>
> *May Your blessing + come upon all who are anointed with oil, that they may be freed from pain and illness, and made well again in body, mind, and soul.*
>
> *Father, may this oil be blessed for our use in the name of our Lord Jesus Christ who lives and reigns with You forever and ever. Amen.*

After the Blessing of the Oil, the sick person was then anointed with oil by the priest on the forehead. The new rite of the Roman Catholic Church for anointing with oil includes the following prayer:

> *Through this holy anointing may the Lord in His love and mercy help you with the grace of the Holy Spirit. May the Lord who freed you from sin save you and raise you up.*[18]

The Practice of Anointing with Oil

There is much to be said for anointing the sick with oil as a function of the healing ministry of the church. We must try to imagine how alienated the sick person feels, especially when in the confines of a

---

[16]Ibid., 21.

[17]Ibid., 56.

[18]Ibid., 64.

ward in the hospital. In speaking with many sick people over the years, I am reminded how lonely their existence is without the companionship of family, loved ones, and fellow members of the church. Visiting with the sick is a helpful practice, but it is only a palliative in relieving these feelings of alienation. By contrast, anointing the sick with oil can be a powerful symbol that the sick person has not been forgotten. It communicates effectively that the church is reaching out to restore the sufferer to health.

We are reminded also by the pericope in James that the anointing of the sick is done in the *name of the Lord.* It should not be lost on us that this is the same Name by which we were baptized and experienced our original healing as God's children. We should also take note that a prayer accompanies the anointing, a prayer of faith for the purpose of restoring the sick person to health. The modern church would do well to consider using this ancient ritual in its ministry to the sick. No conflict need exist between the use of medicine and healing prayer; both methods work in partnership to bring wholeness to the individual.

The Evangelical Lutheran Church of America has published a service for the Laying On of Hands and Anointing the Sick.[19] In this service, the minister lays both hands on the person's head and, following a brief silence, says:

> *I lay my hands upon you in the name of our Lord and Savior Jesus Christ, beseeching him to uphold you and fill you with grace, that you may know the healing power of his love*

If the person is to be anointed, the minister dips a thumb in the oil and makes the sign of the cross on the sick person's forehead, saying:

> *(name), I anoint you with oil in the name of the Father, and of the Son, and of the Holy Spirit.*

---

[19]"Laying On of Hands and Anointing the Sick" in *Occasional Services: A Companion to Lutheran Book of Worship* (Minneapolis: Augsburg Publishing, 1982). Included with the service are these notes of interest. "Preparation for the Service of Anointing: The oil used for anointing is olive oil, to which an aromatic ingredient such as synthetic oil of cinnamon or oil of bergamot may be added. This prayer may be said when the oil has been prepared. *'Lord God, you bring healing to the sick through your Son, Jesus Christ, our Lord. May your blessings come upon all who are anointed with oil, that they may be freed from pain and illness and be made whole. Amen.'"*

The prayer is then said:

> *God of mercy, source of all healing, we give you thanks for your gifts of strength and life, and especially for the gift of your Son, Jesus Christ, through whom we have health and salvation. Help us now by your Holy Spirit to feel your power in our lives and to know your eternal love; through Jesus Christ our Lord.*

Some may object that rituals of healing such as the laying on of hands and the anointing with oil are sought by those who seek quick solutions to their sickness. But such critics fail to understand the nature of whole-person health care. At a time of illness, the needs of the human spirit must be addressed above all else. As mentioned previously, Christian rituals possess a symbolic power by which the deepest mysteries of the faith are communicated. Armed with rituals of healing, the church has a golden opportunity in our modern era to present visible tokens of its compassion for the sick.

A Service of Healing and Wholeness

An effective way to apply the ministry of healing can be to offer a *Service of Spiritual Healing* which is celebrated by the congregation. [20] A Service of Spiritual Healing functions as a means by which the sick are assured that the Healing Christ is present to bring healing today. Consider the powerful impact of love that an ill person feels when surrounded by fellow believers at a healing service. In such a service the opportunity exists for the supplicant to receive the laying on of hands and anointing of oil with prayer at the altar. In addition, the service itself can be an effective means by which the proclamation of the Gospel, the confession of sins, and the intercession of fellow believers can all be compacted in one situation.

The design of a Service of Healing and Wholeness will vary according to the worship style of a particular congregation. I have found that a liturgical service lends itself to the dignity of the occasion when supplication is made for the God of grace to touch the lives of those who are sick. A liturgical service focuses on the Scripture and

---

[20]A sample Service of Spiritual Healing is included in the appendix and can be used without permission.

involves the participation of the congregation, many of whom are not ill but have come to share their faith with the sick. An incredible amount of warmth permeates these services. Those who have attended healing services remark about the outpouring of Christian love that occurs spontaneously on these occasions. Carefully selected music, using the musical gifts of soloists as well as the organist, adds an atmosphere of serenity and joy.

At a specific time in the service, the sick come forward to the altar rail for the laying on of hands and prayer. As the pastor or service leader approaches each supplicant, he bends down to hear the supplicant whisper in his ear the particular need to be addressed. The healing prayer then follows in which the needs of the supplicant are prayed for in the context of a prayer for God's wholeness upon the person. Many of those who go to the altar for prayer are "intercessors" for those sick persons who cannot attend the healing service.

The Evangelical Lutheran Church of America has also published a service entitled "The Service of the Word for Healing."[21] The outline of the service is liturgical, with lessons to be read, the Creed, litanies and prayers for healing, and opportunity for members to come to the altar for the laying on of hands and anointing with oil.

My experience in the healing ministry has convinced me that a healing service can be a dramatic channel of God's healing power. However, the greatest triumphs that these services demonstrate is the deepening of faith in the Risen Christ. It is common to hear participants say that their spiritual growth—in some instances there are conversions to Christ—is the major benefit they have received from these services. Emily Gardner Neal, who once was the leader of a healing service in an Episcopal church in Pittsburgh, has consistently expressed this point of view. A healing ministry is essentially a spiritual ministry because it seeks the wholeness that Jesus Christ gives.

> One particularly dubious minister who had spoken with me some months before, said recently:
>
> "How right you were! Although I must confess that at the start I felt like the blind leading the blind, it was only a short time before people began telling me of the great spiritual benefits they had received from the services—and reports of actual physical healings soon began to trickle in.

---

[21]"The Service of the Word for Healing" in *Occasional Services: A Companion to Lutheran Book of Worship* (Minneapolis: Augsburg Publishing, 1982).

"This ministry has been mightily blessed, and I can only marvel that God has used me as he has."[22]

Do healings of a physical nature take place within a healing service? Certainly they occur. Nor should we be amazed that such manifestations of the kingdom of God take place in our modern age. Mrs. Neal, among others, has reported on hundreds of these remarkable cures of which the following is only a sample:

> Although I never cease to marvel at the manifestations of God's healing power; of seeing with my own eyes a tumor dissolve, or a compound fracture instantly healed, I have in a sense become accustomed to physical healings. . . . Although they amaze me, they no longer take me by surprise. But I have never become in any way accustomed to the healings of the spirit I have witnessed. In them I see, more clearly than ever before, the incontrovertible evidence of the Holy Spirit at work; the undeniable proof that God lives.[23]

Gifts of Healing in the Congregation

We can also speak about the ministry of healing from another perspective, namely, the *gifts of healing* that the Spirit of the church gives to some of its members. Paul discusses this topic in his description of the various functions that members perform within the Body of Christ.

In 1 Cor. 12:9 there is the phrase "*to another gifts of healing by that one Spirit.*" It is significant that Paul speaks of healing gifts in the plural rather than in the singular. Perhaps this is an indication that such gifts comprised many different types of ministries to the sick. A lot of debate has transpired about what these gifts of healing mean, but there is no debate on the purpose of the gifts ". . . the manifestation of the Spirit is given for the common good." What is especially revealing is that *healing* is mentioned among the important activities that take place within the congregation.

Following are some suggested approaches in applying the gifts of healing to congregational life in our modern era. By implementing

---

[22]Emily Gardner Neal, *The Lord Is Our Healer* (Englewood Cliffs, NJ: Prentice-Hall, 1961), 194-95.

[23]Ibid., 5.

these gifts, a compassionate and wholesome spirit of health can be initiated within our congregations.

Ministering to the sick: Among the laity there are some persons who have a particular capacity, by virtue of their faith and personhood, to share the wholeness of Jesus Christ with the sick. The warmth of their personalities, their compelling love for their brothers and sisters, and their ability to communicate the Gospel of reconciliation, mesh together in one succinct package which expresses healing to the sick.

One suggestion is to gather such gifted individuals into the group called *The Fellowship of St. Luke*. After training them in the Christian ministry of healing, entrust to them the responsibility of assisting the pastor in visiting and ministering to the ill. Other congregations may prefer to have the Board of Elders responsible for this outreach. It should be pointed out that such an activity is not creating an independent order of healers in the church. Nevertheless, we need to recognize that there are differences in spiritual gifts. Those who are gifted in ministering to the sick can bring a powerful blessing to the entire congregation and make tangible the fact that God's fellowship is a healing community.

Caring for the sick: Others in the congregation may share their gift of healing by offering works of mercy to those who are sick. This is in keeping with Paul's word of encouragement: "Carry one another's burdens and in this way you will obey the law of Christ" (Gal. 6:2).

By visiting the ill in their homes or at the hospital, by volunteering to assist in the minding of children, by shopping or cleaning, or even by nursing those ill persons who are chronically infirmed, the laity of the church expresses the ministry of the Healing Christ. This type of ministry is referred to as *Diakonia*, the Greek word for "service." Paul mentions, in Romans 12:7-8, the gifts of service, of giving aid, of doing acts of mercy. All of these gifts can be fruitfully applied to the ministry of healing.

Sharon Telleen suggests that the congregation is a caring social network that can provide a strong support system for the sick. She mentions the following specific tasks that the parish can become involved in with the sick person and his or her family:[24] (1) help the individual master his emotional burdens through prayer, meditation,

---

[24]Sharon Telleen, "The Church as a Support to Families under Stress," in *Health and Healing: Ministry of the Church*, ed. Henry Lettermann (Chicago: Wheat Ridge Foundation, 1980), 101-2.

and social contact; (2) share the tasks that need to be done to deal with a crisis, such as providing transportation, doing the shopping, and making necessary phone calls; and (3) provide extra supplies of information, money, materials, tools, skills, and cognitive guidance.

Programs of health and well-being: Many congregations are attracted to the possibility of instructing their members in the stewardship of health and well-being. One such program includes the concept of a *Health Cabinet* which sponsors and supports health-related programs in the parish. Composed of volunteers who are gifted in matters of health—including professional medical people of the parish—the Health Cabinet can help develop strategies, important events, and activities that will sensitize members to health concerns. Activities can include anything from a "Health Fair," in which health checkups are offered, to special seminars on stress and health education, or C.P.R. training. Jill Westberg describes some of the typical functions of Health Cabinets:

> The Health Cabinet assists individuals and families to become more responsible for maintaining and improving their own health and that of their community. While the Cabinet will not be involved in the diagnosis and treatment of individuals, it will greatly step up the promotion of healthy behavior and ensure strong support to individuals who are not well. The Health Cabinet will act as a source of influence in the life of the church community to ensure that the stewardship of health is expressed in worship, education, networks of support, and recreation.[25]

A variation of the Health Cabinet that is gaining in popularity is the Parish Nurse program. In this particular venue, a nurse within the parish is assigned the responsibility of some health care while at the same time promoting health-related programs for the congregation. The Lutheran Church—Missouri Synod officially supports the parish nurse ministry. One important resource offered by this church body is *The Nurse in Public Health Ministry*, which is available from The Lutheran Church—Missouri Synod Health Ministries Unit, 1333 South Kirkwood Road, Saint Louis, MO 63122. Another important organization is the Health Ministries Association, 1306 Penn Avenue, Des Moines, IA 50316.

---

[25]Jill Westberg, "Six Action Models of Ministry," in *Health and Healing: Ministry of the Church*, ed. Henry L. Lettermann, (Chicago: Wheat Ridge Foundation, 1980), 12.

A Postscript

Throughout this book, the theme of the restoration of order has been sounded. It is a worthy theme because it signifies the biblical solution to the quest for health and healing.

In the process of healing itself, we see the handiwork of God's power bringing order where there is disorder, healing in the midst of disease, illness, and sickness. In the ministry of doctors and nurses as they care for the sick, as with others who seek to battle the forces of disease, the hand of God's order becomes magnified. In the compassion of Christian congregations who with their pastors offer a ministry of healing to the ill, God moves to rout the forces of disorder as He provides wholeness.

At the center of this plan to bring restoration to a broken world stands the Healer Himself. He is the author of health and wholeness even as He is author of our salvation. In the kingdom of God, this new order is proclaimed to the world with the promise that a Day is coming when God's plan of restoration will be complete.

The challenge to the church today is to follow the footsteps of Christ, the Healer, and according to the gifts He has given us, to be His hands of healing. For as we do so, we march to the beat of the Drummer who is restoring the order of creation.

Appendix I

A Service of Spiritual Healing

Hymn

Salutation and Collect

Pastor: Grace to you and peace from God our Father and from the Lord Jesus Christ.

People: **And also with you.**

Pastor: O God of Peace, who has taught us that in finding our rest in You we shall be saved, and that in quietness and confidence You shall be our strength: by the might of Your Spirit lift us, we pray, to Your Presence, where we may be still and know that You are God: through Jesus Christ, our Lord. Amen.

The Promises of God

Pastor: Listen to the promises of our Lord Jesus: "Truly I say to you, if you have faith as a grain of mustard seed, you shall say to this mountain, be removed, and it shall be removed, and no thing shall be impossible for you."

People: **Lord, I believe; help my unbelief.**

Pastor: Our Lord Jesus also said, "Heal the sick and say unto the people, the kingdom of God is come near unto you."

People: **Lord, I believe; help my unbelief.**

Pastor: Listen to the words of St. James, the apostle of Christ: "Is there any among you sick? Let him call for the elders of the church, and let them pray over him, anointing him with oil in the name of the Lord; and the prayer of faith shall save him who is sick, and the Lord shall raise him up and if he has committed sins, it shall be forgiven him. Confess therefore your sins to one another, that you may be healed."

People: **Lord, I believe, help my unbelief.**

Intercession

Pastor: Seeing that we have a great High Priest, Jesus Christ, the Son of God, let us come boldly to the Throne of Grace, that we may obtain mercy and find grace to help in time of need.

People: **Our Father Who Art in Heaven . . .**

Pastor: Remember that all of God's children are near and dear to Him, wherever they may be. Let us first pray for those who desire our prayers, many of whom cannot be with us this day. (Here shall be named those who desire prayer to be made for them.)

Blessed Jesus, we bring unto Your loving care and protection on the stretchers of our prayers all those who are sick in mind, body, or spirit. Take from them all fear and help them to put their trust in You, that they may feel beneath them and around them Your strong and everlasting arms.

Cleanse them from all resentments, jealousy, self-pity, pride, or anything else that might block Your healing power. Fill them with a sense of Your loving presence, that they may experience the Kingdom of Love in their whole being. And touch them with Your divine power that they may be healed

according to Your glory and for the building of Your
kingdom upon earth.

People: Amen.

Scripture Reading

Hymn

A Homily on Healing

Litany

Pastor: Father, Son, and Holy Spirit, giver of life, fountain of health
and source of all strength,

People: We praise and thank You.

Pastor: O Son of God who went about doing good and healed all who
came to You in faith and repentance,

People: We praise and thank You.

Pastor: We beseech You to hear us, O Lord: that You will grant
Your healing grace to all who are physically sick, injured, or
disabled, that they may be made whole.

People: We beseech You to hear us.

Pastor: That You will grant to all who seek Your guidance: to all
who are lonely, despondent, or anxious, a knowledge of Your
will and an awareness of Your presence.

People: We beseech You to hear us.

Pastor: That You will bless physicians, nurses, and all who minister
to the suffering: granting them wisdom and faith, skill and
sympathy, tenderness and patience.

People: **We beseech You to hear us.**

Pastor: That You will grant the dying peace and a holy death; and uphold the bereaved by the grace and consolation of Your Holy Spirit.

People: **We beseech You to hear us.**

Pastor: That You will restore to wholeness, brokenness of any kind, in our lives, in our nation, and in the world.

People: **We beseech You to hear us.**

Pastor: Jesus of Nazareth,

People: **Have mercy upon us.**

Confession of Sins

Pastor: Let us humbly confess our sins to God.
In our confession let us think not only of gross sins but sins of disposition as well: bitterness, worry, hurt feelings, resentment, jealousy, spiritual pride, living in the past, self-love, self-pity.

People: **Almighty God, Lord of all, we confess that we have sinned against You in thought, word, and deed. Have mercy upon us, O God. According to Your great love do away with our offenses and forgive us all our sins, for the sake of Jesus Christ. Amen.**

The Absolution

Pastor: The almighty, loving, and merciful God now gives you absolution and remission of all your sins. I therefore proclaim His Peace to you according to His Word.

People: **Amen.**

Anointing and Laying on of Hands

Pastor: The Almighty Lord, who gives power and strength to all who put their trust in Him, be now and evermore your defender. May He instill in you an assurance that there is no other name but the name of Jesus Christ whereby you may receive health and salvation.

(Then shall the people come forward for the laying on of hands and prayers at the altar rail after which they will return to their places.)

Thanksgiving and Benediction

Pastor: Lift up your hearts.

People: **We lift them up to the Lord.**

Pastor: Let us give thanks to the Lord our God.

People: **We do it because we love Your Holy Name, O God.**

Pastor: It is our grateful duty to give thanks to You, O Lord, who gives us health and salvation; whose Son came into the world that we might have life in abundance; who in His love for all people ministered to their infirmities and gave both the power and command to His disciples to heal the sick. We give You thanks and praise that You have continued your healing work among us. May we never forget Your faithful mercies, through Jesus Christ, Our Lord.

People: **Amen.**

Pastor: May God our Father, God the Son, and God the Holy Spirit bless you in your departing, and may He preserve you in body, mind and spirit, until the last day.

People: **Amen.**

Appendix II

My Personal Journal

Within a month after the author delivered this manuscript to the publisher, he was diagnosed with lung cancer. His death came less than four months later. During his last weeks he recorded his "experiences as well as sensations and feelings dealing with" his struggle with his malady. At the request of the author's widow, Marlene, we share Dr. Ludwig's journal. –Editor

During October [1997] I noticed some changes. I experienced a lot of sneezing as if I had been exposed to an allergen. In mid-November I felt winded cycling uphill. When December came, my physical problems escalated. I was tiring easily and becoming short of breath. I finished writing my book in December, gave an important conference presentation, prepared final exams, and completed the academic semester. I also saw my physician and began the testing process. My symptoms and test results baffled the medical professionals caring for me, and it wasn't until February 5th [1998] that a diagnosis was made.

When I wrote in my book, on the very first page, that disease is disorder, the troubler of human happiness, little did I realize I soon would be going through the experience myself.

Garth David Ludwig
February 15, 1998

The Mythology of Disease (February 23, 1998)

We have mythologized disease so as to better come to terms with it and make sense of it. By finding some rational purpose for disease, we hope to dismantle its deadly intentions. One manifestation is to glorify the pain and suffering as if this alone makes us better persons. What blindness we have been cajoled to accept in the name of human understanding. Disease is not nice nor it is God's intentions. It is a parasite and parasites feed on their hosts. My cancer is robbing me of nutrients, of energy, and is sucking me of my body fluids. It also makes me narcissistic, always thinking of myself and my suffering. I can't concentrate on more useful preoccupations. Only music drives away the demon of my illness. There are so few moments of joy and true hope. I look for any tiny sign of improvement, to breathe a little easier, to cough less, to feel good all over. But no day passes without some tragic reminder that a lethal force resides within me, and its aim is to kill me. I fight an entrenched invader who, if I gave in, would control my body, mind, and spirit. But, I will not let it take control of me! Never. I can live with nothing but hope.

My Problem Is Fear (February 24, 1998)

I have always been afraid of pain, of unpleasant events, of bad news. I call myself a dreamer, a searcher of truth and beauty. But is this so much a quest than as an escape from that which makes me afraid? I am locked into the challenges of my life. Truly I am in the valley of the Shadow . . . and damn it, I am afraid. I betray all the symptoms, nervousness, gasping for breath, pulling my ear. I fool nobody, especially Marlene. Only when I relax do I breathe normally. Sometimes I become so agitated, I can barely get my breath, such as when I had to brush my hair this morning.

I believe I have courage but I also have a lot of fears. Only over those particulars I can control do I show courage. But I can't get courage to breathe correctly. Until I do so, I am going to have a difficult time with my cancer.

I am going to have to deal therapeutically with my agitation and fears. The Psalmist's solution is to practice the presence of God. In the midst of fear, know that you are not afraid because you are *not* alone!

The People Who Support Me (February 25, 1998)

The lesson of my illness that has given me the most meaning is the compassionate love of others. And all of it so freely and spontaneously given. Beginning with my own wife and children, the support has been outstanding. No request is too great, no desire refused. They make the sick role, as distasteful as it is, bearable, and in the process, allow me to keep my spirit soaring.

The outpouring from the University, not only faculty but staff and students, has literally been overwhelming. Cards, E-mail, calls . . . not a day goes by without some encouragement.

This has been good for me because I have always fended for myself. Now I experience the other part of the equation. It is a sign of God's gracious love coming to me through others.

What is the lesson? You can only know the grace of God when you stand in desperate need of it. This is the theology of the Cross. God is closest when the night is darkest.

The Healer Within (February 26, 1998)

Hippocrates first spoke about—VIX MEDICATRIX NATURAE —and Albert Schweitzer gave it a popular name: "the healer within." It is our marvelous immune system, an intricate chemical process designed to protect the body from invading germs and pathogens. The amazing feat of the immune system is the real-life fact that we don't become sick or die each day of our lives. I am dumbfounded at the complexity and efficient synchronicity of how B and T lymphocytes work in such uniformity while all the time macrophages and neutrophils scavenge the body for lethal invaders.

And even when the invader seems to have the upper hand, such as when influenza rages, the immune system mobilizes all possible resources to pull the victim through. In this sense, the immune system is the "doctor within." All therapies from professional physicians and all medications are, essentially, aids to assist the immune system to attack the disease and destroy it.

What is now being appreciated is the profound effect of the mind and emotions on the beneficial (or contrariwise, the malevolent) working of the immune system. The link between the two is indisputable, but we just don't know exactly how it works. Or why it works with some and not others.

Can a focused thought, a visual image of healing, dissolve a tumor? Can the prayers of a multitude accomplish the same result? On the other hand, how can radiation or chemotherapy dissolve some tumors but not others? Is it one thing or is healing a combination or multitude of therapies? Here it seems where the mystery of modern medicine now faces its great challenge. Lewis Thomas keeps saying we need more scientific research to find out the deeper intricacies of disease. His mechanical model leaves no room for the processes of mind or emotions. I don't think Thomas is completely wrong. He just doesn't go far enough in his treatment of the person. A person can literally think himself well in certain situations.

The complexity of the human individual is at once the strength and weakness of modern medicine. Modern biochemistry describes the complex interactions that second by second respond to organic functions within the body. Hundreds of medical facts—white blood count, platelet, electrolytes, hemogoblin, etc.—reveal an amazing complexity. But look what happens when a doctor smiles at the patient or says offhandedly, "you're going to make it." That simple, non-complex statement will have an immediate effect on the body's chemistry and change it unalterably.

Hope versus Despair (February 27, 1998)

David Sobel once made the comment that despair is easier than hope because the mind more readily imagines the worst. You have to fight to retain hope, but by giving up the fight you have championed despair. The circumstances of life, as well as significant others, mold us in either of these directions. When I first learned of my tumor, I responded with a surge of hope that was genuine to the core. I am the world's greatest optimist, its champion dreamer. I am anti-reality. The world I have fashioned in my mind's heart is sheer beauty. Disease is non-existent. But I know this other world too, and its rules of operation. The reality of this world, a world of disease and tumors, at time catches my attention. I am brought back to earth. I remember my oncologist saying, "The situation is very serious." Yet I still fervently hope to overcome my disease. I can visualize myself becoming well. But after several months now, it has become a dogfight. The flights of fancy are not so euphoric. Discouragement with my breathing takes some of the edge off my optimism. My daily "struggle" resembles the battle of Britain. I continue to send up the Spitfires to fight the German bombers. I recently read an essay by a colleague who reveals a heart tinged by so much suffering, it has given itself over to despair while struggling to be faithful. I don't want to be like him, although I respect his honesty. I cannot live except I hope in God.

Blessings amidst the Pain (March 1, 1998)

When I was a little child, I used to daydream a lot. I would imagine doing whatever I pleased because there were no other demands on my time. Now that I have all the time in the world—my disease has entered its fourth month—it's not a ball doing whatever I want. For just a moment or two, I would like to feel useful. Tonight Marlene revealed her own pent-up frustrations—"I'm really tired. Your sickness is wearing me out."

At times I myself am sick and tired of being sick and tired. Yet so many helpful blessings have entered my life these past few weeks. Not only the outpouring of love and concern, but the discovery of reading again for pleasure. I truly value Truman Capote's writing—he "underwrites"—and he moves the narrative along. He seeks to report what he hears, what he sees; hence, I would call him a journalistic writer. In many respects, I see myself in the same mold.

Trust in the Healer, Not Yourself (March 3, 1998)

Deepak Chopra once said, "We are the only creatures who can change our biology by what we think and feel." This is holistic health in a nutshell; its truth is demonstrated countless times by those whose attitudes and hopefulness lead them out of the clutches of disease into radiancy of health.

But I am learning that more is at stake here than mere mental and psychical expectancy. My reading of the Psalms, indeed of all Scripture, teaches us that we are healed by a "Healer"—the One who stands apart from us, but is so close in respect to His mercy and compassion.

My illness now is teaching me this vital distinction. Despite my many preparations, visualizations, and imaging, my greatest need is to simply let go, relax in the grace of God, and let Christ heal me as He will. I need to allow Christ's love to flow to the depth of my self and to create health. I need the Healer more than the gift of healing He brings.

Biology Can Tell How We Feel about Ourselves (March 4, 1998)

At the depth of his depression and pain, Job rued the day he was born: "What I feared has come upon me; what I dreaded has happened to me. I have no peace, no quietness; I have no rest, but only turmoil."

The equation works both ways. Our biology can change what we think, feel, and believe. Suffering can do that to a person, engendering bitterness and self-pity along with a sense of justice. No wonder one finds a lot of irritable and irascible sick people. They hurt and vent their feelings on the world.

Magic bullets that can stop pain, the infection, and the suffering are the most welcome nostrums of the healer's kit. But woe to the healer who cannot stem the tide of pain. My doctor told me today that the three human sufferings which cause the most anxiety in humans are (1) burn; (2) breathlessness; (3) pain (actually "itchiness" ranks before pain). I see how breathlessness ranks before pain.

The Many Faces of Cancer Victims (March 5, 1998)

According to Dr. Bernie Siegel, there are three types of cancer patients: (1) The ones who have made up their minds to die—they believe the doctor's prognosis, give up all hope, or else welcome this as an opportunity to leave behind all earthly problems. (2) The majority who are shaken by the news and who faithfully follow all the doctor's orders. These ordinarily also insist on standardized and conventional medical care. (3) The exceptional cancer patient, the feisty person who remains autonomous and in charge, who changes doctors, who disagrees with the treatment, who asks questions, who has an agenda beyond cancer, who makes discoveries during the treatment.

Imperative in fighting cancer is to fight it with love, not hate. Deepak Chopra said it this way, "Conflict does not heal a disease."

When You Want Some Good News but Receive Only Bad News (March 6, 1998)

When I began this Odyssey last December I was characteristically upbeat. I knew something was amiss, but even when I walked into Dr. Johnson's office, I felt confident that what I had was not life-threatening. But my body should—and did—tell myself what my optimistic spirit was denying. Then came bad news in spades: the pulmonary specialist—a malignant tumor-addenocarcinoma; the oncologist—cancer bilaterally in both lungs. Then loss of breath more than ever before, so that I almost need a wheelchair to be transported. Today the internist said I would never have any more lung tissue than I now have, the lowest blow of all. It is a perpetual death sentence. If I don't choke to death, I will die of a heart attack. How I need to hear some good news for a change. What I need is a miracle only God can give.

Weakness—To Be Sick!

When I did my exegetical work on the Hebrew word for sickness, the root word meant to be weak. How poignant that I would ever experience the real meaning of the word I was trying to research. No more descriptive a condition exists than being usurped by a weakness that allows little expression of energy, dependency upon others, difficulty in thinking, depression, frustration, and irritation. It is walking the line between life and death. It is to want so much—but to be denied almost everything. Cancer is a wasting disease because it weakens a person by stages. What I did two weeks ago, I cannot do today. But here is strength in weakness as Paul was reminded by God—for herein comes the grace of God. Let me not forget the weakness that Christ submitted to at the cross!

- Soli Deo Gloria -

Some Final Notes by Marlene Ludwig (April 1998)

By March 21 it was necessary to have Garth moved to the hospital for intensive care and treatment. The cancer that invaded Garth's system was the most aggressive cancer his physicians had ever seen.

I stayed at the hospital through every day and night, returning only twice for a fresh supply of clothing. Our children, presently located in California, New Jersey, and Japan, were called and they along with our new grandchild and daughter-in-law spent every possible moment with their dad.

Many years ago, Garth began a family tradition that we continue still. When we gather together at special occasions—and there are many with a large family—we are each asked to say something when a celebration toast is given or a thanksgiving prayer is said. So at each day's end, as we gathered at his bedside for devotions and prayer, we shared our fondest family memories and thanked him for the inspiration, education, leadership, and love that he gave to us as our pastor, professor, husband, father, and friend.

In his perceived role as an exceptional patient, Garth valiantly battled this disease with every resource possible. Additionally, prayers were offered far and near—prayer chains, congregations, colleagues, friends, family, students and former students—we all wanted him to get better and return to family life, the university campus, and the church community. However, one evening when we prayed, " . . . we are ready to accept Your will for Garth's life, Lord," we could hear through his oxygen mask the ardent and almost jubilant response— *AMEN!*

Eleven days after hospital admission and treatment, Garth was released. He was sent home, attached to oxygen and morphine, in an ambulance. At home, comfortably situated in his den, surrounded by favorite books, pictures, music, and looking out into his garden, Garth said his coming home was *"a dream come true."*

The next day, by mid-afternoon, his symptoms changed and it became evident that it was time to call our pastor and send for children who were still at work. We gathered, as we had done in the hospital, around his bed to pray, share, and take turns holding his hand. This time we sang too. On piano and flute, two of our daughters played his favorite hymns.

The constant presence of Christ was powerful when we sang, with choked or silent voices, the words:

Abide with me, fast falls the eventide,
The darkness deepens, Lord with me abide.
When other helpers fail and comforts flee,
Help of the helpless, oh, abide with me.

At this moment, on April 2 [1998], as Garth struggled with enormous effort to breathe, the Healer came to Garth and blessed him with the gift of perfect health for all eternity.

Hold Thou Thy cross before my closing eyes,
Shine through the gloom, and point me to the skies:
Heavn's morning breaks, and earth's vain shadows flee;
In life, in death, O Lord, abide with me.

God's purpose to never leave us or forsake us is indeed a reality! His presence was with us every day in spirit, power, Word, and especially people. We are deeply grateful to everyone who so generously ministered to us with prayers, messages, gifts, help, understanding, financial assistance, support, food, memorials, and kind words. We are deeply grateful.

Every day I will praise You and extol Your name forever and ever.
Great is the Lord and most worthy of praise,
His greatness no on can fathom. Psalm 145:2-3

Bibliography

Ackerknecht, Edwin. *Medicine and Ethnology: Selected Essays.* Baltimore: The Johns Hopkins Press, 1971.

Alland, Alexander, Jr. *Adaptation in Cultural Evolution: An Approach to Medical Anthropology.* New York: Columbia University Press, 1970.

Amundsen, Darrel W. and Gary B. Ferngren, "Medicine and Religion: Pre-Christian Antiquity." In *Health/Medicine and the Faith Traditions: An Inquiry into Religion and Medicine,* edited by Martin E. Marty and Kenneth L. Vaux. Philadelphia: Fortress Press, 1982.

Anderson, Robert. *Magic, Science, and Religion: The Aims and Achievements of Medical Anthropology.* Fort Worth, TX: Harcourt Brace College Publishers, 1996.

Aulén, Gustav. *The Faith of the Christian Church.* Eng. tr., 2nd ed. London: SCM, 1961.

Baker, Beth. "The Mind-Body Connection: Putting the 'Faith Factor' to Work." In *AARP Bulletin,* 38, no. 7, July/August, 1997: 20-21.

Baron, Richard. "I Can't Hear You While I'm Listening." In *The Healing Experience: Readings on the Social Context of Health Care,* edited by William Kornblum and Carolyn D. Smith. Englewood Cliffs, NJ: 1994.

Belgum, David, ed. *Religion and Medicine: Essays on Meaning, Values and Health.* Ames, IA: Iowa State University Press, 1967.

Benson, Herbert. *The Relaxation Response.* New York: William Morrow, 1975.

Benson, Herbert. *Beyond the Relaxation Response.* New York: Berkley Books, 1984.

Boggs, Wade, Jr. *Faith Healing and the Christian Faith.* Richmond, VA: John Knox Press, 1956.

Bonnell, John Sutherland. *Psychology for Pastor and People.* New York: Harper and Brothers, 1948.

Bonny, Helen. "Music and Sound in Health." In *Health for the Whole Person: The Complete Guide to Holistic Medicine,* edited by Arthur Hastings, James Fadiman, and James Gordon. Boulder, CO: Westview Press, 1981.

Brown, Colin, ed. *The New International Dictionary of New Testament Theology.* Vol. 2. Grand Rapids, MI: Zondervan, 1980.

Cassell, E. J. *The Healer's Art: A New Approach to the Doctor-Patient Relationship.* New York: Lippencott, 1976.

Clark, M. Margaret. "Cultural Context of Medical Practice," In *The Western Journal of Medicine,* vol. 139, no. 6 (December 1983).

Clements, Forrest. *Primitive Concepts of Disease.* Berkeley: University of California Publications in American Archaeology and Ethnology, vol. 32 (#2), 185-252.

Coe, Rodney M. *Sociology of Medicine.* New York: McGraw-Hill Book Co., 1970.

Cousins, Norman. *Anatomy of an Illness: As Perceived by the Patient.* New York: W. W. Norton, 1979.

Deierlein, Kathleen. "Ideology and Holistic Alternatives." In *The Healing Experience for the Whole Person: Readings on the Social Context of Health Care,* edited by William Kornblum and Carolyn Smith. Englewood Heights, NJ: Prentice-Hall, 1994.

Douglas, Mary. "The Abominations of Leviticus." In *Purity and Danger.* Routledge and Kegan Paul Ltd: London, 1966.

Dubos, René. *Man Adapting.* New Haven: Yale University Press, 1965.

Dunbar, Flanders. *Emotions and Bodily Changes.* New York: Columbia University Press, 1954.

Elert, Werner. *The Structure of Lutheranism.* St. Louis: Concordia, 1962.

Foster, George and Barbara Anderson. *Medical Anthropology.* New York: John Wiley and Sons, 1978.

Frank, Jerome. *Persuasion and Healing.* New York: Schocken Books, 1969.

_____. "The Medical Power of Faith." In *Human Nature* (August 1978), 40-47.

Galanter, Marc. *Cults: Faith Healing and Coercion.* New York: Oxford University Press, 1989.

Gordon, James S. "The Paradigm of Holistic Medicine." In *Health for the Whole Person: The Complete Guide to Holistic Medicine,* edited by Arthur Hastings, James Fadiman, and James Gordon. Boulder, CO: Westview Press, 1981.

Graebner, Theodore. *The Practice Sometimes Miscalled "Divine Healing."* St. Louis: Holy Cross Press, 1921.

Green, Judith and Robert Shellenberger. *The Dynamics of Health and Wellness: A Biopsychological Approach.* Forth Worth, TX: Holt, Rinehart, and Winston, 1991.

Grinker, Roy R. *Psychological Concepts.* New York: Jason Aronson, 1973.

Hahn, Robert and Arthur Kleinman, "Belief as Pathogen, Belief as Medicine: 'Voodoo Death' and the Placebo Phenomenon." In "Anthropological Perspective," *Medical Anthropology Quarterly,* vol. 14, no. 4 (August 1983).

Hammer, Ian. "Pastor, the Gene Made Me Do It!" In *Concordia Journal,* vol. 23, no. 1 (January 1997).

Hastings, Arthur and James Fadiman, James Gordon, eds. *Health for the Whole Person: The Complete Guide to Holistic Medicine.* Boulder, CO: Westview Press, 1981.

Hauerwas, Stanley. *Naming the Silences: God, Medicine, and the Problem of Suffering.* Grand Rapids, MI: Eerdmans Publishing, 1990.

Healthy People 2000: National Health Promotion and Disease Prevention Objectives. U.S. Department of Health and Human Services, Public Health Services. Boston: Jones and Bartlett, 1992.

Helman, Cecil. *Culture, Health, and Illness.* Bristol, England: John Wright and Sons, 1985.

Hiltner, Seward. "The Bible Speaks to the Health of Man." In *Dialogue in Medicine and Theology,* edited by Dale White. Nashville, TN: Abingdon Press, 1968.

Hulme, William. "New Life through Caring Relationships in the Church." In *Word & World: Theology for Christian Ministry,* 11, no. 4 (Fall, 1982): 340-52.

Hunter, Rodney J. *Dictionary of Pastoral Care and Counseling.* Nashville: Abingdon Press, 1990.

Irenaeus. *Contra Haeresis* II:32, 4-5.

Jackson, Edgar N. *The Role of Faith in the Process of Healing.*
    Minneapolis: Winston Press, 1981.

_____. *Your Health and You: How Awareness, Attitudes, and
    Faith Contribute to a Healthy Life.* Minneapolis: Augsburg
    Publishing House, 1986.

Kelsey, Morton. *Healing and Christianity.* New York: Harper & Row,
    1973.

Kleinman, Arthur. "The Failure of Western Medicine." In *Human
    Nature* (November 1978): 63-68.

Kleinman, Arthur. *Patients and Healers in the Context of Culture.*
    Berkeley: University of California Press, 1980.

Koenig, Harold G. *Is Religion Good for Your Health?: The Effects of
    Religion on Physical and Mental Health.* New York: The Haworth
    Pastoral Press, 1997.

Kornblum, William and Carolyn Smith, eds. *The Healing Experience:
    Readings on the Social Context of Health Care.* Englewood Cliffs,
    NJ: Prentice-Hall, 1994.

Kreiger, Dolores. *The Therapeutic Touch.* Englewood Cliffs, NJ:
    Prentice-Hall, 1979.

"Laying On of Hands and Anointing the Sick." In *Occasional
    Services: A Companion to Lutheran Book of Worship.*
    Minneapolis: Augsburg Publishing, 1982.

Luther, Martin. *The Freedom of the Christian Man.*

_____. *The Small Catechism.*

_____. *The Large Catechism.*

_____. *Letter to Severin Schulze.* W.A. Br. (letters) XI, M/112.

Majno, Guido. *The Healing Hand: Man and Wound in the Ancient
    World.* Cambridge, MA: Harvard University Press, 1975.

Marty, Martin and Kenneth Vaux, eds. *Health/Medicine and the Faith
    Traditions: An Inquiry into Religion and Medicine.* Philadelphia:
    Fortress Press, 1982.

Marty, Martin. *Health and Medicine in the Lutheran Tradition.*
    Philadelphia: Fortress Press, 1982

Mattson, Phyllis. *Holistic Health in Perspective.* Palo Alto: Mayfield,
    1982.

McElroy, Ann and Patricia Townsend. *Medical Anthropology in
    Ecological Perspective.* Boulder, CO: Westview Press, 1985.

McNeill, William H. *Plagues and Peoples*. Garden City, NY: Anchor Press, 1976.

Meeks, Wayne. *The First Urban Christians: The Social World of the Apostle Paul*. New York: Harper & Row, 1983.

Miller, M. and J. L. Miller. *Encyclopedia of Bible Life*. New York: Harper & Row, 1955.

Miller, Roland E. "Christ the Healer." In. *Health and Healing: Ministry of the Church*, edited by Henry L. Lettermann. Chicago: Wheat Ridge Foundation, 1980.

Moore, Lorna, Peter Van Arsdale, JoAnn Glittenberg, and Robert Aldrich. *The Biocultural Basis of Health: Expanding Views of Medical Anthropology*. Prospect Heights, IL: Waveland Press, 1980.

Neal, Emily Gardiner. *The Lord Is Our Healer*. Englewood Cliffs, NJ: Prentice-Hall, 1961.

Nouwen, Henri. *The Wounded Healer*. Garden City, NY: Image Books, 1972.

_____. *Out of Solitude*. Notre Dame, IN: Ave Maria Press, 1974.

Parsons, Talcott. *The Social System*. New York: Free Press, 1951.

Pattison, E. M., M. L. Pattison, and H. A. Doerr. "Faith Healing: A Study of Personality and Function." In *Journal of Nervous and Mental Disease* 157 (1973): 367-409.

Peterson, Christopher and Martin Seligman. "Explanatory Style and Illness." In *Journal of Personality*, vol. 55, no.2 (June, 1987).

Reisser, Paul C. "Alternative Medicine." In *Christian Research Journal* (Sept.-Oct. 1997): 31-37.

Roehrs, Walter R. *Concordia Self-Study Commentary*. St. Louis: Concordia, 1971.

Sanford, John. *Healing and Wholeness*. New York: Paulist Press, 1977.

Scharlemann, Martin. *Healing and Redemption*. St. Louis: Concordia, 1965.

Schleman, Barbara, Dennis Linn, and Matthew Linn. *To Heal as Jesus Healed*. Notre Dame, IN: Ave Maria Press, 1978.

Selye, Hans. *The Stress of Life*. New York: McGraw-Hill Book Co., 1956.

Siegel, Bernie. *Love, Medicine & Miracles*. New York: Harper & Row, 1986.

_____. *Peace, Love & Healing*. New York: Harper & Row, 1989.

Sigerist, Henry. *A History of Medicine I: Primitive and Archaic Medicine*. New York: Oxford University Press, 1967.

Simonton, Carl, Stephanie Simonton, and James Creighton. *Getting Well Again*. New York: Bantam Books, 1978.

Simundson, Daniel. "Health and Healing in the Bible." In *Word & World: Theology for Christian Ministry*, 11, no. 4 (Fall 1982): 330-39.

Skoglund, Elizabeth. *The Whole Christian*. New York: Harper and Row, 1976.

Taylor, Shelley E. *Health Psychology*. New York: McGraw-Hill, 1995.

Telleen, Sharon. "The Church as a Support to Families under Stress." In *Health and Healing: Ministry of the Church*, edited by Henry L. Lettermann. Chicago: Wheat Ridge Foundation, 1980.

"The Service of the Word for Healing." In *Occasional Services: A Companion to Lutheran Book of Worship*. Minneapolis: Augsburg Publishing, 1982.

Thomas, Barbara. "Health," *Los Angeles Times*, September 22, 1997.

Thomas, Lewis. *The Fragile Species*. New York: Macmillan, 1992.

Tillich, Paul. "The Relation of Religion and Health: Historical Considerations and Theoretical Questions." *Review of Religion* (May 1946).

_____. "The Meaning of Health." In *Religion and Medicine*, edited by David Belgum. Ames, IA: Iowa State University Press, 1967.

Tournier, Paul. *A Doctor's Casebook in the Light of the Bible*. San Francisco: Harper & Row, 1960.

_____. *The Healing of Persons*. New York: Harper & Row, 1965.

Tubesing, Nancy. *Philosophic Assumptions*. Hinsdale, IL: Wholistic Health Centers, 1977.

Twaddle, Andrew. "Sickness and the Sickness Career: Some Implications." In *The Relevance of Social Science for Medicine*, edited by Leon Eisenberg and Arthur Kleinman. Dordrecht, Holland: D. Reidel Publishing Co., 1981.

Van Buskirk, James. *Religion, Healing & Health*. New York: Macmillan Co., 1952.

Watty, William. "Man and Healing: A Biblical and Theological View." In *Contact* (Christian Medical Commission, World Council of Churches, Geneva, Switzerland), vol. 54 (December 1979).

Weatherhead, Leslie. *Psychology, Religion, and Healing.* New York: Abingdon-Cokesbury Press, 1951.

Westberg, Granger E. "From Hospital Chaplaincy to Wholistic Health Center." In *Health and Healing: Ministry of the Church,* edited by Henry Letterman. Chicago: Wheat Ridge Foundation, 1980.

Westberg, Jill. "Six Action Models of Ministry." In *Health and Healing: Ministry of the Church,* edited by Henry L Lettermann. Chicago: Wheat Ridge Foundation, 1980.

White, Dale, ed. *Dialogue in Medicine and Theology.* Nashville: Abingdon Press, 1968.

Wilson, Michael. *The Church Is Healing.* Naperville, IL: SCM Book Club, 1966.

Wolff, Hans Walter. *Anthropology of the Old Testament.* Philadelphia: Fortress Press, 1974.

Zborowski, Mark. "Cultural Components in Response to Pain." In *Journal of Social Issues* (1952).

Index